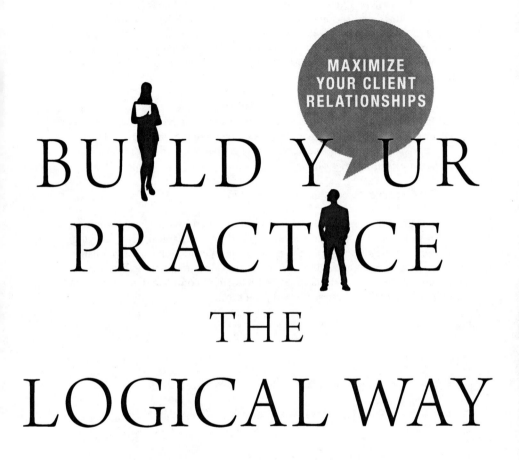

MAXIMIZE
YOUR CLIENT
RELATIONSHIPS

BU LD Y UR PRACT CE

THE

LOGICAL WAY

CAROL SCHIRO GREENWALD and
STEVEN SKYLES-MULLIGAN

FIRST
CHAIR
·PRESS·

D1069371

16 15 14 13 12 5 4 3 2 1

Library of Congress Cataloging-in-Publication Data

Build your practice the logical way : maximize your client relationships/ Edited by Carol Greenwald and Steven Skyles-Mulligan.—1st ed.
    p. cm.
  Includes bibliographical references and index.
  ISBN 978-1-61438-441-0 (print : alk. paper)
1. Practice of law—United States. 2. Attorney and client—United States. I. Greenwald, Carol. II. Skyles-Mulligan, Steven.
  KF311.B84 2012
  340.068'8—dc23

                                                            2012018633

Discounts are available for books ordered in bulk. Special consideration is given to state bars, CLE programs, and other bar-related organizations. Inquire at Book Publishing, ABA Publishing, American Bar Association, 321 North Clark Street, Chicago, Illinois 60654-7598.

www.ShopABA.org

Contents

Chapter 3
Master Communication Techniques to Build a Client-Centric Practice

Chapter 8
Pick the Low-Hanging Fruit—Summary

Foreword

Good clients are at the heart of any successful professional practice. Everyone knows this, but very few professionals take the time and exert the effort to understand who their best clients are, what they really value, how to build deeper relationships with them, and how to replicate those relationships with other clients.

Marketing studies have consistently demonstrated that it takes approximately seven to eight times as much money—and seven to twelve additional meaningful encounters—to acquire a new client as to secure a new piece of business from a client who has worked with you already. In spite of this, law firms often fail to mine their client bases for these "low-hanging fruit" opportunities.

This book is conceived as a how-to guide that will help you tend what is already most rewarding, both intellectually and financially, in your practice: the clients who value you most and with whom you most value working. The steps outlined here are straightforward, strategic, and significantly important for your practice's long-term health and viability.

This book is structured around five core principles derived from the authors' cumulative four decades of experience in helping professionals, especially attorneys, market their practices:

1. Value is defined by the client. In order to be perceived as worth your fee, you must understand what your clients value and deliver it consistently.

2. Communication is central to the delivery of professional services. Attorneys are so accustomed to using their expertise to solve problems for their clients that they may neglect key elements of communication.

3. Creating a loyal client is a process, not a given. No matter how effective your work for a client, without taking certain steps to build loyalty, you likely have, at best, a satisfied client who may or may not be inclined to work with you again.

4. Knowing more about your clients and about your own work preferences will help you build a more enduring practice. Every professional does some things better—and more happily—than

other things. Systematically identifying those things and mapping them to your best clients will have a salutary impact on your bottom line.

5. It is possible to replicate your best client relationships. Once you understand the key characteristics of your best clients, it is easier to seek out and build similar relationships, increasing your professional satisfaction, your overall compensation and your competitive standing in the marketplace.

The authors have endeavored to omit the jargon for which their profession is so frequently—and justly—ridiculed. Where it was necessarily used, a concise explanation has been offered. Like all bodies of knowledge, this one was influenced by, builds upon, and departs from the work of other experts; you will find references to useful works in the footnotes and bibliography.

You may be skeptical about these promises; you probably would not be a good attorney if you are not. Consider this: as competition grows fiercer and as an increasing number of law firms organize more formally along corporate lines and follow corporate business practices, the likelihood of falling behind—or of being forced out of business altogether—will increase significantly.

January 2012

Carol Schiro Greenwald
Larchmont, New York

Steven Skyles-Mulligan
New York, New York

Acknowledgments

The ideas presented in this book took shape over several years of discussion, debate and implementation. Elizabeth Kallen, formerly a professional services consultant, worked with us as we developed the concept. Much of what appears in these pages reflects our "wisdom" obtained through years of hands-on work with clients. Those clients who trusted us to help solve their key business problems, debated strategies with us, and worked to incorporate client-centric practices informed the perspective for this book.

It takes a village for projects such as this, and so we owe thanks to many people who assisted us in a variety of ways. Before we sent the manuscript to our ABA editor, we asked close friends—lawyers and marketing professionals—to review the text. We cannot say enough thanks to Alan Levine, Rita Menz, Dee Schiavelli, and Donna Shaft for their thoughtful suggestions and edits. Special thanks go to Richard Schiro whose trenchant advice and deft edits of early chapter drafts was of immeasurable value, to Donna Drumm who added pungent language and kept us focused on our audience's point of view, and Joshua Bressler whose insights as an attorney who both hires and is hired by other attorneys were critical to helping us shape a spare, accessible narrative.

Other lawyers allowed us to test our perspective in interviews with them, and provided their view of our ideas and, in some cases, "real life" examples to support our ideas. Our thanks and appreciation for their candor and time to Joe Coleo, Bob Danziger, Jon Dorf, Ellen Gesmer, Larry Haut, Larry Hutcher, Andrew Peskoe, and Lou Sherman. In addition, Andrea Prigot, a consultant and expert on legal billing software, helped us adapt real examples of client-centric bills to use as exhibits in the book.

Of course, the book would never have come to fruition without the backing, encouragement, support, and editorial eye of Sarah Forbes Orwig, Executive Editor, Book Development & Publishing at the American Bar Association, who brought our idea to the editorial board of First Chair Press.

Our thanks would not be complete without a heartfelt acknowledgment of the unwavering support of our families, most especially those who bore daily the brunt of our testiness and angst as we endeavored to catch ever-slipping deadlines.

CHAPTER 1

Focus on Clients to Build Your Firm

Your clients will fuel your firm's growth. Consistent, strategic, and sustainable firm growth depends on strong client relationships rooted in practices that are designed to meet not only clients' expressed needs but also their expectations. Individual attorneys fiercely protect their key client relationships precisely because they know that this equation is real.

In a client-centric firm, the organization's resources are aligned "to effectively respond to the ever-changing needs of the customer, while building mutually profitable relationships"[1]

Therefore, any organizational changes need to reflect your client base. The understanding of that base begins with research into your firm, your own growth goals, and the firm in relation to your key clients. This

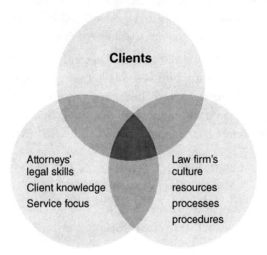

Diagram 1.1: A Client-Centric Firm

1. Craig Bailey, "Becoming Customer Centric," *Customer Centricity Newsletter*, Issue #53, Tuesday, September 14, 2004 (http://www.customercentricity.biz/Newsletters/newsletter53.htm, accessed December 22, 2011).

research looks at the client base today and identifies which parts of it you want to replicate for the future. The resulting firm assessment is then paired with a broader understanding of your key clients, from the perspective of what they do and what they *want* to do in their own world. By combining these two research streams, you are better positioned to decide what services you can offer your clients to help them get where they want to go, and you will also identify what needs to happen in your firm to produce that kind of client-focused value.

Recognize the Convergence that Puts Clients in the Driver's Seat

Today's clients want more than the usual intangible factors that create successful lawyer-client relationships, such as personal chemistry, working style compatibility, and on-point expertise. They demand a proactive approach to their matters based on a deeper understanding of their company, their industry, and the world—local, national, global—in which they operate.

> The fundamental change that has already occurred in the attorney-client relationship is that the market for legal services has become a buyer's market. . . . It is the view of the task force that this shift in the market for legal services—at least for the foreseeable future—will be a durable one. . . . Today clients have greater power to define and demand 'value' . . .[2]

To respond to this trend, firms need to create "stickiness" with clients by "expanding their firms' bonds with clients . . . First, firms must require their lawyers to meet or exceed client expectations about quality, service, cost, and results on every matter—as measured by the client's desire to come back for another matter and to refer additional clients to the firm."[3]

A PERMANENT CHANGE IN EXPECTATIONS AND COMPETITION

The economic downturn of 2008–2010 only accelerated challenges to the practice of law that were already in motion.[4] All indicators point to

---

2. New York State Bar Association, *Report of the Task Force on the Future of the Legal Profession*, April 2, 2011, pp. 20–21.
3. Peter Zeughauser, "Stuck on You," *The American Lawyer*, October 1, 2011.
4. For a thorough analysis of these trends and factors, along with their likely impact and potential remedies, see Richard Susskind, *The End of Lawyers?: Rethinking the Nature of Legal Services* (Oxford University Press, 2009). See also Kate Clifton (ed.). *The Future of Legal Services: Expert Analysis* (Ark Group, 2010).

a more challenging competitive environment: one in which clients will have more choices for how, where, and from whom they receive legal services; fewer dollars overall will be spent on legal services from outside law firms; and law firms will face greater pressure to focus more on budgets, process efficiencies, and transparency.

THE TRADITIONAL FOCUS ON PRACTICE GROUPS INHIBITS CLIENT-CENTRICITY

"It is an idiosyncrasy of the US legal market that while American attorneys may be on the cutting edge of advice to clients, their firms are among the most traditional in the world."[5] Why is a realignment of practice focus and processes so difficult to achieve? Why don't professionals embrace the clients that are most loyal?

One reason is that law firms tend to organize lawyers into practice groups built around the kind of law practiced, rather than around the purpose for which they are working. Corporate attorneys may sit next to litigators, but rarely do they work together. Often, they are unaware of each other's key clients or cases. Such blinders preclude cross-selling of colleagues' services. Sometimes the firm's reward system discourages cross-specialty fertilization, because current client growth is expected rather than rewarded. Also, the way productivity is measured and compensation awarded does not encourage teamwork or technological-facilitated efficiencies.

Clients want to be sure that those working on their matters are familiar with their specific situations and also conversant with the industry, economic, and political worlds in which they operate. They prefer to have continuity in the staffing of their matters. For the law firm, this is often a nice but not essential condition, overlooked when department workloads and priorities require staffing changes, In addition, the way productivity is measured, with its focus on the billable hour, discourages teamwork, fixed project-based fees, and technology-facilitated efficiencies.

---

5. Carolyn Binham, "Business of law: forced to innovate," *Financial Times*, November 3, 2011 (http://www.ft.com/intl/cms/s/0/15c2cb44-044a-11e1-ac2a-00144feabdc0.html#axzz1cljrRyiu, accessed December 22, 2011; registration required).

Build a Client-Centric Practice Based on "Foundation Clients"

A client-focused practice begins by seeing your practice as your clients see it. This means understanding how your client feels about the matter at hand, knowing how intimately the client wants to be involved in resolution of the matter, and thinking about how your work processes and procedures look from the client's perspective.

Key clients are *foundation* clients because they will become the basis for your growth initiatives. Consider them the "low-hanging fruit" of your practice, offering the opportunity for "a course of action that can be undertaken quickly and easily as part of a wider range of changes or solutions to a problem."[6]

Foundation clients use your firm for intellectually interesting work, typically important to them, usually on a frequent basis. This client is usually in your "80/20"—the twenty percent of your clients that provide eighty percent of your revenues. But a foundation client could also be a famous charity or well-known sports or entertainment figure—a client whose reputation places them conceptually in the "80/20" regardless of the actual dollars spent. The foundation client's executives and in-house lawyers and your attorneys usually have compatible work styles and work values.

When you adopt a client-centric approach based on a knowledge of foundation clients' wishes and needs, you create a vehicle for growth that can:

> Invigorate your practice by building a strong client base. The stronger the personal relationship and the broader the practice areas used by the client the more value it brings to both parties. As you work with a client in a number of situations you develop what marketers call "depth of client"—in terms of the breadth of situations you address and your understanding of the whole client. This breadth allows the attorney to become an advisor to the client, which in turn leads to stronger relationships and additional work.

> Strengthen a practice by targeting prospects with characteristics similar to your foundation clients. Your foundation clients present inter-

---

6. World English Dictionary (dictionary.reference.com, accessed December 22, 2011). This is not to be confused with the "fruit of the poisonous tree" doctrine that holds that "evidence discovered through unconstitutional means (such as a forced confession or illegal search and seizure), may not be used as evidence against a criminal defendant." Nolo's Plain-English Law Dictionary (http://www.nolo.com/dictionary, accessed December 22, 2011).

esting legal issues, use services you like to provide, and pay well, so naturally you want more like them. The investment made to understand the world of your foundation clients provides a strong platform from which to approach similar prospects.

> Make the practice of law personally more rewarding by focusing your energies on work you enjoy for clients you like.

Deliver a Stronger Perception of Value to Create Loyal Clients

Creating a loyal client is a process. No matter how effective the work for a client, without creating a relationship that rewards client loyalty, the attorney is working with a satisfied client who may or may not be inclined to work with him again.[7] Satisfied clients can be fickle, swayed by a better deal or a pretty face. Loyalty develops as the attorney and client continue to work together, building a comfortable relationship and a track record of solid results.

There is no right or wrong way to build a client-centric firm. To be successful it must begin from an understanding of your own work preferences. Every professional prefers some aspects of the practice more than others. It may be the counseling part, or the strategic planning, or the win. These preferences help differentiate your services from your competitors and create the service offering your clients like.

A client-centric approach assumes certain principles and practices:

Client empowerment to define and demand increased value imposes upon the attorneys the practical obligation to devise systems that optimize the processes by which they deliver their services, and to communicate that value to the client. . . . attorneys may be required to demonstrate their ability to assess and manage the business risk associated with legal problems, strategically streamline their services based upon those assessments, and measure their results."[8]

Value is defined by the buyer; so to create the value clients want, attorneys need to develop a process that compels the client to share in the development of their legal solutions.

---

7. According to a 2008 BTI study (*BTI Premium Practices Forecast 2008: Survey of Corporate Legal Spending*), fifty-nine percent of in-house counsel said they were considering firing a law firm. In the eighteen months prior to the study two-thirds of large corporate clients replaced one or more of their primary outside firms, amounting to more than five billion dollars in value.
8. NYSBA, *supra* note 2, at pp. 11, 27.

Communication is central to the delivery of any professional service. The service itself is an intangible—a shared experience which is created through language and activities. In a client-centric firm, the shared experience is reinforced through communication guidelines, a client interview program, and shared information initiatives such as knowledge databases and document repositories.

Take an Integrated Approach for Steady Growth

The process constructed here is an end-to-end system for building the practice you really want. Using it, you will move steadily from where you are now to where you ultimately want to be. You may be doing some or even many of the things recommended in this book. However, you are probably *not* doing them consistently as part of a planned and focused marketing system. By showing you how to integrate a client-centric process into your practice, this low-hanging fruit system helps you to build your law business organically without distracting you from the day-to-day demands on your time.

The process works for attorneys in private practice regardless of legal specialty. In most cases, the exercises assume that you work with business entities, but examples show you how to alter the approach if you work primarily with individuals. The size of your firm does not matter; in fact solo practitioners and attorneys in small firms, who form the majority of all those in private practice,[9] have several advantages. First, with fewer people to convince, motivate, and train, the new approach can be implemented quickly. Second, there is probably a shorter learning curve since you already do practice management. And most importantly, you already have tight relationships with your clients.

Difficult as it is to predict, define, and adjust to change—particularly for a profession as immersed in comfortable traditions as law—tremendous opportunities exist for lawyers and law firms that embrace this in-depth examination of their practice and their clients, and then align them to meet client demands.

---

9. According to the 2010 demographics from the ABA, three-quarters of all lawyers are in private practice. Of those in private practice, almost half are solos, fifteen percent are in firms with two to five lawyers, and seven percent are in firms with six to ten lawyers: seven out of ten lawyers works in an environment of ten or fewer lawyers.

CHAPTER 2

Use Value to Create a Foundation of Loyalty

Define Value the Way Your Clients Do

Value is created in the mind of the beholder. It's a feeling that, after all is said and done, what you do for a client is worth more than he pays you to do it. As Warren Buffet explained, "Price is what you pay, value is what you get." As this aphorism suggests, the perception of value is defined by the recipient, not the provider. Value as defined by the buyer is typically outcome-focused and usually relevant to the situation at hand.

The flow of activities in a client-centric firm creates systems that empower a client as an active participant in the lawyering process. Through education and teamwork, clients are able to visualize exactly the value you bring to them.

> [E]very point of contact that the firm has with a client is tailored and unique to that client; making it a valued client experience. . . . A valued client experience entails close collaboration where the firm knows the people, understands their business, understands the particular problem—and constantly asks for feedback about their level of understanding. And most importantly, this level of understanding must pervade the firm.[1]

When clients perceive consistent value over time, they become loyal clients. Your foundation clients should be loyal clients. In this chapter we dissect the features/benefits/value equation, tie it to the advantages inherent in loyal clients, and explain how to use client interviews to develop the feedback that enables a client-centric firm to align its focus with clients' interests.

---

1. The Hildebrandt Institute, whitepaper: *Relationship Intelligence in a Competitive Market*, 2002, p. 5.

$$\frac{\text{Features + Benefits}}{\text{Time}} = \text{Value}$$

Diagram 2.1: The Value Equation

Features are essential—they are the tools in the practice of law; benefits are the reason why lawyers are hired in the first place; value is the inducement that turns a casual client into a loyal client over time, as the relationship expands and deepens. Survey data bear out the strength of this proposition. When corporate counsel are asked why they switch firms, thirty percent say for better value, sixteen percent say for superior client service, and fifteen percent are drawn to a firm with deeper expertise and legal experience.[2]

Legal service providers and clients approach legal services from different perspectives. Attorneys concentrate on the elements that comprise a carefully crafted legal solution: skills, experience, training, and deliverables, such as contracts, motions, and other legal documents. Clients, on the other hand, tend to focus on results first, process second. Clients assume a lawyer's expertise. Some don't know enough about the practice of law to evaluate their lawyer's accomplishments; others know enough and selected you for your experience and reputation. This means that in order to understand what concerns clients you have to talk with them to learn what they think and why.

The concept of client-centricity incorporates an understanding of the difference between features, benefits, and value. Taken as a whole, these elements form a continuum that bridges the gap between the attorney's perspective and the client's view.

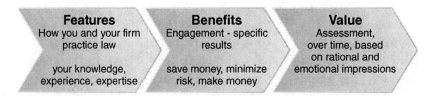

Diagram 2.2: The Value Continuum

---

2. BTI survey findings quoted in, Despina Kartson, "Why Focus on Clients?" *Running a Client-Centric Practice —The Why & How,*" NYC Bar Association CLE, October 26, 2011.

> Features are readily identifiable components of your approach to service, legal experience and expertise, firm attributes, and intangibles such as reputation and your methods and style for providing client service. Features include everything from the location of your office to the legal process management systems incorporated in your approach to your practice.
> Benefits are the consequences of the features: the result you obtained and the process that created the result. Achieving the benefit drove the initial decision to hire you. Typically, benefits are keyed to immediate to mid-term impact.
> Value is the perception created by the cumulative impact of your work and the personal experience of working with you and your firm. The dictionary defines value as "worth in usefulness or importance to the possessor."[3]

Moving from the traditional technique-focused view of client service to a value or value-added view requires a new understanding of clients, an understanding that they are the reason a law firm is in business, and as such, their needs and wishes should be the focal point of the practice. In this chapter use *Form 2.1: Features and Benefits Matrix*, page 26, to balance your practice features against benefits to clients that will influence their ultimate decision as to your value to them.

Enumerate the Features of Your Practice

The first step in analyzing your practice from a client's perspective is simply to enumerate the features: what you do, how you do it, who does it with you, and your record of success. The firm's resources should also be included in a features inventory. Almost anything you might say about how you, your firm, or your colleagues practice is a feature:

> **Knowledge**—Legal training, specialty knowledge of a particular industry, expertise in a particular aspect of the law, such as employment or intellectual property law
> **Skills**—Experienced negotiator, facility in drafting contracts, expertise in structuring organizations, capability in creating trusts

---

3. *The American Heritage Dictionary of the English Language*, Fourth Edition.

> **Accomplishments**—Awards, honors and positions, track record
> **Resources**—Office locations, composition of legal teams, staffing and leverage, technology

Understand the Benefits

Once you have identified the features of your practice, analyze the benefits that accompany them. To do this, consider why a client might care about or be willing to pay for a particular feature. If it is difficult to think about this in general terms, envision a particular client who you believe derives a benefit from the feature. For example:

> Firm geography is a feature. What advantages accrue to clients from your global presence? Or conversely, as a local practitioner, how does your breadth of knowledge about the legal practice in your area benefit your client?
> You are known as an excellent negotiator. How does that benefit a client?
> You have an electrical engineering degree. How does that benefit your manufacturing clients?

Some of the benefits may seem obvious, such as twenty years experience as a patent lawyer or litigator, but note the benefit regardless. Benefits may be tangible, such as money saved or merger documents prepared; some may be a combination of tangible and intangible, such as advice or a review of company manuals or a risk assessment; some benefits are intangible, such as feelings of comfort, safety, being taken care of—all seeds of the emotional aspects that are important to the attorney-client relationship.

Note that there is no strict one-to-one assignment of benefits to features, but every feature must have at least one benefit. Some features, such as expertise in a specific legal area, may have many benefits including efficiency, effectiveness, solid record of success, client comfort in being taken care of by an expert, etc. Some benefits such as efficiency may result from a variety of features, such as expertise, understanding the client, geographic proximity, and such.

Identify Your Value

The difference between features and benefits can appear as stark as the same fact pattern viewed by a prosecutor and a defense attorney—two distinct perspectives. The progression from benefit to value is more nuanced. Benefits are inherent in, and an outcome of, the experience of working with an attorney matter-by-matter. The benefit is the *sine qua non* for a satisfied client. Value derives from an accumulation of benefits over time. The sense of received value grows as a client and attorney work together, but it is more than that. Value is, in a sense, an outcome of the emotional connection that underlies a strong attorney-client working relationship, which ultimately creates the loyal client who will give you repeat business and refer others to you.

As with benefits, there are both tangible and intangible elements of value.[4] Tangible elements of value are typically outcome focused—a realized result, such as case dismissed, divorce granted, contract signed, deal completed. "For the GC, value is as much about exposure, budgetary constraints and indemnities as it is about winning."[5] Tangible results emerge when an attorney helps a client defend herself from an outside threat, minimize risk, grow her business, solve a problem, enhance an opportunity, or maximize asset value.

Intangible elements are intrinsic to the goal or strategy behind the legal activity, or to the achievement of the client executive or family member who was affected by the legal decision. Intangible elements also include aspects of client service delivery such as the lawyer's ability to:

> Make a client feel comfortable throughout the process.
> Respond to client inquiries within the client's time parameters.
> Recognize the client's budgetary constraints and abide by them.
> Anticipate problems and propose solutions before the client asks.
> Understand and work with the client's definition of success.

---

4. There is a substantial amount of literature, much of it in the form of client surveys, on how clients value their relationships with attorneys and the work that attorneys do for them. Staffing firm Robert Half and *Inside Counsel* magazine both publish regular surveys.
5. Mary B. Clark and Jay Dinwoodie, "The Volley over Value-Based Pricing," *Strategies*, October 2003, p. 11.

Many of the intangibles are a direct result of the lawyer's time and effort to understand the client and create a service experience that mirrors his needs and values.

Another factor that contributes directly to the client's perception of value is the lawyer's ability to align the legal strategy with the value the client places on the matter. The more important the situation to the client, and the greater the available client resources, the higher the value to him. In a routine situation the client may be less interested in having his lawyer deploy the vast array of resources which may take more time and money than the client wishes to spend. For a routine situation, your client may be reluctant to bear the financial, emotional, and opportunity costs associated with a "leave no stone unturned" level of effort. However, for a more important matter, that same level of effort would have greater value to your client.

See the following summarizing the Association for Corporate Counsel Value Index and presenting a case study of it in use.

Case Study—The ACC Value Challenge

In 2009, the Association of Corporate Counsel (ACC), the professional organization for in-house counsel, released a set of measurements and supporting materials intended to drive a restructuring of the relationship between internal law departments and the external firms they hire. Called "The ACC Value Challenge," the program is designed to create a dialogue between corporate counsel and their outside law firm providers around the subject of value.[6] Implementation of challenge initiatives includes initial meetings between outside counsel and internal lawyers to agree on stages in the work process and a budget and to set expectations (see chapter 6).

One component of the program that can apply to anyone interested in creating a more pro-client service posture is the *ACC Value Index* which in-house counsel designed to rate the performance of their outside counsel at the conclusion of each engagement. The index consists of six criteria:

1. understands objectives/expectations
2. responsiveness/communication
3. legal expertise

---

6. See *ACC Value Challenge* (http://www.acc.com/; accessed December 22, 2011). The site has information about various elements of the Value Challenge, as well as the survey. There are also publically-available survey results, which provide some insights as to how other firms' relationships went well or badly.

4. predictable cost/budgeting skills
5. efficiency/process management
6. results delivered/execution

Of these criteria, two relate to communication, one to legal expertise, and three to changes in the methods of delivering legal services to make the process more transparent and the costs more predictable.

The criteria reflect the growing pressure on in-house counsel from CEOs, CFOs, and boards of directors to reduce costs and demonstrate business value at every turn. The *ACC Value Index* directs outside counsel toward desired behaviors—such as cost control, efficiency, and project management—and also imposes some measures of success for each matter. And not coincidently, it encompasses the values and focus of a client-centric firm.

Even if a significant portion of your client base is not comprised of other attorneys, you may find the *ACC Value Index* useful in helping you manage your client relationships. While smaller firms and solo attorneys may not wish to formally discuss the Value Index with their clients, it may prove a helpful road map as the practice moves toward client-centricity. For example, when you begin working with a client consider how your approach would change if you were to be rated on each of the Value Index benchmarks.

ACC Value Challenge Covenant with Counsel

The ACC Value Challenge also suggests a two-part covenant between the client and the law firm, the outside counsel portion of which appears below.

As outside counsel, our firm will:

> Learn your business and strategic objectives and apply that understanding to your matters.

> Give honest feedback on whether your objectives in a matter are realistic and attainable.

> Use the most appropriate staffing and tell you if we don't have the needed expertise.

> Designate one lawyer to serve as our relationship manager, whose time will not be billed for this role.

> Proactively offer value-based alternative fee structures.

> Provide budgets and estimates for specific engagements up front and advise you immediately if there may be any material changes.

> Understand that we are responsible for our budgets and estimates and that our experience forms a basis for accuracy.

> Seek to reduce our costs creatively and constantly, and share those savings with you.
> Understand that you seek neither elegance, new law, nor perfection unless these provide value consistent with your company's objectives.
> Train our associates efficiently and effectively without imposing additional and unwarranted costs on you.
> Never "reinvent the wheel;" we will look first to past work product and encourage efficiency and continuous improvement.
> Not ask for blanket conflict waivers and discuss with you any client or issue conflicts.
> Use technology to our mutual benefit, including billing.
> Meet deadlines and keep in touch.
> Continue our commitment to pro bono and diversity activities.
> Work hard to retain and reward personnel that embrace these concepts, and ensure every member working on your project walks this talk.

Not every benefit will be of value to every client or to any one client all the time. For example, you may settle a case or get it thrown out of court thereby saving your client the potential dollar value if he lost. That financial savings represents an immediate benefit, but the long-term value may be saving the company's reputation or eliminating a potentially time-consuming case thereby freeing up the legal department to focus on other concerns.

On the flip side, it is also possible to create a negative perception of value, particularly on the intangible level, when you do not meet the established expectations, such as:

> higher than projected bills
> longer than expected response times
> insufficient knowledge of the client's decision-making context as it relates to the engagement
> problems related to the implementation of the case
> your personal value proposition

Once you have completed *Form 2.1* you have the necessary information to craft your own value proposition for each of your clients, especially your foundation clients. These should be outcome-focused and relevant to the specific client. Use your value statement to make your value visible to your client. Use *Form 2.2: Your Value Proposition*, page 27.

Make the Transition from Vendor to Trusted Advisor

Lawyers don't see themselves as similar to paper supply companies and electricians, as one lawyer said when exclaiming about a letter his firm received from a large bank that began, "Dear Vendor."[7] However, all professionals—including attorneys, bankers, consultants, financial advisors, physicians, and risk managers—begin every client relationship as a vendor, hired for a very specific task or set of tasks. Typically when a firm begins working with a new client they are seen as a vendor (i.e., a competent professional called in to solve a specific problem).

Today, the pressure to reduce costs has led some large companies to include procurement in the law firm hiring process which moves selection from the cozy world of referrals to a focus on "cost, deliverables and metrics."[8] At the same time that cost pressures are leading to commoditization of law firm hiring procedures, the complicated reality of clients' global worlds is leading to an increased need for attorneys to be more than legal technicians. Clients want a dialogue between experienced attorneys and senior business executives as to how they could respond to marketplace and economic trends.

A trusted advisor is one of the first people a client calls when a significant event happens, whether or not it appears to be in the attorney's specific area of expertise. A corporate attorney in a mid-size full service firm when asked about his advisor role said:

> Our job is to be an advisor and not just another vendor/service provider to clients in whatever way helps them the most. . . . When a client wants to do something and we disagree, I often offer advice, a second opinion, by saying 'x' doesn't make sense to me.

David Maister, who coined the term "trusted advisor" sees this far-reaching level of involvement as a trust-based relationship that encompasses both personal and professional issues and "requires an integration of content expertise with organizational and interpersonal skills."[9]

---

7. This is not an uncommon reaction. In an article by Martin Collins, "Monetizing Gains and Avoiding Commoditization," *Inside Counsel*, February 2011, he says, "I can still recall the first time, as outside counsel, that I was referred to as a 'vendor.' Me, a $600 an hour professional with 15 years experience, being lumped in with janitorial services and copier maintenance? That hurt."
8. *Financial Times* Report: *A New Dawn: Lessons for Law Firm Management in the Post-Crisis World*, 2011. p.12.
9. David Maister, *The Trusted Advisor* (The Free Press, 2000) pp. 8–9.

When an attorney invests in a relationship over time and becomes a trusted advisor, there is a much broader scope for making a contribution to the client's well-being. The rewards—financial, intellectual, and personal—are commensurate.

The relationship from vendor to advisor moves through a succession of steps. The diagram below shows how the client/advisor relationship evolves from vendor to trusted advisor.[10]

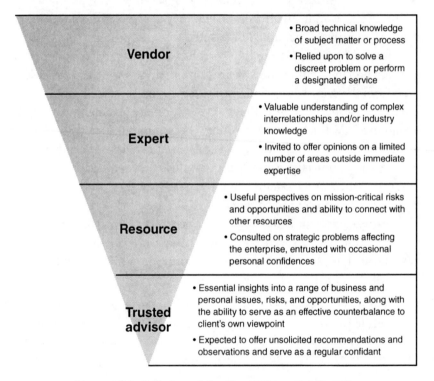

Vendor

- Broad technical knowledge of subject matter or process
- Relied upon to solve a discreet problem or perform a designated service

Expert

- Valuable understanding of complex interrelationships and/or industry knowledge
- Invited to offer opinions on a limited number of areas outside immediate expertise

Resource

- Useful perspectives on mission-critical risks and opportunities and ability to connect with other resources
- Consulted on strategic problems affecting the enterprise, entrusted with occasional personal confidences

Trusted advisor

- Essential insights into a range of business and personal issues, risks, and opportunities, along with the ability to serve as an effective counterbalance to client's own viewpoint
- Expected to offer unsolicited recommendations and observations and serve as a regular confidant

Diagram 2.3: Evolution of the Client/Advisor Relationship

The broader, more strategic nature of today's conversations between lawyer-advisors and their clients means that lawyers need to be involved with the C-suite—the top executives who make the strategic decisions. Outside lawyers' inside counterparts are also assuming a more proactive advisory role with their business colleagues. "There is a recognition that

10. *Id.* This book contains the most comprehensive discussion of the trusted advisor. The diagram follows the broad outlines of Maister's concept of the evolution of a professional relationship, augmented by the authors' own experience.

unpredictable times call for a deeper conversation where senior members of both client and law firm can engage in a dialogue about broader market and strategic issues."[11]

At the same time as they are seeking broad, conceptual input, business executives say they also want pragmatic, targeted, and pointed answer to their questions—advice they can apply immediately.

> The provision of timely, accurate and in-depth knowledge is emerging as a competitive differentiator. And there is a growing desire among companies for the relationship with their law firm to broaden beyond the purely legal.[12]

Private companies place similar value on advice from their lawyers. Solos who serve as outside counsel for small and family-owned businesses often see themselves as consigliere and want to be included in clients' discussions about next steps. Family law practitioners need to know all about the extended family situation in order to resolve guardianship claims effectively. Tax lawyers need far broader dealings with their clients facing an IRS audit than the immediate cause of action. Litigators acting only on the basis of a pleading may not know enough to seek the most appropriate solution for the client.[13]

Align Your Perspective Through Client Interviews

One of the most important initiatives in a client-centric firm is the client satisfaction interview.[14] These are not the same as the meetings and conversations attorneys have with clients on a regular basis. These are designed to find out "How's business?"—what's happening with the client in the coming months and years: their growth goals, strategic plans, potential competition, and growth opportunities. Lawyers typically include "How'm I doing?" questions at the end, but these events are intended to focus on the client's assessment of upcoming opportunities and threats which may or may not have a legal component. It provides a

---

11. *Financial Times* Report, *supra* note 7, at pp.20–21.
12. *Financial Times* Report, *supra* note 7 p. 24.
13. Using the research approach outlined in Chapters 4 and 5 will give you the knowledge base you need to work effectively within your client's culture and in tune with your client's goals and aspirations.
14. For a comparison with BtoC business' use of client feedback, see the whitepaper, *Capitalizing on Customer Feedback*, Pepper & Rogers Group, 2010 (http://www.allegiance.com/resources/papers/prgvoc .php; registration required; accessed December 22, 2011).

venue for lawyers to deepen their knowledge about their client's internal and external challenges.

The interview serves as an opportunity to build on your informal discussions and event-driven advice and provides a foundation for the law firm to proactively help the client avoid pitfalls and capitalize on opportunities. Not incidently, it also gives outside firms the chance to find out what clients think about the value they deliver, the resource mix they offer the client, and the expectations surrounding their service delivery.[15]

Client interviews cement relationships and create an effective base for future dialogue. They enable the attorney to reiterate their shared values. The evaluation of past work for the client creates a road map for improvement in the relationship going forward. Typically discussion topics lead to new matters, and relationships strengthen when the law firm fixes any service problems that are brought to their attention in the interview.

Clients universally appreciate the fact that their outside law firm takes the time to meet with them to consider their plans and how they can help them move forward with those plans. In a 2011 study of client feedback initiatives, over half of the respondents felt that client feedback programs returned real value to their firm. Eighty-two percent agreed that such programs have a positive impact on client relationships.[16]

Lawyers who handle consumer bankruptcies, DWI citations, divorce, tax issues, medical malpractice, and personal injury cases often don't see these kinds of interviews as appropriate since there may be no post-matter relationship. The consumer-focused lawyer can still consider two client feedback options:

1. Immediately after the matter closes, schedule an "exit interview" to discuss how the client perceived the case resolution process and any changes they would like to suggest. The conversation also provides an opportunity to explain the kind of referrals the lawyer would appreciate, and offer his services as a resource even if the next problem relates to a different area of law.

---

15. LexisNexis Martindale Hubbell/Wicker Park Group, *Global Client Feedback Initiative*, 2011, p. 30. Seventy-eight percent of US respondents felt that their firms uncovered valuable information about the clients' needs.
16. *Id.*, pp. 27-29.

2.   Send an email survey at the end of the calendar year using one of the online free survey tools to clients served in that year, asking questions about their perceptions of the service, their life since the case, and their willingness to refer the lawyer.

Lawyers engaged in personally traumatic or dramatic legal areas such as divorce, guardianship, family law, personal injury, and medical malpractice can also make it a practice to call the client three to six months after the matter closes to find out how the client is doing and see if they can be a resource in terms of connecting the client to specialists in whatever areas are now important. This reinforces the client's impression that she was more than a number to her lawyer, and at the same time, positions the lawyer as a counsellor to be called when the next legal problem arises.

The formal, annual, scheduled client feedback interview process has four components:

> who to interview
> who to select to be the interviewer
> interview content and structure
> interview follow-up

Select Clients to Interview

Interview clients reflective of where you are now and where you want to be. The choice of clients to interview is very important. "The firm should choose clients key to the existing market position of the firm as well as its desired future."[17] Because of the time investment, it is usually impossible to interview all clients. Typically firms interview three categories of client: foundation clients, future foundation clients, and problem clients with potential.

Firms rarely hold interviews with difficult clients and clients not integral to the firm's growth strategy. However, when these interviews unearth negative perceptions and the attorney corrects the problems, the client becomes engaged and loyal rather than leaving the firm.[18]

---

17. Stephen M. Peterson and Kelly A. Fox, "Focus on Clients," *San Francisco Daily Journal*, November 2, 2001.
18. "Dissatisfied customers whose complaints are taken care of are more likely to remain loyal, and even become advocates, as those that are 'just' customers." Strauss & Seidel reprinted in "50 Facts about Customer Experience," *Return on Behavior Magazine*, October 2010.

Your foundation clients can be indispensable sources of information about your firm's performance. An integral part of building a strong relationship is a frank, but structured, discussion that covers the client's values, goals, and aspirations going forward, and that also evaluates your relationship with them. Consider scheduling these face-to-face meetings annually for the purpose of listening to them.

When interviewing business leaders, it is effective to go to the client's place of business. The choice of venue indicates your interest in knowing more about them and may make your clients feel more relaxed and in control. One managing partner in a corporate law boutique says that he always learns something when he visits the client. For example, when he visits a doctor client and sees the office sign without its "Inc." or "P.C." he knows he needs to alert them to the potential liabilities. Lawyers interviewing individual clients might also want to meet in a neutral space such as a club or restaurant, or at the client's home in order to set the client at ease.

A formal annual interview affords a unique opportunity for feedback and conversation. The structure of the conversation is important; advance preparation is necessary and follow-up is essential. Also, unlike a typical conversation where each participant carries equal weight, in a client interview your client should be doing most of the talking. When you schedule one of these sessions, make it clear that you are not charging for it because it is part of your investment in a valuable client relationship.

Determine Who Should Conduct the Interview

There are two views as to who should conduct the interview: a member of the firm or an outside specialist in executive interviewing. Most firms use someone from the firm; typically the managing partner or chairman of the firm handles the interview, sometimes accompanied by the relationship partner. Sometimes the relationship partner is the interviewer. In some firms, a second person, often the marketing director, accompanies the attorney to take notes. In recent years some firms have hired client relationship managers specifically for the purpose of conducting client interviews.[19]

---

19. In "Calling All Clients: Client Interviewing Weathers Economy," *The Legal Intelligencer*, June 17, 2011, Gina Pasarella cites three firms that have appointed full-time client interviewers.

Another avenue is to hire an outside consultant or survey firm to manage the entire interview process from scheduling to the interview itself, the report write-up, and presentation to the partners. These professionals are skilled, trained interviewers who know how to follow the question guideline (written in conjunction with the firm that hires them) and still pursue interesting conversation sidepaths when they arise.

Having a lead attorney[20] conduct the annual client interview may serve to deepen loyalty as the client perceives the personal investment in the relationship. At the same time it may impede honest evaluations; the client may be reluctant to be candid if the lawyer has become a personal friend. The attorney may be in a better position than an outsider to ask highly specific questions about a particular matter and will certainly have better access to institutional memory about the client's objectives over time and history with the law firm.

A survey of law firms and clients showed that both greatly preferred to have the relationship partner, rather than a managing partner or lawyer not involved in their work conduct the interviews.[21] The interviewer's job is to draw out the client's view of past events, sense of current risks, and vision of future possibilities. Your firm should select the person objectively best prepared to do that.

Structure the Interview

Client interviews are highly structured conversations. The person conducting the interview should be well-prepared, and the entire client team should be ready to assist in the effort.

Use *Form 2.3: Client Interview Preparation*, page 29, to help you research both internal and external situations to provide a starting point for discussion in the interview. You may want to prepare an agenda in advance and ask your client if they wish to add anything. To ensure the interview will be valuable in terms of enriching your relationship, dur-

---

20. See the "client teams" section of Chapter 6 for a discussion of different team roles. "Lead" attorney in this case can refer to either the person managing the relationship or the person managing the work; both will have been intimately involved with the client and various matters.

21. *Financial Times* Report, *supra* note 7. One-third of clients responding to the *Financial Times* Report said they would prefer to provide feedback via informal discussion with a lead partner, as opposed to thirty percent of attorneys. The next most popular option ("structured discussion with a lead partner") was favored by twenty-nine percent of clients, but only sixteen percent of attorneys agreed.

ing the meeting, make sure to tell the client how much you and your colleagues enjoy working with them and how much you value the relationship. Be sure to thank them for taking the time to have this interview conversation.

Follow Up

Make it a point to follow up with your client on issues raised and ideas discussed. After the interview, it is important to follow up with a conversation summary to the client and discussions with the appropriate members of the client team as to next steps. Any remedial actions should be reported to the client. Any changes that will incur billable charges should also be clarified, and if possible, clients should know what the anticipated cost will be. Use *Form 2.4: Client Interview Follow-Up Guide,* page 33, as a guideline for this final step in the annual interview process.

See the following on Leonard Street and Deinard's "Client Conversations" Initiative.

Leonard, Street and Deinard's "Client Conversations" Initiative

In 2009, Leonard, Street and Deinard, a 178-lawyer firm headquartered in Minneapolis, MN, undertook a firm-wide initiative to implement the ACC Value Challenge. They developed a turnkey program called "Client Conversations," designed to increase the number of in-person client interviews. The program included training, an interview implementation toolkit, a way to report outcomes and incentives for participation. The toolkit included talking points for scheduling the interview meeting, key interview questions, conversation best practices (be prepared, asked open-ended questions, listen more, talk less), and the ACC Value Challenge Guidelines ("Meet. Talk. Act.").

Over one hundred client conversations were completed by forty-seven attorneys during a three month period in 2010. Participating attorneys were recognized at an off-site event. "The firm shares that the program is now embedded in the fabric of the firm."[22]

---

22. Jill Weber, "Value Practice Profile," Leonard, Street, and Deinard, *ACC Value Challenge Tool Kit Resource,* October 2010 (http://www.acc.com/advocacy/valuechallenge/toolkit/loader.cfm?csModule=security/getfile&pageid=1176981&page=/valuechallenge/resources/index.cfm&qstring=&title=%26%2339%3BClient%20Conversations%2C%26%2339%3B%20Value%20Billing%20and%20Budget%20Programs%20and%20Alternative%20Task%20Force%20Practices%20at%20Leonard%2C%20Street%20and%20Deinard, accessed December 22, 2011).

Leonard, Street and Deinard's Client Covenant

The covenant, created more than a decade ago, makes five promises to clients:

> We will serve as a seamless extension of your business and its strategy.

> We will understand your business.

> We will communicate effectively.

> We will manage your fees and costs.

> We will request your feedback.

"The Covenant is the firm's pledge to meet the service expectations of its clients . . . [and] is an organizational principle of the firm's culture. . . ."[23]

Know the Difference Between Satisfaction and Loyalty

Most clients are satisfied, but have you ever considered that satisfaction might not be enough to develop the practice you envision? Certainly it is better to have satisfied rather than dissatisfied clients. However, satisfaction is no guarantee that a client will hire you again. Satisfaction is based on past experience, so satisfied clients are susceptible to competitive forces that range from lower pricing to more appealing packaging of services.[24]

By contrast, the concept of *loyalty* embodies emotion, a sense of faithfulness, as compared to *satisfied* which merely connotes approval of the status quo.

> [Loyal clients] believe that one organization's product/service offer remains their best option. . . . A loyal relationship is an exchange. The organization provides the loyal customer with products and services they desire. These loyalty customers consider the product/service offering to be superior to that of the alternatives offered by competing organizations. The more unique it is and the closer it matches to customer needs, the stronger the loyalty relationship with the customer.[25]

---

23. *Id.* See also Leonard, Street and Deinard's "Client Covenant" (http://www.leonard.com/about/client-covenants, accessed December 22, 2011).

24. Numerous market studies have corroborated this. One of the starkest is a 2007 survey by MMResearch for a financial services firm which revealed that, while 90% of its customers professed to be satisfied, 41% of them could be persuaded to switch firms if fees were lower or interest rates higher.

25. The Loyalty Research Center, "What is Customer Loyalty and Loyalty Analysis," 2004–2005, pp. 1–2 (http://mktg.uni-svishtov.bg/ivm/resources/Customer%20Loyalty%20Measurement.pdf, accessed December 22, 2011).

In 2007, the Gallup organization began promoting what it called a "customer engagement" metric and pegged it to projections of a business's financial performance.[26] According to further studies from Gallup, an organization's top tier of customer (what they call "fully engaged") spent forty-six percent more money than those who were merely satisfied. What accounts for the difference? Gallup describes this top tier customer as "emotionally engaged and rationally loyal."[27]

Steve Jobs, founder and CEO of Apple Computer, was a loyalty lodestar. His goal was to give people what they would want—what they desired but couldn't express—and in return they adored him. His ability to envision the desires that consumers were unable to articulate created Apple's raving, engaged fans who promote and defend their chosen brand.

> "Jobs' cause was us—the people—consumers and users of the technologies of computing, communication and connection. . . . [When he pushed employees to be great] he was acting not only as a mercurial visionary, but as one of history's greatest consumer advocates. . . . And he created unprecedented loyalty in doing so.[28]

Loyalty has an emotional component—part need, part expectation, part inchoate desires. It is this emotion that creates the positive tie with you and your firm. At the satisfied level, clients are still focused on a firm's features and immediate benefits. As clients continue to be satisfied with their lawyer's performance and results, they begin to see the advantages—professional and personal, physical and emotional—of continuing to develop their relationship. This commitment, an emotional attachment reinforcing the rational decision to hire,[29] creates loyal clients.

$$\text{Quality (service} \times \text{results)} + \frac{\text{Value}}{\text{Time}} = \text{Loyalty}$$

Diagram 2.4: The Loyalty Equation

26. An overview of this metric and its applications is available on Gallup's Web site: (http://www.gallup .com/consulting/49/customer-engagement.aspx, accessed December 22, 2011).
27. Id.
28. Jim Sullivan, "What Steve Jobs Taught Us About Loyalty," *Return on Behavior Magazine*, October 17, 2011. See also "Stop Listening to Customers . . . Sometimes," experiencematters blog, August 29, 2011 (http://experiencematters.wordpress.com/2011/08/29/stop-listening-to-customers-sometimes/, accessed December 22, 2011).
29. "75% of the purchasing decision is based on emotion." In Nadji Tehrani, "Loyalty Marketing . . . Because Companies Live Or Die By Repeat Business," *Telemarketing*, November 1995, p. 2.

$$\frac{\text{Features + Benefits}}{\text{Time}} = \text{Value}$$

Diagram 2.5: The Value Equation

Features plus benefits when built on a platform of individualized service for foundation clients and their counterparts create a value that forms a bond between the attorney and the client. In a client-centric firm this one-to-one relationship expands out to include multiple players at both the client and the law firm.

As the relationship expands and deepens, the combination of service, process, and results creates a value that over time creates a loyal client.

Loyal clients are the backbone of a law firm's business. These are the repeat players who turn again and again to "their" firm for strategic advice from their trusted advisor, or for help with a specific problem. Loyal clients recommend their lawyer to colleagues, family, and friends. Loyal clients contribute to a firm's growth and the lawyer's own practice in a number of ways:

> They are more enjoyable to work with because you have created a strong working relationship with them and enjoy the legal issues they ask you to resolve.
> The relationship itself becomes more effective and efficient as both parties acclimate themselves to working together.
> They yield more profit to your firm because they provide recurring business, and often pay higher fees because of the complexity of the issues presented.
> Depth of client presumes the ability to cross-sell appropriate services to meet needs as they are uncovered; and when trying these new services, loyal clients tend to have less price sensitivity than merely satisfied clients.
> They will be open to opportunities to work with you again.
> They make requests, rather than demands, on your time and expertise.
> They are less likely to be upset by minor mistakes.
> They recommend you to their friends and associates. In the online social network world they are your WOM (word of mouth) advocates.

As with any extended effort, there are also costs involved:

> financial—management and technology investments required by these clients
> intangible—the nonbillable hours spent to maintain the relationship
> structural—the client's requests for certain personnel and specific approaches to practice

It makes sense to focus efforts on the foundation clients that will grow the firm in the direction you want to go.[30]

The combination of a rational reason for a client to place confidence in a professional and a genuine interpersonal relationship between client and attorney is very powerful.[31] The commitment goes both ways. In a client-centric firm you have chosen to create a culture and process that caters to clients' needs and preferences. As you deepen your relationships, you will need to continue to develop practice tools that reinforce the benefits and value your firm offers these clients.

Forms

Form 2.1: Features and Benefits Matrix

Use the form below to list all of the features of your practice, the benefits a client may gain from each feature, and specific benefits that particular clients received as a result of that feature. List even the benefits that seem obvious. A feature might be that you have litigated product liability cases related to automotive parts for twenty years. So the benefits to automotive manufacturers and distributors include industry knowledge, case knowledge, trial expertise, and such. Other examples of benefits to a particular client include:

> How does having offices in the same cities as client 'x' benefit the client?
> What advantages have your seasoned negotiating skills offered client 'y'?
> How has your industry knowledge helped client 'z' implement a mergers and acquisitions program?

---

30. See John Atkinson, "Eight Steps to Client Loyalty" for a client loyalty/profitability matrix. (http://www.lawmarketing.com/pages/articles.asp?Action=Article&ArticleID=126, accessed December 22, 2011).
31. In *Relationship Marketing* (John Wiley & Sons Canada Ltd., 1998), Ian Gordon went so far as to state, "Relationships are the only real asset of the enterprise . . . . A relationship . . . provides the company with long-term, lower risk revenues and the opportunity to grow both revenue and profit in many ways."

Features of your practice	General benefits	Benefits obtained by specific clients you may want to reference when you discuss your work

Form 2.2: Your Value Proposition

This two-part form will help you develop a working value statement. The first section is a self-assessment of your own approach to client service. The second part consists of a two part exercise to help you untangle the value proposition from the service and results you provide. The conclusions you form at the end of the exercise should become part of an "elevator pitch" and be broadcast throughout the firm as a "motto" to help all personnel stay focused on why you are in business.

Part 1: Self assessment: Complete the assessment below considering how you generally function while handling matters for clients. Be as critical and honest with yourself as you can. Insert statements relevant to your particular practice in the two blank spaces.

My approach to my work and my client service (words in parentheses are the benefits associated with the activity)	Proactively	Consistently	Usually	Infrequently	Never		
Bill within parameters established with the client (cost-conscious/efficient).	❑	❑	❑	❑	❑		
Respond to telephone and email inquiries within two to three hours. (responsive).	❑	❑	❑	❑	❑		
Anticipate issues and propose solutions (proactive/creative).	❑	❑	❑	❑	❑		
Understand the client's industry and market challenges (industry expertise/global context).	❑	❑	❑	❑	❑		

My approach to my work and my client service (words in parentheses are the benefits associated with the activity)	Proactively	Consistently	Usually	Infrequently	Never		
Understand the client's goals, needs and concerns (relevant/act as an advisor).	❏	❏	❏	❏	❏		
Develop legal strategies that are appropriate to the level of urgency the client places on the matter (goal/process).	❏	❏	❏	❏	❏		
Respect the client's personal, emotional responses to a situation. (empathic).	❏	❏	❏	❏	❏		
Add other characteristics that you want to include in your value statement.	❏	❏	❏	❏	❏		

> Statements rated "proactively" or "consistently" indicate values you offer your clients.

> Statements rated "usually" indicate immediate opportunities to develop additional value.

> Statements rated "infrequently" or "never" indicate longer-term opportunities to develop additional value, or elements that are unlikely to form part of your value proposition.

Part 2: Tangible values: Rank the tangible values list below in numerical order, from most to least relevant for your practice. On the blank lines, add tangible values germane to your work that are not already listed.

Rank	Benefits
	Minimize risk
	Take advantage of opportunities
	Eliminate problems
	Increase the worth of assets

Rank	Benefits
	Add revenue

Part 3: The working value proposition: Take the top two tangible values from Part 2 and combine them with your best three service features from Part 1. (For example: I manage risks and help my clients increase the worth of assets. My approach to my work is cost-effective, creative, and relevant).

I work with my clients to [first tangible value] and [second tangible value]. My approach to my work is [first service feature], [second service feature], and [third service feature].

Form 2.3: Client Interview Preparation

Use this form to help you prepare for and conduct annual interviews with your foundation clients.

Part I: *Preparation*

1. Review of matter(s) handled since last in-person meeting:
    a. Areas/measures where previous matter(s) went well from the client's perspective:

    _____

    _____

    b. Areas/measures where you did not meet client's expectations on previous matter(s):

    _____

    _____

    c. Changes you made to meet client's expectations

    _____

    _____

2. Current client-related news:
    a. Major stories impacting client's industry:

    _____

    _____

    b. Major stories regarding client's growth, plans, or financial health:

    _____

    _____

c.   Stories involving legal issues, client's use of other law firms:

_____

_____

Part II: Revisiting Prior Matters

> Plan to discuss those areas or measures that went especially well or poorly on matters handled since your previous client interview.
>   ○ Also note any follow-up from the last meeting.
> Review your service against the client's service-related requests and the service performance standards you implemented for the engagement.
> Typical questions about your ongoing relationship include:
>   ○ What did you see as the strengths and weaknesses when we worked together on our last matter?
>   ○ Are there any changes you would like in the team, the work process, or our invoicing practices?
>   ○ What benefits have you seen from working with our firm?
>   ○ What value do you think our firm provides? How could we add more value?
>   ○ Did our firm meet or exceed your expectation? If not, how can we improve in this regard?
>   ○ How can our firm help you move forward with your concerns?
>   ○ What do you know about our other capabilities?
>   ○ Could you introduce us to _____?
> Consider asking context-focused, work-related questions:[32]
>   ○ What legal work is now being done by outside counsel?
>   ○ Who makes the decision as to which firm to use?
>   ○ If there were one thing our firm could do to deepen your relationship with us, what would it be?
>   ○ What is the general image you and your colleagues have regarding our firm? How do we compare to our competitors?

---

32. See *ACC Value Challenge*, "Meet. Talk. Act" questions to discuss with in-house counsel (http://www.acc.com/advocacy/valuechallenge/toolkit/upload/VC-Meet-Talk-Act.pdf, accessed December 22, 2011). See also, David Maister, "Questionnaire for Client Feedback," (http://davidmaister.com/index.php?nav=resources&data1=20&data2=36, accessed December 22, 2011), and William J. Flannery, Jr., "20 Questions You Should Ask Current and Prospective Clients," *Texas Lawyer*, September 23, 1991.

Snapshot	Poor	Fair	Neutral	Good	Excellent	Notes/Follow-Up
Demonstrated understanding of objectives and expectations.	❏	❏	❏	❏	❏	
Was appropriately communicative and responded in a timely manner.	❏	❏	❏	❏	❏	
Brought legal expertise to bear effectively.	❏	❏	❏	❏	❏	
Client team members worked well with their in-house counterparts.	❏	❏	❏	❏	❏	
Client team members were responsive.	❏	❏	❏	❏	❏	
Budgeted and billed appropriately.	❏	❏	❏	❏	❏	
Managed matter timeline efficiently.	❏	❏	❏	❏	❏	
Delivered desired results.	❏	❏	❏	❏	❏	
Other:	❏	❏	❏	❏	❏	
Other:	❏	❏	❏	❏	❏	

Part III: Client's Aspirations, Goals, Etc.: One way to structure the conversation about your clients' goals, opportunities, and concerns is to use a variation of the SWOT (Strengths/Weaknesses/Opportunities/Threats) analysis covered in Chapter 5 (see below). Questions keyed to your SWOT assessment could include:

> What do you see as the major trends in your industry landscape in the next year or so?
> Are there new competitors that will impact the way your business operates?
> What opportunities do these developments pose to your company?
> What risks do you see as most important during the next year?
> How might we help you prepare to meet these opportunities or risks?

Abbreviated SWOT Analysis

Area	Opportunities	Threats	Steps Needed to Prepare
Client's Industry Landscape • Competitors • Industry trends • Global problems			
Client—External View • Geographic expansion • Product/service expansion			
Client—Internal View • Personnel issues • Finance issues			
Legal Needs • Pending matters • Anticipated matters • Budget/investment • Selection criteria			
Client relationships • Changes in personnel • Key people involved in new initiatives			

Direct Questions Approach: Use news items about the company, the locations, and the industry as lead-ins to discuss current activities and future plans. Make sure you do not ask your client for information that could have been obtained from the news, the company Web site, or other readily-available sources. Typical open-ended questions include:

> Are you satisfied with how your business is doing?
> What are the most important factors affecting [line of business] next year?
> What do you see as major opportunities for next year? Major obstacles?
> Where do you think growth will come from?
> Has your competitive situation changed in any way this year? Are you expecting any changes next year?
> Will the structure of the company change in the next one to two years? If so, in what way?

Part IV: *A strong finish: Note here anything your client wanted to discuss that was not on your agenda, along with opportunities you want to pursue or strategic ideas you have concerning expanding the relationship.*

_____
_____
_____
_____
_____
_____

Discuss the best way to move forward on specific issues such as:

> Performance issues related to previous matters
> An issue or opportunity raised during the SWOT analysis
> A point made during the discussion of your services

Form 2.4: Client Interview Follow-up Guide

A prompt follow-up and thank you for the time is the usual next step. You may also want to include specifics related to the interview in the follow-up, such as:

> Discuss performance issues from previous matters. Explain how you plan to address those issues going forward and solicit feedback about whether the issue has been corrected to the client's satisfaction.
> Review educational pieces or news items related to any industry or enterprise trends you discussed, along with your sense of how that might affect your client.

> Offer further thoughts about how you can add value in to the discussion of risks or opportunities.
> Propose how you plan to implement 'next steps' such as responses to specific questions or requests for information left open at the conclusion of your meeting.

A well-positioned follow-up is one of the strongest signals you can send that you are committed to the relationship—and to your client's success.

CHAPTER 3

Master Communication Techniques to Build a Client-Centric Practice

Communication is the essence of legal practice, whether it involves conferring with a client, speaking to a jury, or resolving a problem in a mediation forum. The ABA's *Model Rules of Professional Conduct* are essentially a catalogue of the responsibilities lawyers have to communicate with their clients, protect the confidentiality of client communications, and represent clients truthfully and honestly to the best of their ability. Communication is the instrument that builds a positive professional experience.

Credibility is the foundation of good lawyering; judges expect it when lawyers argue before them, juries rely on it when they are balancing the future of your client, and your clients depend on it when you tell them that this is the best information available at the time. Each communication transaction is a building block of integrity, and every one that is not credible, authentic, or truthful tears away at that essential foundation of a lawyer's practice.

The number one reason clients leave a law firm usually centers around communication issues: "they don't understand me," "they didn't do what I wanted," and most often "they don't return phone calls on time."[1] This is a typical customer reaction to poor service. A recent survey found that eighty-two percent of U.S. consumers said they stopped doing business with an organization due to a poor customer service experience, and seventy-nine percent "said they blabbed about the negative customer experiences in public and amongst friends."[2]

---

1. This has consistently been true for at least the last decade. See Marci Krufka, "Corporate Legal Officers Have Spoken . . . Are Law Firms Listening?" *Report to Legal Management*, Altman Weil, 2003 (http://www.altmanweil.com/dir_docs/resource/9b161425-6d12-4c8f-820f-9195c49b1764_document.pdf, accessed December 22, 2011). BTI surveys corroborate these views.
2. Lora Kolodny, "Study: 82% of U.S. Consumers Bail On Brands After Bad Customer Service," October 13, 2010 (http://techcrunch.com/2010/10/13/customer-service-rightnow/, accessed December 22, 2011).

Intangible communications such as empathy, personal chemistry, and working style compatibility are the building blocks of successful lawyer-client relationships. Of course, they vary with each client, each lawyer, each matter, and each firm. These intangibles are communicated through both actions and words, but often the impact of a firm's or a lawyer's communication style goes unnoticed. Communication disconnects reflect this reality: few firms or attorneys take the time to really analyze how they communicate, create a communication policy in their firm, and establish a personal communication protocol that focuses on what is important to their client base.

Grasp the Whole Picture: 360° Communication

Diagram 3.1 illustrates the concept of 360° communication—a concept that encompasses the full range of information-sharing relationships from one-on-one talks with a client to supporting the client's own marketing and sales efforts through joint marketing activities. In this chapter we focus on four areas:

1. an expanded definition of the standard one-on-one relationship between an individual lawyer and his client
2. professionalism as a component of communication
3. technology-enhanced communication initiatives that facilitate knowledge sharing, contact management, and billing statements
4. client-lawyer reciprocity in terms of shared marketing initiatives and mutual referrals

COMMUNICATION IS THE KEYSTONE OF CLIENT-CENTRICITY

Client service is an intangible that becomes real to the client as it takes place. As you and your client work together, the way you treat your client and your ability to explain legal options in language the client understands will either create a strong relationship or destroy one. Attorneys can use discussions with the client to set clients' expectations of the legal process and both the desired and possible result options. Clients, for their part, compare your treatment of them and their situation to their own approach to client service and their experience with other service

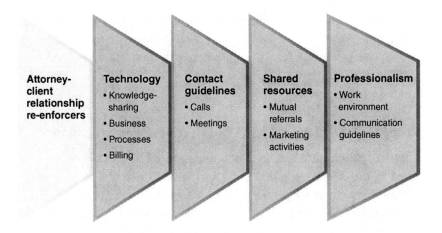

Attorney-client relationship re-enforcers	Technology	Contact guidelines	Shared resources	Professionalism
	• Knowledge-sharing	• Calls	• Mutual referrals	• Work environment
	• Business	• Meetings	• Marketing activities	• Communication guidelines
	• Processes			
	• Billing			

Diagram 3.1: Aspects of 360° Communication

providers. Communication becomes a key component in their evaluation of their attorney and the success of the relationship.

"Very little in life is as disconcerting as being involved in a lawsuit. . . ."[3] David Maister draws an analogy between service provided by a lawyer and a car mechanic.[4] For both, the potential client may be unable to judge the technical expertise of the service provider, worried about the appropriate solution and its cost, and anxious for a quick resolution. The client's perception of service excellence comes to rest more heavily "on the quality of service rather than the quality of work. Because of the ambiguity that surrounds technical excellence (and the difficulty the client has in appraising it), the personal relationship between the client and the provider takes on great significance. . . ."[5]

Lawyers working with in-house counsel presume that the emotional part of the equation is less relevant because both parties are legal professionals. Yet, in-house attorneys often hire expensive famous firms even while requesting cost reductions because they can fall back on that firm's reputation should something go awry. This protective rationalization has a large emotional component. Focusing on the emotional component,

---

3. Stephen E. Schemenauer, "What We've Got Here . . . is a Failure . . . to Communicate: A Statistical Analysis of the Nation's Most Common Ethical Complaint," 30 *HAMLINE L. REV.* 619, Summer 2007, p. 631.
4. David Maister, *Professional Service Firm Management*, 5th ed., Maister Associates, 1992, p. 65–66.
5. *Id.*

a rainmaker partner discussing relationships with in-house counsel said: "People do business with people they like. Personality and services are the keys to creating a relationship where the client likes you and feels comfortable calling you. Clients need to feel you are an advisor and not just a document person."

Recognize the Characteristics of Effective Communication

Effective communication is the foundation of the relationship outlined in the ABA's *Model Rules of Professional Conduct*.[6] The bedrock of the attorney-client relationship is an association of equals who agree together on a course of action. The lawyer is charged with educating the client as the matter evolves so that the well-informed client can participate in key decisions. "Rule 1.4 and the comments that follow emphasize the attorney's multi-faceted role as advisor, consultant, and agent of the client, providing guidelines for ensuring good attorney-client communications."[7]

Model Rule 1.4a [3] prescribes the level of information as appropriate to a "comprehending and responsible adult." The level of information appropriate for a general counsel and the victim of a hit and run accident may be worlds apart. The attentive lawyer will adjust the amount of detail needed to keep the client informed. He will consider variables such as the legal process itself, the amount of time available in which to make the decision, the client's familiarity with legal issues and prior legal experience, and the amount of involvement the client wants to have.

As stated in Model Rule 1.4a [5], "the guiding principle is that the lawyer should fulfill reasonable client expectations for information consistent with the duty to act in the client's best interests, and the client's overall requirements as to the character of representation."

Open communication builds the trust relationship at the center of the client-lawyer relationship. Trust builds through the small daily activities and office procedures that demonstrate each attorney's unique

---

6. Relevant *Rules* are excerpted in Appendix 1. The complete *Rules* can be found online at http://www.americanbar.org/groups/professional_responsibility/publications/model_rules_of_professional_conduct/model_rules_of_professional_conduct_table_of_contents.html, accessed December 22, 2011. The *Model Rules*, adopted by the ABA House of Delegates in 1983, form the basis of most state ethics rules. Many states have added ethical restrictions and client service standards or rules of professionalism that also apply to lawyers admitted to practice in the specific state.
7. Stephen E. Schemenauer, *supra* note 3, p. 649.

approach to client service. These can be as seemingly unimportant as the amount of lapsed time between a client call and your response, or as large as the decision to settle or litigate a bet-the-company dispute.

Emotion is a fundamental component of the attorney-client relationship, paving the way to commitment, trust, loyalty, and continued business. One managing partner calls it "simple math. Understanding leads to trust which leads to efficiency because you know what the client needs which leads to profitability." The communicator-attorney will show empathy, concern, and an awareness of the sensitivities, emotions, and politics that complicate the client's situation—from a general counsel's role in a major merger to a father's role in a nasty divorce. Clients want their attorney to smooth the worries, absorb the hassles, and teach them not to be afraid.

The managing partner of a fifty-attorney firm explains that "the key requirement to build business is empathy. The client needs to feel that the connection to them is not just about money, that you see them as more than a revenue source and take their case seriously. You need to show them you are with them for the long haul—you are looking for a relationship, not a matter."

The managing partner of a small firm says that the basis of a relationship is "connectivity. It doesn't happen overnight. It means getting to know your client as a person. You need to invest the time to know the person behind the title. Trust comes from understanding who your client really is."

A real estate lawyer says his clients place a high value on four aspects of service: "responsiveness, advocacy for them, quick turnarounds, and judgment as to what is important and what isn't."

Lawyers can demonstrate these sensitivities by paying careful attention to the language and tone of their communications. Sometimes it's just a matter of attitude. When clients' calls are viewed as an opportunity to cement a relationship, then the attorney who smiles as he says "hello" projects an attitude of friendliness and accessibility, and makes the client feel special.

A key part of effective communication involves thinking ahead about what the client will need. This is both a mindset and a timing issue. A corporate attorney says, "I don't want a client to call to remind me of something left undone or late. I want to be ahead, be faster than they need."

Understanding the clients' objectives and worldview allows the attorney to anticipate obstacles of importance to them. Suggesting alternatives while there is still time to respond will position the lawyer as a valued advisor working for and with the client. For example, while visiting a client to review their pension plan, a partner initiated a conversation about how the owners, both in their 60s, wanted to handle succession planning. A far-ranging discussion led to a subsequent meeting with the owners' accountant, and the firm is now drafting the company's succession plan.

View Client Complaints as an Opportunity

The most common complaint against attorneys is the failure to communicate with clients, a violation of Model Rule 1.4 which establishes the attorney's obligations vis-à-vis clients.[8] In 2006 the Maryland Attorney Grievance Commission reported that twenty-two percent of its cases arose from a lack of diligence or communication.[9]

Not only do unhappy clients leave; they will vent to friends. "A dissatisfied customer will tell between nine and fifteen people about their experience. . . . Happy customers who get their issue resolved tell about four to six people about their experience."[10] When clients call to express concerns or complain, consider their willingness to vent as a demonstration of the strength of the relationship and address the issues in a positive manner. Sometimes the complaint is prelude to a negotiation on the size of the bill or an unexpected rebuff from opposing counsel. Often unexpected silence on the part of a client suggests the need to probe for problems.

Complaints and misunderstandings call for active listening skills which focus on the client's verbal and non-verbal communication. By controlling your own response and staying positive, you can defuse the situation and guide the client toward an amicable resolution. For example, when a firm's partner learned that his staff person had failed to meet the deadlines of a referred client after the referral source complained to him about it, he took immediate remedial action and saved his relation-

---

8. *Id.* pp. 646–649, 655.
9. Robert Zaniel, "How to Keep Your Clients from Turning Against You," CLE video (http://learn.lawline.com/video/what-are-the-most-common-complaints-about-lawyers/, accessed December 22, 2011).
10. Attributed to the White House Office of Consumer Affairs in James Digby, "50 Facts about Customer Experience," *Return on Behavior Magazine*, October 2010.

ship with the client and the referral source. See the following on active listening below.

The Art of "Active Listening"

Effective communication begins with paying attention. With all the client demands on an attorney's time, it is very easy to concentrate on the urgent and ignore less pressing matters. When meeting or speaking with a client, try to exclude distractions. Make it a point to tell the client that you will turn off your phone and ask your staff not to interrupt you unless absolutely necessary.

There are two reasons for this. First, such interruptions send a powerful, unspoken signal that you do not regard the client as important. Your client may not consciously register the interruption when it first happens, but your lack of client focus will create an underlying doubt about whether you care about him. If it happens repeatedly, that doubt can grow until it undermines your ability to become a trusted advisor to your client. An advisor who cannot be relied upon to listen carefully and completely ultimately will be called upon only for his technical expertise.

Second, interruptions make it harder to pay attention to the unspoken, physical, and emotional communications that accompany the spoken conversation. Regardless of the circumstances, the spoken words convey only a fragment of the story. Attending to the whole picture requires the use of "active listening." This is more subtle, but if you are a litigator you understand the need to focus in on the full body communication and listen for what is being conveyed but not said. Interruptions disturb your ability to fully comprehend all the various elements of the client's narratives.

Keep in mind that interruptions are not only external. Your professional training taught you to be a highly focused problem-solver. As your clients speak, you may need to guard against a well-learned tendency to formulate actionable solutions too quickly. The following pattern may be familiar to you:

> Your client begins to describe a situation or matter to you.

> While your client is speaking, your mind leaps ahead to the legal implications and begins to consider what you can do to help.

> As soon as the client finishes or pauses you begin asking a quick series of questions or presenting your analysis of the situation.

> Your client responds.

> While your client is responding, you are already working out the next segment of your strategy.

> The last two items repeat until the conversation reaches some conclusion.

This pattern shows a strong bias toward action and may seem an effective use of time to some clients who appreciate a "take charge" attitude. On the other hand, paying more attention to next steps than to your client's message—both spoken and unspoken—can interfere with your opportunity to develop a fuller understanding of your client's concerns. With a more complete understanding of the whole situation you may want to develop a more comprehensive solution. Shortcutting the discussion also denies both of you an opening for further development of your relationship.

Imagine a different approach. Suppose that your client comes in and begins to speak about the matter she wants you to handle. Instead of merely presenting a fact pattern, she seems to want to present you with the whole story, nicely polished. To get the most from the conversation, you might adopt the following steps:

> Allow a few seconds between the time your client finishes speaking and the time you begin to speak.

> Restate what you thought you heard and wait for agreement.

> Ask a few probing questions to make sure you have all the information you need.

> Ask if your client wants your help and ask permission, if she does, to discuss potential courses of action. (Sometimes clients don't want to hear a legal answer, particularly if the recommended option will be expensive to implement.)

> Identify possible courses of action.

The "active listening" approach completely changes the conversation and positions you as a strategist, advisor, and confidante instead of a technical problem solver.

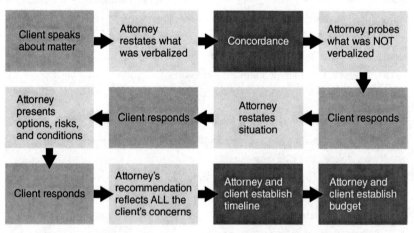

Diagram 3.2: An "Active Listening" Conversation

Understand Client Communication Preferences

A communications maxim says it is the communicator's responsibility to ensure that the message is received. How do you do that in an effective way when you—and your clients—are so busy? Ground rules can be helpful. Three areas are particularly important: communication preferences, client involvement, and responsiveness.

Determine Each Client's Preferred Communication Method

You almost certainly have a favorite communication tool—one that suits your style, personality, and work habits. Your clients do, too. Some will concentrate only in face-to-face meetings; others prefer the immediacy of their mobile phones; and still others want to read details at their leisure. Some prefer to read traditional documents and memoranda; some like email summaries. Some value the instantaneous nature of text messages, while others find them off-putting or inaccessible.

An easy way to ensure successful communication is to ask clients how they prefer to be contacted. For example, one national litigation counsel sends a general counsel he works with "short, sweet emails" requesting a few minutes for a phone call. With another in-house counsel, he combines meetings and social activities: "We brought up and disposed of more important issues at Yankee games than anywhere else."

Establish communication preferences early in the client dialogue. Ask your clients what they prefer:

> What is your preferred point of contact—office number, direct line, fax, mobile phone, email, mail, text message?
> What is your preferred time to receive communications?
> Is it important to you to have your attorney's personal phone numbers?
> Do you want to be called on evenings or weekends?
> For meetings, do you prefer in-person meetings, video conferences, Skype, or phone conference calls?

This discussion is also a good time to let the client know if she will or will not be billed for quick questions in emails or calls.

Asking about communication preferences does not imply that you always will be able to follow the guidelines. Obviously, if you are in court when they call or, conversely, if you need to speak to them immediately regarding a new development, your call may not fit within the guidelines. However, by asking these questions you are establishing the groundwork for a collegial relationship of equals in which each person plays her assigned role: the attorney as the legal expert in charge of execution of the client's wishes; the client as the final decision-maker regarding an acceptable resolution of the case.

This courtesy can be extended beyond clients to colleagues and others in your business network. Attorneys who work together regularly can set these ground rules. Associates can make similar agreements with the partners they work for. Solo practitioners who use an answering service can give instructions to tell callers when they will be available. Solos can also put a message on their phones that explains when they will pick up these messages and when they will return the calls. The purpose in all these situations is to use rules to smooth the edges of interpersonal relationships.

Use *Form 3.1: Communication Preferences Checklist*, page 69, to record the preferences, and note the date of agreement and dates when the plan is modified.

Concur on the Degree of Client Involvement in Matter Decisions

Another key aspect of the attorney-client relationship is the degree of client involvement in matter decisions. Clients want you to listen to them, respect their input, and allow them to be an important part of the process. Of course, at the same time, some clients hand off all the details and responsibility to the attorney. So, ask your client, "What level of involvement do you want?" Is the client comfortable delegating most decisions to you or is he interested in every detail of the matter? Have you had initial discussions that explained the legal course of action and set the client's expectations as to the various activities and time frames relevant to his matter?

Sometimes a client tells his attorney to move forward on an issue and handle everything, but changes his mind midway. To prevent this kind of situation, a New York–based patent attorney likes to give clients advance notice of important actions: "Opposing counsel has asked for an extension, and I am going to give it to them in accordance with the way we agreed to handle the matter unless I hear otherwise from you."

Part of the initial conversations might include questions designed to ascertain the client's psychological approach to problems and problem-solving. Legal issues are often stressful for clients because of the potential for unanticipated situations and the business or personal impact of the case. Questions to consider include:

> Does the client respond to action requests within a reasonable timeframe?
> Does the client have reasonable expectations about the matter—its options, timings, and outcome?
> How does the client respond to your ideas and approach?
> How well does the client evaluate and tolerate risk?

Be Responsive

A frequent cause for misunderstandings and dissatisfaction between client and attorney is over the question of promptness. One person may think a call returned within twenty-four hours is timely, while another thinks two hours is too long. Ask clients how they handle response time in their own businesses. Explain how you integrate callbacks into your work schedule. Then draft an agreement that sets out when you will return calls and emails, and who in your office will handle the client's questions if you are not available. Return to *Form 3.1: Communication Preferences Checklist* to note these preferences.

Clients know that their attorney works on multiple matters simultaneously, so a failure to respond within their definition of promptness is often seen as a sign that their matter is less important to the attorney. For some clients the decision to hire a lawyer underscores the importance of the matter; for others it means giving away some of their control in order to get the issue settled. Whatever the reasons for turning to an attorney, clients parse your behavior for signals that you know it is their time and money.

Initiating a communications ground-rules discussion and setting communication guidelines positions you as a reliable communicator who will accommodate your service posture to meet the work habits and preferences of your client.

Assess Communication Content and Style

Although many people suggest that good communication practices boil down to accessibility and availability—e.g., answer your phone—the content of the communication is equally important. The content and purpose of your interactions need to be focused on the client's objectives and be relevant to his issues.

Clear communication involves a translation process from the terminology of legalese to English. Clients want language that is practical, jargon-free, and solution-driven. Speaking laymen's language while focusing on their concerns creates forward-thinking conversations about how and when the client will act on the advice given.

Sometimes when attorneys are using legal terms of art the client doesn't fully understand the implications. This can raise later issues when work has to be redone, or the client has unreasonable expectations because he did not understand the legal situation. You can check the client's assumptions by asking him what he understands about the process, the goals, and his role in it. This gives the attorney an opportunity to correct misunderstandings, avoid future roadblocks, and at the same time, create a more harmonious relationship with the client. A frank exchange of views at the beginning of an assignment can avoid misunderstandings as the case unfolds.

Ensure Informed Consent

Model Rule 2.1 states "the lawyer must make reasonable efforts to ensure that the client or other person possesses information reasonably adequate to make an informed decision." Client conversations may cover the specific facts and circumstances of the situation, but they might also include advice concerning bigger picture issues. (See Appendix 1, Model Rule 2.1) The key question in proactive advice is whether it is in the client's best interests to acquire information that, while relevant to the situation, may be disquieting in regard to potential risks, unpleasant facts, and uncomfortable alternatives.

While the attorney, as expert, controls the legal process, he is required to consult with the client regarding the means to attain the agreed-upon ends. According to Model Rule 1.2, the attorney should abide by a client's decisions regarding:

> the purpose and objectives of the representation
> the means by which the objectives are pursued
> whether to settle a civil matter
> the kind of plea to enter, the question of waiving a jury trial, and whether the client will testify in a criminal case
> authorized expense parameters
> impact on other people who might be adversely affected

Clients normally defer to their lawyer on technical questions and issues of law. Sometimes they disagree. They then need to work it out or end the representation. For example, a litigator was approached by a businessman to handle a dispute with a bank over debt. The businessman felt the bank was totally in the wrong and wanted a broadly-based set of allegations filed immediately. It was important for him to see some action because he was worried, angry, and losing sleep over the situation. The lawyer, taking a more reasoned, calm approach, wanted to pursue some fact-finding and discovery to corroborate the facts. They parted ways. The businessman said, "I don't agree with your approach," and hired someone else who would follow his direction.

Create Opportunities for Communication

Updates

The ABA *Model Rules* say lawyers should keep the "client reasonably informed about the status of the matter." Model Rule 1.4 requires that a lawyer act with reasonable diligence and promptness in terms of relevant communications, not only because they may affect the legal situation, but also because unreasonable delay may lead to increased client anxiety and potentially undermine the client's confidence and trust in the lawyer. Busy lawyers often forget to make time to stay in touch. Avoid this by scheduling call times during work on a matter. Set a time to talk every week just to check-in with the client. Set aside a time every day to connect with inactive clients and far-flung colleagues. Point the call to their ballpark by asking, "How's your business?" or "What's new in your business?"

Some attorneys think the act of calling is a nice thing to do to stay top of mind. Others think that unless it is relevant to the client, it will be a waste of time for two busy people. A recent trend is to email or text someone you want to talk to, asking if they would like to take a call, and if so, when would be a convenient time. Rather than just intruding on someone else's day, this approach is both courteous and sensitive to their schedule.

Communicating comes naturally when you are working actively on the client's matter. Consider the client's perception when long lapses occur due to circumstances beyond your control. To keep the client tuned in during such a hiatus, call just to remind them of the reason for the lull—perhaps you are waiting for the other side to respond to a query, or a court date has been postponed. Status update calls are gracious and courteous, but more importantly, they solidify the client relationship by reaffirming the importance of the matter even in the absence of activity. Such calls are welcomed by most clients because they ease the anxiety of waiting.

In-Person Communications

Some occasions suggest an in-person meeting rather than a call, text, email, or even a written note. "It's easiest to influence when we're together. . . . email is one dimensional, phone two dimensional, meetings three dimensional. . . . Enthusiasm is contagious when we're face-to-face."[11]

The point is to show clients that in a service world they always come first. There are many ways to do this:

> Invite new clients to join you and your legal team for a welcome lunch.
> Meet on a regular basis during an engagement just to touch base about the client's world—what's happening both at work and home.
> Celebrate the end of a matter with a social activity.
> Call a few weeks after a matter is settled to see how everything worked out.
> Between matters, drop by to say hello when you are in the neighborhood, or share a social occasion.
> Visit the client in their home or office between engagements. Use the opportunity to schedule a client loyalty interview focused on their

11. Alan Weiss, "In Case You Were Wondering What I Was Thinking. . . . ," *Alan's Blog* (http://www.contrarianconsulting.com/2011/11/page/2/, accessed December 22, 2011).

objectives and concerns and also their relationship with your firm and you.

> Support the client's charitable interests whenever possible by buying a program ad or a table, or joining them for their fund-raiser event.

> Ask how your client documents its internal policies, procedures, and guidelines. If any of the work you have done for your client impacts how the company's employees perform their jobs, propose outlining guidelines for that specific area. If appropriate, do a complimentary preventive audit.

Courtesy

Positive communication is the sum of little things. One "little thing" that is often overlooked is courtesy. It is important to thank clients for their business, thank referral sources for their assistance, and thank colleagues for helping you improve your service to clients. The most appreciated thank-you note today is the old-fashioned handwritten kind that shows you took the time to write. Courteous service includes making life easier for clients:

> Give clients an office directory with everyone's direct dial numbers and email addresses so they have easy access to whomever they need in the firm—include support staff.

> Instruct others who answer your phone to always give their name when they answer, e.g., "Hello, this is Linda, John's assistant. He is in a meeting, may I help you?"

> Send an anniversary card on the anniversary of the day someone first became your client.

Convey Professionalism in Every Communication

The first impression of a person occurs within seven seconds of meeting her. You want to be sure everything about your practice sends the message you want to send. You need to consider how you dress, how your staff present themselves, the look and feel of your office environment. The attitudes and demeanor of the attorneys and staff, and the office environment must be professional.

The client-centric firm should create and publicize a set of communication standards that govern all staff and attorney interactions with clients. The purpose is to create a foundation of mutual expectations as the basis for the relationship. One way to communicate client-centricity is to hand every new client a copy of the firm's standards and their bar association's statements of client rights and responsibilities. See the sample client service standards and sample statements of client rights and client responsibilities, see below.

Sample Client Service Standards

Basic Assumptions

Clients are entitled to:
> be treated with courtesy and consideration at all times
> expect attorneys' independent, professional judgment and undivided loyalty, uncompromised by conflicts of interest
> have their questions and concerns addressed in a prompt manner
> be kept informed as to the status of their matter
> receive sufficient information to participate meaningfully in the decision-making process concerning their issues

General Communications

> Telephone messages will be returned as soon as possible, certainly within the same day.
> If you cannot return the call personally, your secretary or assistant should do so, to say you are unavailable and set a time to return the call.
> Every individual will check email, voice mail, and personal PDAs frequently during the day.
> During meetings and with clients, smartphones should be turned off as a matter of courtesy and an indication of the client's importance to you.
> If a smartphone must be kept on, explain to the group/client why this is necessary.
> Client correspondence will be handled promptly.
> Maintain regular communication with clients, updating them according to the agreed-upon parameters set out in the initial planning meetings.

Communication Commitments

> We will consult with clients about the means by which their objectives are to be accomplished and provide sufficient information so they can make informed decisions.

> We are committed to taking the time to learn about and understand each client's issues and needs so as to provide reliable, trustworthy advice.
> Our goal is to be as accessible as possible.
> We will keep clients informed of seminars and educational programs that might be relevant to them.
> We will seek ways to assess client satisfaction, and always welcome client feedback and input.
> We have designated _____ to serve as an ombudsman for all clients.
> _____ is available to address any concerns.

Billing

> Bills will be clear, easy to understand, and in line with the expectations set with the client.
> Clients will be informed of all unanticipated charges or budget overages.
> Bills will be sent in a timely manner.
> Billing issues will be resolved promptly.

Attorneys should train all their staff from receptionist to COO in the significance of these guidelines. After all, the most important first impression is made by the staff person answering the phone—often the office receptionist. A gum-chewing, frowning, PDA-focused receptionist sends a visceral message about the culture of the firm. Instead of affirming the client-attorney relationship, such a message undermines the relationship.

Your firm should remind all personnel to introduce themselves with a direct look and a firm handshake. Offering guests a welcome drink is a considerate gesture. Some firms issue clothing guidelines as part of professional comportment rules. These typically ask everyone to abstain from overly casual or revealing clothes.

Lawyers are also mindful of the bad impression extravagance can make on clients who feel it is their money being spent on offices more splendiferous than their own. Kramer Levin was mindful of the need to toe this fine line when the firm moved to new offices in 2005. They wanted the space "to appear as very substantial and professional. And they want to stack up with their competitors," without coming across as ostentatious or excessive.[12] You don't have to be a large firm to create a

---

12. Teri Karush Rogers, "A Law Firm's Ideal Home: Substantial but Not Lavish," *The New York Times*, July 31, 2005, p. 28

cultivated, yet commercially solid, impression. A small litigation boutique conveys a sense of both solid professionalism and out-of-the-box thinking in an office with curved walls, glass-walled conference room, granite top conference table, a subtle color scheme, and a diverse selection of interesting art.

Reception areas should be neat, attractive, and stocked with a thoughtful selection of newspapers and magazines that reflect clients' interests. Plants should be fresh, not drooping and in need of water. Firm promotional material may be available but should not be the only reading option. Semi-public spaces such as the coffee area should be neat and clean. Individual's offices should be well-organized. A disorganized space suggests a disorganized approach to work.

Conference rooms especially need to be cleaned after each use. It contradicts the attorney-client confidentiality pledge to see another person's legal documents still in the conference room after the meeting is concluded. Clients may be uncomfortable at the thought of their private correspondence scattered in a public room, and an un-wiped white board can present a strategic advantage when opposing attorneys walk into your offices.

> People cannot see your service. So . . . they judge your service by what they can see. Look at your business card. Your lobby. Your shoes. What do your visibles say about the invisible thing you are trying to sell? **Watch what you show.** [emphasis in the original][13]

Implement Technology to Facilitate Communication

> Technology has dramatically changed many aspects of the practice of law including client expectations, time demands. . . . In particular, electronic communication has fueled a culture in which clients want more legal information, answers on the spot and lawyers who can interpret, rather than simply provide, information.[14]

Technology, with its smartphone immediacy and infinite research resources, reinforces clients' demands for immediate responses. Not only do clients want answers, they may fail to differentiate between easy and

---

13. Harry Beckwith, *Selling the Invisible*, (Warner, 1997), p. 186.
14. NYSBA, *Report of the Task Force on the Future of the Profession*, p. 13.

difficult answers. Establishing agreed-upon communication guidelines including response times at the beginning of a matter, sets client expectations regarding the way in which you practice. Then, when you take the time to consider a complex question instead of answering immediately, the hiatus is seen as responding appropriately to the issue rather than as a sign of indifference to the client.

Communication is enhanced by the rapidly growing trend for lawyers to use personal devices such as smartphones, tablets, and iPads for work purposes. Two personal injury attorneys in Arizona gave iPads to their major clients so that the clients could access an email account that contains their case documents and contact the attorneys whenever they wanted information. The attorneys use the tablets to create presentations with embedded video, interviews with key witnesses, and animated re-enactments of the accident that help settle a case before it goes to trial.[15] At the other end of the firm size spectrum, more than two-thirds of CIOs of the largest law firms agreed on the top four "biggest benefits" of mobile technology: increased flexibility (ninety-one percent), better client service (eighty-seven percent), increased productivity (eighty-three percent), and improved access to data (sixty-nine percent).[16] Similarly ninety-nine percent say their firms use videoconferencing, and fifty-seven percent say clients are invited to use the system for their own needs.[17]

Technology is particularly important as a competitive differentiator for the small and medium size firm. Using cloud computing allows small firms to be technologically competitive with larger firms. Cloud computing is basically a set of outsourced computer resources accessed through the Internet and "providing the hardware, software, human resources and business model required to deliver, store and manage digital data offsite. The outside service providers in turn achieve economies of scale, lowering the cost to all their customers."[18]

For smaller firms and solo practitioners, cloud computing adds resources that facilitate data management, information access, and client service. An attorney can work from anywhere on any kind of hardware,

---

15. Johna Berry, "iPads bring new levels of connection to lawyers, clients; tablet use adds quality to presentations," *The Arizona Republic*, July 7, 2011.
16. "Law Firm Technology 2011: All about the Connections," *The American Lawyer*, November 2011.
17. *Id.*
18. Jonathan Redgrave and Andrew Cosgrove, "Ready to Litigate in the Cloud?" *Legal Times*, April 27, 2009.

store documents, collaborate on work products, and communicate with almost anyone, almost anywhere in the world. One small firm that has grown in part due to its early adopter use of technology now employs four staff personnel in billing because of the need to match invoices and billing to a wide variety of client preferences.

Technology, especially in the cloud, provides enormous flexibility and facilitates 24/7 responsiveness to clients. It provides predictability and stability in terms of costs and scalability and comfort for clients who know that smaller firms can have access to the resources needed to handle their matters. Phone systems, information stored in your office computers, and emails are always up-to-date and accessible when you use an enterprise communications system that allows you to access documents and information from anywhere and respond to clients from anywhere in real time. Modernizing the law firm's business functions using Internet resources allows an attorney to meet and exceed clients' communication expectations.[19]

Knowledge Management

Knowledge management as a business function emerged in the early 1990s, facilitated by the ability of technology to capture and distribute a wide variety of information. It can be defined as "a range of strategies and practices used in an organization to identify, create, represent, distribute, and enable adoption of insights and experiences. Such insights and experiences comprise knowledge, either embodied in individuals or embedded in organizations as processes or practices."[20]

> Law firm leaders recognize that the relationships their lawyers have with clients and others are a crucial resource. . . . Relationship Intelligence, the knowledge a firm has about the collective relationships of its lawyers and staff, is a critical component of the firm's intellectual capital and a key to future success.[21]

This kind of knowledge base is a precondition for client-centric practices. It makes it possible for an attorney to coordinate and integrate

---

19. See Alan Cohen, "Drawing the Line," *The American Lawyer*, November 2011, and the Law Firm Technology Survey Highlights in the same issue.
20. "Knowledge Management," *Wikipedia* (http://en.wikipedia.org/wiki/Knowledge_management, accessed December 22, 2011).
21. Hildebrandt International, whitepaper: *Relationship Intelligence in a Competitive Market*, 2002.

knowledge about the client, attorneys' knowledge of the client, information about the client's world and, of course, the work and accompanying activities related to each client.

Large firms have many knowledge-sharing systems, but smaller firms can create a similar end result by requiring attorneys to log the details related to any contact, from a call to a completed matter, in a client folder so that anyone can see who knows whom and what they've done together. Solos can keep a similar contact-specific log. As a relationship builds, it is important to remember past activities and work products in order to refer to them again as the relationship becomes stronger and deeper.

Microsoft® Outlook™ has fields where you can enter personal information about clients such as birthdays, family member names, assistants' names, and other facts that come up in casual conversation. There are also an increasing number of apps to remind people of key dates, add notes to documents, store articles in client folders, and do many other tasks that facilitate client-centricity.

Marketing initiatives such as articles, alerts, email newsletters, blogs, and podcasts provide opportunities to present up-to-date information concerning court decisions, legislation, and regulations that may impact your clients. A 2010 survey of corporate executives found that clients like electronic alerts on the following topics:

> eighty-four percent want original research on topics important to them
> eighty-four percent want industry updates
> eighty-two percent want summaries of recent cases relevant to their industry
> eighty-two percent want invitations to seminars or events
> seventy-nine percent want legislative or regulatory updates[22]

These knowledge management vehicles can be sent to both past and present clients with a personalized note pinpointing the parts most relevant to them. Even if your technology includes intranets or extranets that give clients access to your knowledge centers, it is still important to send a personalized email inviting them to review the newest piece. A

---

22. Larry Bodine, "Executives Rely on the Internet to Find Lawyers," December 15, 2010, summary of Greenfield/Belser survey: *Digital Marketing 2010* (http://www.lawmarketing.com/pages/articles.asp?Acti on=Article&ArticleCategoryID=13&ArticleID=1109, accessed December 22, 2011).

knowledge management system, used in a thoughtful, relevant manner, is a vibrant and important tool for strengthening the bond between lawyer, law firm, and client.

Billing

Invoices are a powerful marketing communications tool that show the client how you implemented the plan set out in the initial planning sessions in terms of tasks and associated dollars. Engagement letters, invoices, and any other materials that spell out what you will do and when are communication pieces that reinforce the expectations you've set in your engagement letter or statement of work. The structure and language in the invoice allow the attorney to show clients how the expectations set at the beginning of the matter have been met. It says "We did what we promised."

Invoices also report on the work done for that month. It helps the client track the process and recall past discussions if the invoice tells the story of how the work was done and by whom in an easy to understand narrative. A corporate lawyer explained, "What clients usually want to understand is how the time was spent in business terms." It makes sense to note activities that took place but were not charged to the client. For example:

> A corporate lawyer says he never charges for spontaneous calls from clients because he feels that if the client thinks any call will cost money "they won't talk freely about their issues."

> A patent attorney says when he has long conversations with clients, he shows the full time of the call on the bill, but only charges for the minutes actually spent on work.

> Even if you don't charge for them, you might want to note the time spent to discuss DWI laws with client's brother-in-law, lunch with client's daughter to discuss law school options, and copies of a brief sent to the client's vacation home.

Clients today are thriftier and looking for lower fees, but they also crave predictability and transparency—a sense of what the final bill will be and how the money is being spent. If it turns out that the dollar amount is larger than anticipated, a client-centric approach would suggest phoning the client first to let them know to expect a larger bill, or writing a cover letter or email explaining why it is larger. In the same manner, when a bill is less than expected, highlight the reason why and the actions you took in order to reduce the bill.

The sample invoices in the following show how an invoice as described above would look, and how an invoice based on a time and billing system report could also be adapted to tie time and money to tasks.

Communicating Progress and Value through Invoices

"Billing is an easy way to distinguish yourself from other firms, and most attorneys do not take advantage of the opportunity," says an intellectual property lawyer and former general counsel of a social media firm. As in-house counsel, he sometimes found it difficult to consider the reasonableness of a bill for services rendered when he was not the primary contact on the matter. For example, if an invoice noted 1.8 hours spent to "prepare letter to opposing counsel," the information provided was insufficient to enable him to evaluate whether counsel took too long to write a routine, straightforward letter, or counsel did a stellar job crystallizing numerous difficult arguments and points in that short an amount of time. He would then have to confer with the in-house legal point person, and not infrequently call the firm to inquire about the entries. The results: lost time and added aggravation for all attorneys involved and a general counsel wondering why the company's outside counsel didn't seize its own opportunity to remind him how great it is. In extreme cases he would be left with a feeling that, at best, the outside firm was oblivious to his bill review responsibilities, and at worst, the firm was trying to hide billing inefficiencies.

When he founded his own firm, he determined that sending the kind of invoices he wished he had received when he was in-house would be an easy way to distinguish himself. He sends clients highly detailed bills with a summary page and thorough listing of tasks undertaken, arranged by date, but keyed to specific activities. He shows time spent but not billed to emphasize value, and concludes with a client-friendly note. His point is that

> the work and value that you provide your clients often is tremendous. Seize the chance every month to show and remind them why they are lucky to have you. Yes, more effort is required to prepare that invoice, but why would you spend any less effort on the single document that gets you paid than you would crafting your letter or brief to the Court to achieve that client's

objective? I want to deliver invoices that are understandable, even by someone other than the client's point person, that tell a story, and that do not
prompt clients to wonder or seek more information. If I spend two and a half
hours writing a letter to a judge to win a motion, I'm going to take the additional two minutes to explain the content and importance of that letter in the
invoice, rather than just list it cryptically as 'letter to judge.'

The hypothetical invoice Sample 2 shows what these techniques look like in practice, while invoice Sample 1 shows a different approach to using an invoice to communicate value while making use of information available from a time and billing
system.

Work with the client at the onset of the engagement to find out what
software they want you to use, to whom the bills should be sent, and
what information should be included. Work with your technology team
to create a standard billing system that will be compatible with your
foundation clients, or design such a system yourself.

Collating time entries by task helps a client see the steps taken in each
segment of the matter. If you plan to group by activity, use the descriptions to show progress. Use action verbs and include details that remind
the client what happened, as compared to a listing that merely says you
attended a meeting or sat in on a conference call. Many time and billing
systems automatically track computer usage (emails, research, writing,
etc.) and assign it directly to client accounts; often a smartphone app
will do the same for individual attorneys.

Some firms explicitly add marketing material to billing statements.
They use the opportunity to enclose a separate summary of the matter
highlighting what they did and the value received by the client. Other
firms include promotional material regarding a new whitepaper or
upcoming webinar, or "how are we doing?" surveys in the invoice, and
ask the person who receives the bill to pass it to the appropriate person.

Develop Shared Communication Activities

Communicating with clients *in* their world and *about* their world is both
a way to keep abreast of what's important to them and a way to reinforce

your connection with them. It deepens relationships, keeps you and your skill set top of mind, and supports the attorney-advisor role. This, in turn, can lead to more business and transform a casual client into a foundation client.

Successful communicators never take their clients for granted. They keep in touch between engagements, and look for ways to provide forward-thinking services. If you work with public companies, listen in on their quarterly earnings calls. In fifteen minutes, you will learn what high points and pain points are for your client right now.

Some lawyers subscribe to Internet news gathering services to keep up to date on cases, laws, and regulations that will impact key clients and then share the information with the appropriate clients. Other attorneys make a habit of forwarding news items to clients when appropriate, with a note explaining why the item is relevant.

Thought Leadership

"Thought leadership" refers to your role in the marketplace conversation. Do you add substantive content to LinkedIn group discussions? Do others refer to comments by you or other attorneys in the firm, or send your materials to others? If they do, you are a thought leader in your field—like McKinsey on strategy, Seth Godin on social media, or Steve Jobs on innovative leadership.

Being an intellectual resource and commanding a presence in the discussion of issues relevant to your clients reinforces your connection. Some major firms initiate surveys on attitudes or actions related to a specific issue or trend, and use the results to move the direction of the conversation. Many firms, large and small, host webinars or sponsor seminars. A client-centric attorney might also offer to do a keynote presentation at a client's industry conference.

Many firms overlook the importance of their Web site as a means of sharing knowledge. A 2010 survey of executives found that eighty-five percent considered professional service firms' Web sites important sources of information. They look for specific industry expertise.[23]

---

23. *Id.*

For solo practitioners and members of small firms, this may seem one task too many to add to an already over-stuffed schedule. Fitting these activities into a workday is partially a matter of attitude. Consider what you are working on and reading right now, and think about some small facet of it that might interest your clients or colleagues. For example, a lawyer in a small firm uses his Facebook account to share a factoid learned at a recent CLE seminar. He reminds his Facebook friends in same sex marriages that they will pay New York taxes as "married/joint," but federal taxes as "single" because the federal government has not yet recognized same sex marriage.

If you like to write, you might want to submit an article to your local bar association's newsletter, then upload it to your Web site and send it out in a distribution email to the clients who would be interested in the topic. Client-centric sharing might mean offering in-house seminars at a client's location either for in-house attorneys or for executives. For individual clients, an educational event could be held at a community center or place of worship. The more knowledge clients gain from you, the more likely they are to seek your advice as new issues arise.

Shared Marketing

One of the most ubiquitous relationship-building mantras says "What goes around, comes around." Sharing visibility and networking opportunities with clients is an indirect way to validate your high opinion of them and the importance of the relationship. Again, implementation of this idea is more a matter of attitude than firm size or marketing budgets. For example:

> Highlight foundation clients in your own information activities. Ask them to be on a panel you host or sponsor, contribute to an article in your newsletter, or provide a quote for your blog.

> One firm highlights an important business client in each quarterly newsletter, then converts the article into a plaque and presents it to the client at a celebratory champagne dinner.

> Attorneys who deal with personal situations could invite a client to contribute thoughts on how to manage child visitation schedules or the work/parent time trade-off, or a similar kind of personal experience.

> Invite clients to visit your firm to explain what they do to your client team or practice group, or perhaps sit on a panel at a firm retreat to discuss their view of good client service.

> Explore co-authoring a whitepaper, feature article, or book with your client.

Contribute to Their Marketing Efforts

Much of this chapter has been about the abundance of information in contemporary business life and how to manage it within the context of building two-way communication with your clients. Another part of this process is actually generating information that will be useful to clients in their efforts to reach their marketplace. Every business has to market these days, and the most effective marketing is based on educating prospective buyers. As an attorney who has worked on some of the most intricate issues related to your clients' businesses, you are in a unique position to help them educate their prospective customers. Look for topics that are of fundamental importance but easy to discuss in the form of tips, FAQs, or short articles.

> Find out if your client has a newsletter, blog, or other regular information-based marketing vehicle to which you can contribute an occasional article on a legal topic of interest to their customers—but not legal advice which would be against the *Model Rules* requirements.

> Determine whether your client regularly contributes articles to industry newsletters, blogs, or information sources. If so, consider whether it would make sense for you to co-author an article.

> Offer to appear in a video or participate in a podcast if these are part of your client's marketing program.

You can also help clients by publicizing what they do and who they are. Support your clients by buying their products or promoting their services whenever possible. Most law firms maintain accounts at the banks that hold their lines of credit. Look for similar ways in which you can demonstrate your clients' importance to you by supporting their interests. If your client is Kraft or Coca-Cola or Dell, do you use their products and tell them how much you enjoy them? Do you recommend them to others? If you are running in a charity marathon do you wear their logo on the back of your race T-shirt? During a meeting to discuss additional work, one attorney told a personal goods company about all the products their company manufactured that she used when she brushed her teeth, bathed, washed her hair, changed the baby's diaper, etc. It showed the client, explicitly, that she took the time to research their products, and implicitly, that as one of their customers she has a high opinion of the company.

Nominate your client for a "best of . . ." award and let them know how pleased you are to be able to promote their successes. Most importantly, ask them to define their "good customer" and then try to make introductions that will help them grow their business. Use *Form 3.2: Shared Communication Activities Tracker*, pages 70–72, to track your initiatives.

Many lawyers mention that a key aspect of the advisor role, of being close to the client in their business and as a friend, is to add value through mutual introductions. One managing partner says, "I am a constant resource for whatever ails them [his clients]. Today I had four emails by noon each asking me for resources to address non-legal needs." Another lawyer said, "I see referrals as solving a need—helping others to do their job. A good referral makes a client happy." Solos who work with attorneys in complementary practice areas can create a referral network, thereby aiding each other and those who need their services.

Participate in Their Organizations

One of the easiest ways to enhance your involvement in your clients' world is to ask them what organizations they belong to and which industry leaders they respect for their views. Your primary focus should be on organizations directly relevant to the clients' interests as discussed in Chapter 5, but you may want to look at their charitable interests as well. Then ask the client to take you along to a meeting. If you find it useful, you may want to join as an associate member, and over time become active on the group's committees.

If an important client is not active in any professional organizations, you may want to bring an organization to him.

❯   Research the organizations that serve the client's industry segment.

> Evaluate the likelihood that a particular organization will advance your client's overall business goals.

> Recommend that you attend a meeting together to scout it out.

Take Another Look: 360° Revisited

All the aspects of 360° communication reinforce each other. As you apply this expanded concept of communication links to your foundation clients you will create deeper and broader relationships that morph from matter/vendor one-offs to sustaining relationships.

Sample Statement of Client's Rights and Statement of Client's Responsibilities[24]

Statement of Client's Rights

(As adopted by the Administrative Board of the Courts)

1. You are entitled to be treated with courtesy and consideration at all times by your lawyer and the other lawyers and personnel in your lawyer's office.

2. You are entitled to an attorney capable of handling your legal matter competently and diligently, in accordance with the highest standards of the profession. If you are not satisfied with how your matter is being handled, you have the right to withdraw from the attorney-client relationship at any time (court approval may be required in some matters and your attorney may have a claim against you for the value of services rendered to you up to the point of discharge).

3. You are entitled to your lawyer's independent professional judgment and undivided loyalty uncompromised by conflicts of interest.

4. You are entitled to be charged a reasonable fee and to have your lawyer explain at the outset how the fee will be computed and the manner and frequency of billing. You are entitled to request and receive a written itemized bill from your attorney at reasonable intervals. You may refuse to enter into any fee arrangement that you find unsatisfactory. In the event of a fee dispute, you may have

---

24. These samples from the New York State Bar Association were taken from its Web site (http://www .nysba.org/Content/NavigationMenu/PublicResources/ClientRightsandResponsibilitiesDeclaracin DeLosDerechosDeLosClientesyResponsabilidades/Client_Rights_and_Re.htm, accessed December 20, 2011).

the right to seek arbitration; your attorney will provide you with the necessary information regarding arbitration in the event of a fee dispute, or upon your request.

5. You are entitled to have your questions and concerns addressed in a prompt manner and to have your telephone calls returned promptly.

6. You are entitled to be kept informed as to the status of your matter and to request and receive copies of papers. You are entitled to sufficient information to allow you to participate meaningfully in the development of your matter.

7. You are entitled to have your legitimate objectives respected by your attorney, including whether or not to settle your matter (court approval of a settlement is required in some matters).

8. You have the right to privacy in your dealings with your lawyer and to have your secrets and confidences preserved to the extent permitted by law.

9. You are entitled to have your attorney conduct himself or herself ethically in accordance with the Code of Professional Responsibility.

10. You may not be refused representation on the basis of race, creed, color, age, religion, sex, sexual orientation, national origin, or disability.

Statement of Client's Responsibilities

Reciprocal trust, courtesy, and respect are the hallmarks of the attorney-client relationship. Within that relationship, the client looks to the attorney for expertise, education, sound judgment, protection, advocacy, and representation. These expectations can be achieved only if the client fulfills the following responsibilities:

1. The client is expected to treat the lawyer and the lawyer's staff with courtesy and consideration.

2. The client's relationship with the lawyer must be one of complete candor and the lawyer must be apprised of all facts or circumstances of the matter being handled by the lawyer even if the client believes that those facts may be detrimental to the client's cause or unflattering to the client.

3. The client must honor the fee arrangement as agreed to with the lawyer, in accordance with law.

4. All bills for services rendered which are tendered to the client pursuant to the agreed upon fee arrangement should be paid promptly.

5. The client may withdraw from the attorney-client relationship, subject to financial commitments under the agreed to fee arrangement, and, in certain circumstances, subject to court approval.

6. Although the client should expect that his or her correspondence, telephone calls, and other communications will be answered within a reasonable time frame, the client should recognize that the lawyer has other clients equally demanding of the lawyer's time and attention.

7. The client should maintain contact with the lawyer, promptly notify the lawyer of any change in telephone number or address and respond promptly to a request by the lawyer for information and cooperation.

8. The client must realize that the lawyer need respect only legitimate objectives of the client and that the lawyer will not advocate or propose positions which are unprofessional or contrary to law or the Lawyer's Code of Professional responsibility.

9. The lawyer may be unable to accept a case if the lawyer has previous professional commitments which will result in inadequate time being available for the proper representation of a new client.

10. A lawyer is under no obligation to accept a client if the lawyer determines that the cause of the client is without merit, a conflict of interest would exist, or that a suitable working relationship with the client is not likely.

Demonstrating Value in an Invoice

Sample 1: Single-page format from a small firm with multiple personnel, single matter, multiple tasks

Data from the time-tracking system that was used to generate the invoice appears below. Most time and billing systems have the capability to produce a basic report like this that shows the data for a blended rate analysis.

Willis & Henderson, P. C.
133 S. Main Street
Suite 1402
Essex, MA 01929

Invoice submitted to:

March 01, 2012

ABC Corporation
17 North Thunder Way
Suite 1001
Boston, MA 02114

In Reference To: ABC v. Bismark
Invoice #10009

Professional Services

		Hours	Amount
Analysis/Strategy			
2/17/2012 DAB	Travel to/from archived document site to review court of appeals action; analysis of file material, including correspondences, memos, briefs, rulings, and court orders. Analysis of file documents to determine what will need to be copied. Analysis of additional motions filed at county court to prepare for appeal.	6.00	2,850.00
2/21/2012 PG	Copied and reviewed documents, marked them by topic, added to Case Map.	2.50	412.50
SUBTOTAL:		8.50	3,262.50
Research			
2/16/2012 SJS	Met with Mr. Whitley to review details not discussed in the original meeting.	4.00	1,500.00
SUBTOTAL:		4.00	1,500.00
Trial and Hearing Attendance			
2/24/2012 DAB	Court appearance with Mr. Whitley.	7.00	3,325.00
SUBTOTAL:		7.00	3,325.00
For professional services rendered		19.50	$8,087.50

Timekeeper Summary

Name	Hours	Rate	Amount
David A. Brickley	13.00	475.00	$6,175.00
Steven J. Santos	4.00	375.00	$1,500.00
Paula Grant	2.50	165.00	$412.50

Client	Matter	Task	Timekeeper	Level	Date	Time Spent	Rate Value	Total Value
ABC	Bismark v. ABC	Analysis/ Strategy	D. Brickley	Partner	2/24/2012	6.0	$475.00	$2,850.00
ABC	Bismark v. ABC	Analysis/ Strategy	P. Grant	Paralegal	2/25/2012	2.5	$165.00	$412.50
ABC	Bismark v. ABC	Research	S. Santos	Associate	2/16/2012	4.0	$375.00	$1,500.00
ABC	Bismark v. ABC	Trial and Hearing Attendance	D. Brickley	Partner	2/17/2012	7.0	$475.00	$3,325.00
								$8,087.50

Sample 2: Multipage format from a solo firm, multiple matters, and multiple tasks

BresslerLaw PLLC

3 West 35th Street, 9th Fl · New York, NY 10001
917/869.4343 | 917.591.7111
jrb9@rblaw.com · www.jrblaw.com

October 5, 2011

Via e-mail: client@greatclient.com

Mr. Client
Great Client Inc.
100 Legal Matter Avenue
New York, NY 10000

Invoice for legal services rendered, as described more fully below, from September 1, 2011 through September 30, 2011:

Total hours:	6.6
Hourly rate:	$425
Legal fees:	$2,805
Less courtesy reduction:	($595)
Disbursements:	$0
Total due:	$2,210

Bressler Law PLLC Federal Tax Identification Number (EIN): 99-9999999

CREATIVE COUNSEL FOR INNOVATORS™

Mr. Client
Great Client Inc.
October 3, 2011
Page 2 of 3

www.xhlaw.com

Date	Description	Time (hrs)
September 4, 2011	Teleconference with Mr. Client concerning maintenance filings for pre-existing U.S. trademark registrations, trademark issues concerning TRADEMARK1 and potential new U.S. trademark applications	0.5
September 5, 2011	Teleconference with Mr. Client concerning maintenance filings for pre-existing U.S. trademark registrations and concerning potential new U.S. trademark applications; USPTO registration availability research for TRADEMARK2 and TRADEMARK3	1.1 (0.5)
September 6, 2011	Teleconference with Mr. Client concerning maintenance filings for pre-existing U.S. trademark registrations and potential new U.S. trademark applications	1.5 (0.5)
September 11, 2011	Prepare Sections 8 and 9 filing for TRADEMARK4 (Class 25); prepare U.S. trademark application for TRADEMARK3 (Class 10); correspondence with Mr. Client concerning same; prepare U.S. trademark application for TRADEMARK5 (Class 10); prepare U.S. trademark application for TRADEMARK2 (Class 10); teleconference with Mr. Client concerning prospective TRADEMARK1 license agreement	1.8
September 12, 2011	Correspondence with Mr. Client concerning Sections 8 and 9 filings for U.S. trademark registrations	0.1
September 13, 2011	Teleconference with Mr. Client following up on strategy for maintenance filings and proposed new U.S. trademark applications; revise draft TRADEMARK3, TRADEMARK2 and for TRADEMARK5 trademark applications per Mr. Client comments; complete and submit TRADEMARK1 Sections 8 and 9 filings (Classes 10 and 25); complete and file the TRADEMARK3 and TRADEMARK2 trademark applications	1.2
September 24, 2011	Correspondence with Mr. Client concerning Sections 8 and 9 filings acceptance for TRADEMARK4 (Class 25); review TRADEMARK4 clothing Section 8 and 9 acceptance	0.1

CREATIVE COUNSEL FOR INNOVATORS™

Mr. Client
Great Client Inc.
October 3, 2011
Page 3 of 3

www.xhlaw.com

Date	Description	Time (hrs)
September 26, 2011	Correspondence with Mr. Client concerning status of Sections 8 and 9 filing (Class 10) (no charge)	0.1 (0.1)
September 29, 2011	Correspondence with Mr. Client concerning edits to Non-disclosure Agreement ("NDA") (no charge)	0.1 (0.1)
September 30, 2011	Correspondence with Mr. Client concerning edits to NDA (no charge)	0.1 (0.1)

Total hours	6.6 hrs @ $425/hr = $2,805
Less courtesy reduction	(1.4 hrs) @ $425/hr = ($595)
Total legal fees	5.2 hrs @ $425/hr = $2,210
Disbursements	$0
TOTAL	$2,210

Notes:

Please feel free to inquire at any time about the services, fees and disbursements. I appreciate the opportunity to assist you, and I hope that you continue to be pleased with the quality, promptness and value of services rendered.

Forms

Form 3.1: Communication Preferences Checklist

> *Preferred mode of contact* ranges from email to in-person, and covers a variety of phone options. The client might also want to vary the mode of contact depending on the nature of the conversation.

> Many people set aside a specific time of day to take calls. For international clients, consider setting call time parameters taking their workday and yours into consideration.

> *Turnaround time* varies widely. Many attorneys think twenty-four hours is reasonable, but many clients think more than two hours is unreasonable. Discussing expectations may avoid problems down the road.

> *Preferred type of meeting:* Clients dealing with personal issues may want to meet in person, while business people may prefer to save time and use videoconferencing or conference calls instead.

> *Client's level of involvement* may change as a matter progresses, or as new information raises the stakes. Documenting the client's directions as to their level of involvement may provide a jumping off point if communication issues occur mid-matter.

Names: Attorney Client Contact	Client's Preferences	Date of discussion: Date accepted: Date of last review/update:
Preferred mode of contact		
–2nd choice		
Time of day to take calls		
–2nd choice		
–Weekend calls?		
–Evening calls?		
Turnaround time for calls		

Calendared routine call:
  –how often
  –day of week/time of day		

Preferred type of meetings		

Names: Attorney Client Contact	Client's Preferences	Date of discussion: Date accepted: Date of last review/update:
–2nd choice		
Coverage when primary attorney is not available		
Client's assistant's name (if applicable)		
Person to talk to if client is unavailable		
Client's preferred level of involvement in the matter		
Points at which client wants to be contacted about a decision		

Form 3.2: Shared Communication Activities Tracker

Activity	Purpose	Date	Responsibility of	Evaluation / how measure results
In-person activities				
–visit their location				
–celebrate the end of a matter				
–client loyalty interview				
–educational seminars at the client's location				
–preventive audit of client's policies				
–meetings between matters				
–other				

Activity	Purpose	Date	Responsibility of	Evaluation / how measure results
Thought leadership				
–topic / legal issue				
–audience				
–purpose				
–format				
–publication venue				
Education				
–seminar at the firm				
–seminar at the client's				
–webinars				
–podcasts				
–videos				
Shared marketing				
–speaking opportunities				
–visibility opportunities				
–in newsletters				
–online				
–other				
–joint publicity				

Activity	Purpose	Date	Responsibility of	Evaluation / how measure results
Support for client's business				
–referrals				
–use their products/ services				
–support their charities				
–promote their successes				
–other				
Other activities				

CHAPTER 4

Research to Understand Your Current Practice

Growing a client-centric practice built around the services provided to foundation clients (sometimes called "key," or "top," or "best" clients) begins with serious research into clients in the context of your practice and your firm's practice capabilities and as a participant in each client's own world.

Selection of the clients that will be most important to the firm is a major strategic decision because it will affect the way the firm grows and the type of service delivery procedures put in place. Research provides facts to balance emotional factors such as "like to work with," "challenging legal work," or "rewarding results." Chapter 4 defines the client in the context of the legal practice; Chapter 5 looks at clients in their worlds.

Gather the Most Relevant Information about Your Firm: "The Five Cs"

How do you concentrate on "need to know" vs. "nice to know"? What facts are relevant to building a client-centric firm?

A classic mnemonic, The Five Cs, provides a framework for understanding the "what" and "why" of client's needs, expectations, and wishes, and the capabilities of the law firm to meet clients' requirements. The Five Cs, shown in *Diagram 4.1*, move outward from the law firm and its attorneys to include clients and outside influences—collaborators, competitors, and context. Let's define each category in more detail.

Diagram 4.1: The Five Cs, Firm View

1. *Company/firm analysis:* This analysis should focus on you and your firm. It's important to understand the features of your practice which include both the legal services you offer and the way you perform services. Taken together, these create the service package that clients buy.

   ❯ What are your key practice areas, services, and products? How do your services fit in the marketplace—are they top of the line, competitively-fine, or commodity-ordinary?

   ❯ What is the staffing pattern in your firm? What kind of leverage do you have? If you are a solo, do you use any outside staffing services? As a lawyer responsible for staffing several teams said, "Clients want [staff] consistency because familiarity is extremely important."

   ❯ What is your reputation with your clients and in the marketplace?

   ❯ What are your competitive advantages—the distinctive characteristics of the way you practice law? What are your core competencies?

> How are you using technology to improve efficiency and effectiveness? How can you pass technology efficiencies on to your clients?

> Who are your clients? What do they want and need? What do you do that fulfills their wants and needs? Do you practice law in a way that meets or exceeds their expectations? Can you increase profits by changing the way services are provided to clients?

> How does pricing affect your competitiveness? Which costs are variable and which are fixed? Are you profitable? Do you offer alternative fee arrangements?

> Do you know your costs at a granular level—in terms of how you go about practicing law? For example, in litigation, do you know how much time it takes to do a deposition, draft and file a simple motion, respond to an interrogatory?

2. *Client/customer analysis*: This involves a 360° view of the client from the perspective of the client as a component of your practice, and the client as an independent entity with needs related to the environment in which it operates. Key questions include:[1]

> What is this client—a business entity, government agency, not-for-profit? How is it organized? What is its global reach? Do you know the annual revenue and financial resources of the client? What are its core competencies and competitive advantages?

> What does it sell? To whom? In which markets?
>   ○ Does it sell primarily B-to-B (business to business) or B-to-C (business to consumer)?
>   ○ Does it engage one-on-one with customers or through channels such as retail stores, wholesalers, or the Internet?

> Who are the key advisors and decision-makers? What are their leadership/management/decision-making styles?

---

1. These questions seem to apply primarily to business entities rather than individuals or family groups, but the questions can be adapted to life cycle issues as well. See Forms 5.2A-5.D-1 in Chapter 5 for a discussion of research on individuals.

> How many employees does it have and where are they located? Who are the main competitors? What problems are on the horizon?

> Clients buy products and services to secure a benefit or resolve a problem, then make a cost-benefit analysis that determines if the benefits will match the cost. What are the buying motivators for your key clients? Have their reasons for seeking legal assistance changed in the last two years?

> Are you using your knowledge about the most important clients to create a dialogue around their wants and needs? Are you a proactive advisor? Are you as beneficial to them as you can be? As you should be?

> How are you using technology to link to your clients? Do you share common software?

3. *Collaborator/channel analysis:* This invites a broader view of client service than just that focused on a practice area or specific matter. It centers on relationships with other attorneys (both inside a firm and in other firms) with complementary expertise, other professional and financial advisors brought into the same deals, and your own vendors, any of whom may be able to offer needed services to clients. "Channel" is a marketing term that means the technique used to reach others, ranging from networking to a Web site.

> Which of the other professionals who service your foundation clients do you know?

> Which ones do you work with now?

> Who could you work with in order to be able to help your client in more areas?

> Where do you see collaborative marketing opportunities?

> What marketing outreach channels do you use to sell your services (e.g., Web site, Internet attorney publicity/selection sites, newsletters, whitepapers, video, podcasts)?

4. *Competitor analysis:* Competitors include not only other law firms but also non-legal businesses that offer service alternatives such as banks, employee benefits specialists, brokers, and outsourcing companies. Internet and do-it-yourself capabilities may also offer competition in terms of their service offerings and price points.

> Who competes with you in terms of your services?

> What are the threats in terms of specific practice or geographic areas?

> Who competes with you for specific clients?

  ○ What is your share of each foundation client's work vis-à-vis your competitors?

> What are your competitors' core competencies and strategic advantages?

> Are you aware of any potential competitors that might emerge in the next few years?

5. *Context/climate analysis:* Nothing happens in a vacuum. The importance attached to problems, opportunities, and risk is conditioned by the context in which both your clients and you operate. Knowing the context allows you to be relevant advisors for clients because you know which issues are germane. It provides a background for understanding the circumstances related to a specific issue. For example, it is more useful to read a pleading about an anti-trust violation when you know the context—industry trends, relevant laws, precedents, and the client's competitive situation. Context also applies to the growth potential of an individual attorney's practice or a firm's expansion.

   Climate refers to the atmosphere in which decisions are made both within a client and in the client's milieu. For many businesses today the climate is economically uncertain.

   > What trends are affecting the way you practice law?

   > How does the macro-economic and political climate affect your clients and their relationship with you?

   > For example, think of the practice balance seesaw between bankruptcy and mergers and acquisitions practices; typically when one is "hot" the other is not.

In this chapter, we focus the Five Cs on you—first on firm, yourself, and your respective goals. The data collection begins with a quick overview of the organization, structure, practice focus, and profitability. Then we ask you to look at your "80/20" clients in the context of your firm—revenue generated, practice areas used, relationships between client personnel and attorneys, and potential to grow your relationship with and services for the client.

Most of the data reside somewhere in your law office business systems—new matter forms, accounting and time systems, client contact lists, client relationship management systems reports, and if you have a marketing staff member, in her data. It may seem like an overload of research that will take too many hours, so perhaps do one segment every day or every week. The data, once collected, becomes information that will drive decisions about your own practice trajectory and the growth direction for your firm. Key patterns will emerge regarding: clients' use of practice areas, staffing arrangements and average cost per matter, profitability by area and staff person, and attorney areas of non-legal expertise to be built into marketing programs.

The results will enable you to create fact-based plans for growth in specific areas, with specific kinds of clients, using specific attorney teams. This kind of targeted approach takes less time and resources to implement successfully than more general, unfocused approaches to growing your practice.

1ST C: COMPANY/FIRM ANALYSIS— ### AN OVERVIEW OF YOUR FIRM

A useful overview is to look at your firm's resources in two ways:

1. as a snapshot of where you are today
2. as a perspective to use in anticipating clients' needs

Firm Basics: This information then becomes the framework for making decisions about the firm's growth and direction. Use *Form 4.1: Firm Basics*, page 93, to set down basic information about firm structure, personnel, office locations, practice areas, revenues, pricing policies, technology, and clients categorized by kind of client and your reputation.

Practice area and service products: The traditional focus on specific areas of law can inhibit an understanding of your client's view of the services offered. One reason for this is that professional service firms' practice groups usually are defined by the kind of law practiced, rather than the purpose for which their kind of law will be used. That narrow focus often leads to silo practices. In a silo practice setting, a corporate attorney could be friends with the litigator whose office is next door, but may not be knowledgeable enough about the details of his practice to introduce him to clients who may need his services—e.g., to offer litigation services to a corporate client when the deal goes sour and the client wants to sue. By contrast, retailers often organize their goods around the buyer's needs. For example, Walmart sells basic first aid products in the hunting and fishing equipment department.

Clients often equate size with expertise: if a firm has fifty litigators and ten corporate attorneys, they may conclude that its expertise lies in litigation. Conversely, when a solo or two-partner firm lists ten practice areas, a potential client may feel that the attorneys are not sufficiently expert in the area the client needs. Clients want their lawyers to be extremely knowledgeable and experienced in their legal area. Some clients want to know where the practice area expertise is located. They may not want to pay to "fly in" specific attorneys from another office or they may want local counsel because they prefer in-person meetings. Clients want to know the following:

> What services do you offer?
> Who works in which practice areas? If you are a solo or small firm, do you team with others to provide a full array of services?
> Do you have any service "products" where you have combined separate practice areas into one client-centric package? For example, mergers and acquisitions could reside in the corporate practice area and bring in tax, real estate, trust and estates, litigation, and employment law as needed, or you could create a packaged mergers and acquisitions "product" which introduces the client to attorneys in all these areas as part of the complete service required for a successful merger or acquisition.

In terms of anticipating client needs as a means of deepening client relationships, a practice area's contribution to revenue is a quick indicator of its strength within the firm. Understand where you make money, and where your most skilled attorneys practice. Declining revenue suggests problems that may reflect economic trends, client disinterest in the service, client ignorance that a particular service is available, or client dissatisfaction. Rising practice area contributions to revenue suggest the kind of trends or client situations that are driving growth. In the latter case, the strategic question is how to maximize and extend the growth, and in the former situation, the strategic question is how to make the practice area more relevant.

Use *Form 4.2: Firm-Wide Distribution of Practice Area Resources*, page 95, to analyze the relative strength of your practice areas.

Knowledge database of product and industry expertise: Every client thinks that his own situation, his industry, and his product are unique. Clients want to be sure their attorney already understands the context in which they operate for two reasons. They don't want to pay for a lawyer's time to get up to speed. They use knowledge of their world as an indicator of the lawyer's legal expertise; if he is not well-versed about the client's industry, they extrapolate and think he will be the same in his law practice.

Clients buy your experience in their industry and your understanding of their business. This also includes knowledge about the products themselves. A corporate lawyer may have expertise in international trade agreements between automobile manufacturers that includes specific knowledge about automobiles. A litigator with product liability cases related to domestic-use cleaning products will have explicit knowledge about the chemicals used in the products. A lawyer's practice may focus on cross-border transactions that leads to geographic expertise and familiarity with the laws of the country across the border—Canada or Mexico.

The importance of non-legal knowledge is highlighted in the *Financial Times'* survey[2] of international company clients and their law firms: three-quarters of the large company executives said that CEOs are primarily responsible for appointing a law firm. For complex work, approximately half of these executives singled out "understanding of industry" followed by "international focus" as the most critical factors, while almost two-thirds of the lawyers felt that "specialist legal expertise" was most important.

Use *Form 4.3: Knowledge Database of Product, Industry, and Geographic Experience*, page 96, to determine areas in which each attorney in your firm or with whom you work on a consistent basis has product, industry,

---

2. "Lessons for law firms: Putting clients at the heart of your management," *Financial Times* presentation for roadshow, June 2011. The BTI Consulting Group's 2011 survey data show the primary reasons corporate counsel give for hiring a specific firm are: They understand my business, and they understand my company's needs.

or geographic expertise. When you aggregate the expertise of individual attorneys, you may be surprised at the breadth of knowledge in certain industries, products, or business practices. These areas of strength can be just as important to certain clients as legal expertise.

Fees and profitability: Large fees and multiple hours spent on certain kinds of engagements may not equate to profitability. There may be insufficient leverage, more extensive preparation than the client wants to pay for, or too many write-offs. So, while you are investigating the "innards" of your practice areas and your lawyers' areas of expertise why not analyze engagement and matter profitability at the same time? There are many ways to approach profitability.[3]

Data can always be aggregated, but once it is, sometimes the building blocks of analysis get lost. The suggestion here is to select a reasonable number of billing records from a variety of engagements and analyze them at the matter level, looking at timekeepers and daily time records in order to develop a task-level hours and money cost. Use *Form 4.4: Profitability Analysis by Task*, page 96, to break down a legal process into its time and money components by task.

Once you have isolated these specifics for a number of matters you can average the hours and costs associated with each task in order to get ballpark figures to use when developing alternative fees. In the staffing levels and hourly rates columns, note the people who are performing each task and their hourly rates.

To determine matter profitability, add profit and overhead percentages to the total time cost and compare that number to the actual amount you billed. Once this analysis is completed, the data can be combined in various ways to calculate the profitability of specific services and specific clients.

To determine profitability per client, use *Form 4.4: Profitability Analysis by Task* again for specific clients in your "80/20." Then add in profit and overhead cost percentages and subtract write-offs to come up with

---

3. For other approaches see Edward Poll, *Law Firm Fees & Compensation: Value & Growth Dynamics,* (LawBiz Management Company, 2008); Edward Poll, *The Business of Law: Planning and Operating for Survival and Growth,* 2nd ed., (American Bar Association 2002); ACC Value Challenge (http://www .acc.com/valuechallenge, accessed December 22, 2011); Foonberg, Jay G., *How to Start and Build a Law Practice,* 5th ed., (American Bar Association, 2004).

a rough sense of the average matter value and the profitability of these specific engagements.

2ND C: CLIENT ANALYSIS—
TWO APPROACHES TO YOUR CLIENT BASE

There are many ways to segment clients in terms of their potential to be growth clients for the firm. We will discuss two of the most productive approaches:

> Pareto's Law "80/20" clients: the handful of clients (twenty percent or less, usually much less) that provide eighty percent or more of your revenues.
> A, B, C, D, client segmentation: the principle that puts clients into value buckets based on criteria such as revenues from client, type of work, and compatibility, and uses these criteria as a basis for determining the long-term value of specific clients.

Pareto's Law "80/20"

The first step is to identify and understand your most important clients. Importance can be tied to the symbolic value of the client, its prestige, or the kind of work you do for them. These clients usually reinforce your value to them by paying good rates promptly, with recurring opportunities to work on interesting issues. They, and clients like them, should become the focus of your "low-hanging fruit campaign." The handful of clients you define as foundation clients usually comes from this group.

You begin by analyzing these top revenue providers. Looking at the last five years, identify the firm's top clients in order to understand the characteristics of your client base, and focus on the parts of it you want to replicate for the future. Because the data reside internally in separate systems it is rarely aggregated and analyzed for planning purposes. Use *Form 4.5: "80/20" Client Analysis*, page 98, to collect the following data:

> gross revenues, per client, per year
> practice areas used
> firm's staffing patterns
> relationships with client
> client characteristics

An analysis of these data will reveal drivers of your practice including industries, demographics, location, and clients' needs. The data also identify patterns in terms of practice areas used, staffing, relationships between attorneys and client contacts, and contribution to firm revenue. Patterns related to longevity and change in the "80/20" indicate the "churn level"—the attrition level among your top clients. If the churn level is high, it suggests client service problems; if it is low, it suggests reliance on too few clients.

The forms provide a broad view of the foundation-class of clients in the context of your firm. They can also be used to analyze the total relationship with individual clients.

> Revenue per client coupled with profitability of the work you do for them imply the importance of your relationship to the client and the client's continued satisfaction (or not).

> A review of practice areas used, compared to areas which could have been used is an indicator of depth of client—the fewer the services, the narrower your relationship with them.

> An analysis of your staffing patterns often discloses areas for increased efficiency. Clients like familiarity. They want to work with the same people from matter to matter. This analysis shows where this is happening.

> Relationship patterns let you see whom you know versus whom you should know to fully understand your client and deepen your working relationship.

When aggregated, the data indicate the levels of risk and opportunity associated with each key client.

Relationship at Risk

In a hypothetical example, imagine that a biotech company client uses the firm for employment contracts, patents, and immigration law, but not for any corporate or litigation work. Although it is a large ("80/20") client for the firm, the work represents less than twenty percent of the client's outside spend on legal services. Because the three practice areas are so disparate, there is little staffing overlap. In addition, each group looks at the client only from their narrow perspective. Separate partners control each practice area and rarely consult about general client concerns.

These facts suggest that, although the client has paid relatively large fees over the past five years, the firm is in danger of losing the client to a firm that can create a coordinated approach focused on the total company. The lack of corporate and litigation work suggests that work is not coming from the department head, but rather from associate counsels in separate areas. To turn this client into a loyal client willing to give the firm a larger percentage of their work will require major changes in the firm's culture.

Analysis of the "80/20" clients adds specificity to the general patterns developed in *Form 4.2: Firm-Wide Distribution of Practice Area Resources* and *Form 4.3: Firm-Wide Knowledge Database of Product and Industry Experience*. It suggests areas that lend themselves to the creation of industry or product/service groups for business development purposes.

One firm found twenty partners with expertise in facets of the energy industry scattered among six practice areas. The firm created a business development group focused on their energy industry experience and increased their industry client base by twenty percent. As trends emerge that are relevant to these clients, practice areas can combine services such as real estate and corporate finance working together in the area of foreclosures and securitized mortgages.

A, B, C, D, Client Buckets

Not all clients are comfortable to work with. They don't all pay on time or offer interesting work. Some are irksome because they spin your wheels, whine, or demand instead of request. Assigning clients to A, B, C, D value buckets provides a guideline for deploying the firm's resources. How do you divide your clients into A, B, C, and D buckets? The category particulars are flexible and should reflect your own client list, but the concept remains the same:

> "A" clients form the support structure for your firm and your personal practice. They offer the opportunity for interesting work, are easy to work with, share similar values, pay on time, and provide a foundation for current and future growth. Most A clients will be in the "80/20," either for the firm as a whole or for specific offices or practice areas.

> "B" clients are good clients that can be grown into As. They offer interesting, quality work. Often they are too small to need a full range of services. Some may be important reputational clients, such as museums or charities, but limited in their revenue potential.
> "C" clients are typically commodity clients—nice enough, average clients using basic services at lower rates. They may also be "B" clients that are on a declining trajectory in terms of working with your firm—perhaps because of bankruptcy, merger, or personnel disputes.
> "D"clients are those you wish you didn't have. Typically they are argumentative, unprofitable, slow payers. They cost more to service than you can charge them. Sometimes they are clients taken on for their potential, which is not realized.

To fill the buckets, give every partner a list of their clients and ask them to assign them to buckets. Then merge individual lists into one firm-wide list and have the management committee (or similar leadership committee) edit the list. Most firms will end up with a handful of pure As, some Bs, and a large number of Cs and Ds.

The prudent path is to spend maximum focus and time with A clients, educational and growth time with B clients and some Cs, minimal face time with most Cs, and to hand off D clients. The time saved by not spinning your wheels with D clients can be spent on A clients and business development. Use *Form 4.6: Looking at Segmented Clients by Practice Area*, page 101, to provide an overview of practice areas in terms of the quality of the clients served. The data should highlight practice areas used by top clients and suggest areas where there is a disconnect between your perception of a practice area's value and your clients' use of it.

3RD C: COLLABORATOR/CHANNEL ANALYSIS

Working with collaborators can be looked at in a variety of ways. In Chapter 3, we discuss ways to use communication channels to share matter-related work, knowledge-sharing and marketing activities with your foundation clients. In Chapters 6 and 7, we look at ways to use collaborators and various communication channels to create tighter relationships with foundation clients and add new clients like your foundation clients. Here we look at close ties to complementary professionals and your own vendors who can provide resources that enhance a client-centric firm. Some collaborators are excellent referral sources; others become resources to share with others in your network. As one rainmaker lawyer explained, "I make business connections for businesses and investors and introduce them to people for [non-legal] services they need."

Use *Form 4.7: Collaborator Relationships*, page 101 to begin to see who knows whom.

4TH C: COMPETITOR ANALYSIS

Everyone shares markets and marketplaces with a variety of competitor firms and businesses. As you create a realistic picture of the arena in which your practice and firm operate, it is important to understand what competitors offer so you can differentiate your firm from the others. Everyone practices law a bit differently because every personality operates differently. These differences become part of your marketplace reputation and your service promise to clients. Use *Form 4.8: Competitor–Practice Area Matrix*, page 102, to outline the most important current competitors (both law firms and non-legal businesses) and on-the-horizon threats to your practice.

5TH C: CONTEXT/CLIMATE ANALYSIS

Your role as client advisor requires an attorney to understand not only the legal matter at hand but also the context in which it arose, because changes in the client's world affect the purpose of and use for the legal solution. Use *Form 4.9: Context Factors Looking Out Twelve Months*, page 102, to identify trends, laws, rules, regulations, and possible court decisions that your clients would want to know about.

Legal Context and Relationship Development

A recent forecast of major trends in corporate governance "based its list on formal and informal client surveys, market trends, and analysis of legislative and regulatory issues at the federal and state levels."[4] The trends include growing threats from whistleblower "bounty hunters" because of the incentives for employees to report wrongdoing: a need to demonstrate not only that a company has compliance guidelines in place but also

---

4. Shannon Green, "Forecasting Governance and Compliance Trends for 2012," *Corporate Counsel*, December 2011.

that the programs are effective and companies will follow up on issues employees raise. Noting this information, employment lawyers can talk to their clients about compliance processes and whistleblower policies; corporate lawyers can discuss governance and risk issues such as directors and officers liability, and how the board should handle the increased focus on governance. Litigators can use the trend information to update clients on recent court decisions related to these issues.

Put It Together: The SWOT Analysis (Strengths/Weaknesses/Opportunities/Threats)

Chapter 5 explores the foundation clients' worlds from their perspective. When this research overlays the research about the firm, you will be able to create a strategic road map for growth using foundation clients as the rallying point. Before turning to the clients' worlds, it is important to summarize and interpret the collected data. The basic tool for such analysis is a SWOT (see *Form 4.10: SWOT Analysis Matrix*, page 103)—a one page review of the Strengths, Weaknesses, Opportunities, and Threats that impact your practice and firm.

SWOT sounds like a military acronym, but it is really just a basic tool for creating a research-grounded strategy to grow your firm. We are using it in this chapter to summarize your competitive situation. Under *strengths* and *weaknesses*, group the data about internal attributes. Under *opportunities* and *threats*, collect the specifics of the external conditions in which you and your firm compete for clients. This SWOT organizes the data regarding who you are, what your firm looks like, what the firm does well, and the kind of clients you want to work with. Using this tool suggests answers to such questions as:

> where to concentrate your growth efforts
> which clients to categorize as foundation clients
> areas of overlap and divergence between your firm's resources and strengths and your key clients' needs
> your place in the larger marketplace
> opportunities to pursue immediately
> threats to plan for

As you fill in the quadrants of *Form 4.10: SWOT Analysis Matrix*, think about your firm as others see it: What do your clients think of you and your firm? What kinds of services do they think you offer? How do you differentiate yourself in their minds?

Strengths

Strengths include attributes such as what you do, how you do it, and where you do it, as well as intangibles such as your clients' perceptions of your service and its quality. Consider the following questions:

> What differentiates you from your competition?
> How do your clients see you?
> How do your services benefit your clients?
> How do your competitors see you?
> What attributes of your firm are most important to your clients?

Weaknesses

Weaknesses are related to gaps in your service offerings or office resources that you will need to create a client-centric firm focused on your foundation clients' needs. Consider the following questions:

> Have you lost any new work from key clients because of gaps in your service offerings?
> Does the marketplace categorize you as weak in certain areas vis-à-vis your competitors?
> Do you have the appropriate personnel and leverage ratios?
> Do you have appropriate technologies?
> Do you have sufficient capital to make the changes required to facilitate growth?

Sample scenarios: A major client is moving to Chicago but you only have a New York office. Or your client, a chip manufacturer, is buying a software company with a large patent portfolio and you have only a small intellectual property group.

Opportunities

Opportunities arise when you can leverage trends, court decisions, or new laws ("context" in the Five Cs). Opportunities are also created from your relationships with collaborators and from marketing outreach to client communities. Consider the following questions:

> What political, economic, or market trends make your services more compelling to your key clients?
> Is anything happening to one of your competitors that provides opportunities for you to add new attorneys or expand a practice area?
> How can you team with your collaborators to attract more business?

Threats

Threats are factors in the marketplace that may affect your growth. Consider the following questions:

> Are any of your competitors threatening any of your practice areas?
> Is there growing price or service delivery competition?
> Which current legal rulings or economic conditions might inhibit the growth of your firm?

After you have filled in the quadrants, rank the various factors in each quadrant and prioritize them. Consider organizational issues such as financial stability, leadership strength, employee morale, and engagement with the firm's goals. Think about the client sectors you want to grow and consider what investments your firm needs to make, such as additional staff, another office in a different location, or an alliance with lawyers who have expertise in areas complementary to yours. Balance your strengths such as industry knowledge, practice areas, and experienced attorneys against the impact of weaknesses and threats.

> Which strengths do you want to build up first?
> Which ones are most important today as compared to six months or a year from now?
> How will you maximize their potential?
> How will you handle areas of weakness?
> > O   Do you need to upgrade technology? Expand office space? Re-align leverage ratios?
> How quickly must you remediate weaknesses or ameliorate threats?

The outcome of the research should be a one-page assessment that identifies areas to grow, areas to de-emphasize, opportunities to leverage, and threats to circumvent. Use the assessment as a starting point for establishing goals for your firm, as well as for specific practice areas and individuals. Goals should be specific, measurable, and realistic. Goals can include the following:

> increased revenue from clients and from strategic enhancements to the firm's resources
> growth grounded in office enhancements, personnel changes, technology requirements, or business development strategies
> client development goals based on existing and potential foundation clients
> personal goals such as intellectual or subject matter challenges related to new areas you want to cultivate, current knowledge you want to update, relationships you want to initiate or deepen, or skills you want to acquire

Now that you know where you want the firm to go you have a baseline against which to measure change as you implement service arrangements and work processes that focus on your most valuable clients. The ultimate objective of client-focused change is to develop deeper, broader relationships with clients in order to foster loyalty, friendship, rewarding work, and growth.

Identify Your Foundation Clients

There is a strange dichotomy in prevailing views on how to grow a firm. One view is that it is easier and less expensive to get more business from current clients with whom you have a solid relationship than to troll the waters for new clients. Consider the following statements from experts:

> "It costs six to seven times more to acquire a new customer than to retain an existing one."[5]
> "The probability of selling to an existing customer is sixty to seventy percent. The probability of selling to a new prospect is five to twenty percent."[6]

---

5. Attributed to Bain & Company in James Digby, "Facts about customer experiences and referrals," *Return on Behavior*, October 2010.
6. *Id.*, attributed to Marketing Metrics.

The other approach is to focus on finding new clients rather than growing through client retention and expansion:

> "A survey asking which is the most important marketing objective, shows that thirty percent think it should be customer acquisition and twenty-six percent think that it is customer retention. However, sixty-two percent admit that they concentrate on customer acquisition with only twenty percent focusing on customer acquisition."[7]

> "Fifty-five percent of current marketing spend is on customer acquisition. Thirty-three percent of current marketing spend is on brand awareness. Only twelve percent of current marketing spend is on customer retention."[8]

Law firms tend to follow the acquisition model rather than the retention model. Attorneys are rewarded for large books of business as measured by quantity of clients rather than quality of the relationship. The premise of "low-hanging fruit" is that it makes more economic sense and saves attorney time and money to build a business around your best clients. Statistics illustrate this:

> "Eighty-one percent of companies with strong capabilities and competencies for delivering customer experience excellence are outperforming their competitors."[9]

> "A two percent increase in customer retention has the same effect as decreasing costs by ten percent."[10]

> "Customer profitability tends to increase over the life of a retained customer."[11]

Over the long term, most growth comes from a flow of steady clients. How do you focus your efforts to strengthen that flow? The answer is by identifying a core group of the best clients—clients we call "foundation clients." Foundation clients are "low-hanging fruit" in the sense that there is additional work from them waiting to be picked by service providers who have a broad understanding of these clients' needs and preferences.

---

7. *Id.*, attributed to Emarketer.
8. *Id.*, attributed to McKinsey.
9. *Id.*, attributed to Pepper and Rogers, *2009 Customer Experience Maturity Monitor.*
10. *Id.*, attributed to Emmet Murphy and Mark Murphy, *Leading on the Edge of Chaos.*
11. *Id.*

Consideration of the growth plans that emerged from the previous analysis also comes into play when selecting foundation clients; you want to choose a handful of clients that fit your growth plan.

After analyzing the collected data, there should be sufficient information to enable selection of foundation clients. The number can be flexible, but as the next chapter shows, these clients require ongoing strategic research and thought, which can be time consuming. The number one rule of thumb suggests one to three foundation clients in a small firm, perhaps one per practice area in a mid-size firm and approximately twenty in a large firm as your foundation clients. These become the focus of your client-centric practice.

Use *Form 4.11: Foundation Client Contacts*, page 104, to catalogue your foundation clients.

Revisit the Five Cs

Working through the five Cs can produce a multi-layered picture of your firm, captured in your SWOT analysis and a one-page plan to move forward.

> *Company* (your firm) sets who you are and what you do.
> *Clients* segments your client base into more and less desirable clients.
> *Competitors and context* reflect the reality of the world in which you compete for reputation and growth.
> *Collaborators* highlights people and institutions outside the firm that you might partner with to serve clients better.

Brought together in a SWOT analysis, this research lays the foundation for growing your own version of a client-centric firm.

Forms

Form 4.1: Firm Basics

Category	Firm/attorney characteristic
Year founded	
Legal form	
Number of offices	
HQ office	
Geographic reach	
Number of partners Equity/non-equity	
Associates	
Paralegals	
Staff—in your office	
Staff—outside resources used	
Staff by office breakdown	
Revenues for last fiscal year	
Major practice areas	
Minor practice areas	

Categorize your services by competitive level in the marketplace:
 	
Which services fit in each category:
   –bet the company
   –bread and butter competitive
   –commodity	

Attorney breakdown by practice area—# of attorneys in each practice area	
Revenues for previous year	

Category	Firm/attorney characteristic
Pricing: do you use only the billable hour formula or do you use other kinds of fee arrangements?	
If you use alternative fee arrangements, which ones and why?	
What other kinds of arrangements?	

Would you characterize your firm as
  −technologically advanced
  −technologically mid-stream
  −behind the technology curve
Why?	

What are the main technologies used currently?	

What is the category breakdown of clients
  −corporate
  −Fortune 500
  −large middle market
  −small to medium middle
   market
  −family-owned
  −start-up
  −professional firm
  −government
  −not-for-profits
  −individuals/family	

What five words do you think the marketplace associates with you and your firm?	
What five words do you want people to use to describe your firm?	
What is your reputation with your clients?	
How well known are you in your market? How do you make this judgment?	
What makes you different from your competition?	

Category	Firm/attorney characteristic
What are the five main points you make when you talk about you, your firm, your practice?	
Other characteristics you think are important to round out the basic picture of your firm.	

Form 4.2: Firm-Wide Distribution of Practice Area Resources

This chart shows the distribution of your practice areas and products in terms of staffing patterns, office locations, and contribution to revenue. Under practice areas, drill down below the top-level description of a practice. For example, a corporate practice could include asset protection, mergers and acquisitions, directors and officers policies, securities and capital markets, white collar crime, and other sub-areas. Including all the specific practice segments enables you to find differentiators in terms of what kinds of law you do best and what services clients find most useful.

If you have a small firm or a solo practice, under "personnel" note when you use outside resources such as contract attorneys, or law school interns.

Year _____

Practice areas services and products	Contribution to revenue			Personnel distribution [#]			Location HQ Branches
	2011	2010	2009	Partners	Legal staff	Non-legal staff	
Continue to add practice areas							

Form 4.3: Lawyer Knowledge Database of Product, Industry, and Geographic Experience

Across from each individual's name list the primary industries and product areas in which he or she has expertise. In the last column identify the key clients for whom the attorney uses the expertise. Think back three to five years.

> In the *industry* category identify separate industries, e.g., manufacturing with specific kinds of manufacturing noted, banking, agriculture, car dealers, government, and so on.

> Under *product* expertise list separate products each attorney has worked with, e.g., automobiles, airplanes, tires, nanotechnology, medical devices, and such.

> *Geographic* expertise includes not only specific country knowledge but also global expertise related to clients who sell through the Internet.

Individual lawyer names	Industry expertise	Specific product expertise	Geographic expertise
Continue to add lawyers			

Form 4.4: Profitability Analysis by Task[12]

Approach the process of determining matter profitability by concentrating on task-level data. Break down selected engagements into matters and matters into specific tasks. Then note the timekeepers on each task

---

12. One way to figure profitability is to use headcount and billing rates. See the ACC Value Challenge model for an Excel spreadsheet that provides a way to determine law firm profitability (http://www.acc .com/valuechallenge/resources/economicmodel.cfm?Iagree=1, accessed December 22, 2011).

by level, hours worked, and cost per hour. Finally, incorporate data to determine the time and money required for each task. Individual tasks and kinds of matters can be aggregated to get an average cost. With this snapshot of costs, time parameters, and leverage for each task, you have data-based flexibility in your approach to setting fees.

Kind of matter _____

Name of client _____ **Dates covered** _____

Time and money	Task 1 define	Task 2 define	Task 3 define	Continue to add tasks as needed

Staffing levels
  Partner
  Associate
  Paralegal
  Non-legal support				

Hourly rates for
  Partner
  Associate
  Paralegal
  Non-legal support				

Date—hours billed
  Partner
  Associate
  Paralegal
  Non-legal support				

Date—hours billed
  Partner
  Associate
  Paralegal
  Non-legal support				

Continue to add dates and hours as needed				
Total hours of all personnel				
Overhead percentage				
Desired profit margin				
Total cost for all hours				

Form 4.5: "80/20" Client Analysis

These are typically the top revenue generators for the firm, for a practice area, or sometimes for an individual partner. This exercise works for any sub-set of clients such as reputation, specific service used, client characteristics to replicate in target clients, etc.

4.5A: Client Analysis by Revenue to the Firm

Client Name	2008 $$	2009 $$	2010 $$	2011 $$	2012 $$	Client Relationship Partner	Strength of Relationship Today[13]
Continue to add client names							
Total firm revenue							
Total revenue from "80/20"							
Percent (%) of total revenue from "80/20" clients							

13. Use a basic 1 to 5 scale with 1 = troubled relationship today and 5 = strong, solid, growing relationship.

4.5B: Client Analysis by Practice Area Penetration

Again, break the area down into the kinds of matters you actually work on.

"80/20" Clients One name per line	2008 List practice areas used	2009 List practice areas used	2010 List practice areas used	2011 List practice areas used	2012 List practice areas used	Total number of different practice areas used 2008–2012
Continue to add client names						

4.5C: Client Analysis by Staffing Patterns

In the service team breakdown columns, indicate the number of people working on each client's account by partners, associates, paralegals, and administrative staff. If multiple offices are involved, you may want to show both a total number and staffing patterns by office.

Client Name	2008 service team breakdown	2009 service team breakdown	2010 service team breakdown	2011 service team breakdown	2012 service team breakdown	Names of key partners 2008–2012
Continue to add client names						

4.5D: Client Analysis by Your Firm's Relationships with Each "80/20" Client

Complete this chart for the most recent year for each client on the "80/20" list. If there has been significant change in your staffing patterns with a client, you may want to do this form for earlier years as well.

Client Name _____ Year _____

Names of firm personnel	Client attorneys he/she knows	Client C-suite execs he/she knows	Locations where he/she has contacts	People he/she needs to know
Number of people in your firm working with client Write answers in the cell below	Total Number of ATTORNEY Contacts At Client Write answers in the cell below	Number of C-SUITE EXECU-TIVE Contacts At Client Write answers in the cell below	Number/percent (%) of client's branches / divisions you work with[14] Write answers in the cell below	Technologies you share with client[15] Write answers in the cell below

4.5E: Client Analysis by Client Characteristics

Client name	Type of entity	Primary products/ services NAIC/SIC[16]	Their customers	Their major markets	Their competition	Geographic locations— for offices and sales	Number of locales you work with
Continue to add client names							

---

14. If the client has only one location, put NA [not applicable].
15. In the 21st century compatible technologies are a key contributor to the strength of attorney-client relationships.
16. NAICs and SICs correlation table can be found online at http://www.census.gov/epcd/www/naicstab.htm, accessed December 22, 2011.

Form 4.6: Looking at Segmented Clients by Practice Area

This chart provides data for evaluating each practice area's strengths and weaknesses so when you decide what your ideal client will want in the way of legal services, you can see immediately whether you already have the capability or will have to develop more robust practice areas.

Practice Area/ Specific Service Total number of attorneys in practice area	2011 Total number of clients served	2011 Total number of clients in your "80/20"	2011 Total number of 'A' and 'B' clients not in the "80/20"	2011 Total number of 'C' and 'D' clients	2011 Total $$$ revenue from practice area	2011 Percent (%) of total firm revenue	2011 Practice area $$$ revenue from "80/20" & A and B clients	2011 Percent (%) of practice revenue from "80/20" & A and B clients
Bankruptcy								
Corporate								
Employ-ment								
Litigation								
Add additional practice areas								

Form 4.7: Collaborator Relationships

Across from each attorney's name insert the names of the two or three people they rely on most often for assistance in each of these areas. Financial industry includes commercial and investment bankers, factors, lending agencies, etc. Vendors include a range of service providers from telecom and printers to IT consulting and executive search. Use this list again as you implement your client focus program.

Year _____

Attorney names	Financial industry	Accountants	Contacts in other industries	Vendors
Continue to add names				

Form 4.8: Competitor–Practice Area Matrix

Consider current and near-term (within twelve months) competitors.

Year _____

Practice Area	Legal Competitors	Reasons why	Non-legal competitors	Reasons why
Appellate practice				
Bankruptcy				
Corporate				
–contracts				
–M&A				
–D&O liability				
Continue to add areas				

Form 4.9: Context Factors Looking Out Twelve Months

Think broadly as you fill out this form. *Factors* includes trends, rules and regulations, judicial decisions, and the economic situation. For example, if you have a financial institution client you would want to monitor the *Dodd-Frank* law, federal and state regulations that implement its directives, staffing of the new agency created to oversee the law's implementation, as well as economic conditions here and abroad, proposed legislation and court decisions that will affect these clients.

> *Time frame* refers to the time you think your clients have to prepare for, take advantage of, or insulate themselves against the factor.
> *Clients* refers to those clients currently affected and those you need to advise about potential repercussions.
> *Practice areas* refer to the practice groups that will benefit from changes like these.

Factor	Time Frame	Clients affected and how	Impacts which practice areas

Form 4.10: SWOT—Strengths/Weaknesses/Opportunities/Threats Matrix

The purpose of a SWOT analysis is to spell out on one sheet of paper all your advantages and disadvantages in terms of your practice, your firm, and the market context in which you practice. The process of creating a SWOT will force thoughtful, strategic, creative thinking about the what, why, where, and how of your approach to building your practice.

Purpose of this SWOT analysis _____

_____

Participants _____

Date _____

STRENGTHS	WEAKNESSES
What are you good at?	*Where can you improve?*
What advantages does your firm have?	*What resources do you need to compete more effectively?*
Why do people hire you?	
In what ways is your firm / practice different?	*What mistakes have you made that create buying obstacles?*

Consider also:
    Firm resources—people, geography, technology
    Financial stability
    Reputation—of firm and individual attorneys
    Unique selling proposition
    Practice area strengths
    Leadership commitment
    Work flow/staffing procedures promoting efficiency
    Leverage
    Client service style
    Client base overview: most prevalent . . .
        type of entity
        industry or demographic
        geographic location
    Foundation clients [names]
    Successes/track record
	Consider also:
	    Gaps in your/your firm's expertise/experience
	    Gaps in your product/service offerings
	    Gaps in your client service implementation
	    Financial area weaknesses
	    Leadership/personnel/leverage issues
	    Resource inadequacies
	    Technology inadequacies

STRATEGIES *for capitalizing on strengths*	***STRATEGIES*** *for minimizing or remediating weaknesses*

OPPORTUNITIES	THREATS
What trends lend support to your strengths?	*What challenges do you face?*
What is your practice's expansion potential over time?	*Who are your competitors?*
	What are your competitors doing?
How, when, and where will you grow your practice?	*What trends hurt your selling proposition?*
Market trends	Market trends
Size of market share	Demand curve—clients' company business cycle
Client needs	Size of market share
Context trends, e.g.:	Fee pressures
Economic	Context trends, e.g.:
Political	Economic
Legal	Political
Globalization	Legal
Lifestyle changes/consumer tastes	Globalization
Role of the internet/social media	Lifestyle changes/consumer tastes
Environmental issues	Role of the internet/social media
Pace of technological change	Environmental issues
	Pace of technological change
STRATEGIES *for leveraging opportunities*	**STRATEGIES** *for eliminating or minimizing threats*

Form 4.11: Foundation Client Contacts

Foundation client name, address, telephone number	Key contact at client	Key contact at firm	Number of years w/ firm	Reasons selected as foundation client

CHAPTER 5

Research to Understand Your Foundation Clients' Worlds

Chapter 4 focused on key clients within the context of your practice and your firm's practice. In this chapter, the focus is on the whole client in its world. This kind of broad understanding is a precondition for acting as an advisor and alerting the client to opportunities and pitfalls before they occur. Clients want their lawyers to be proactive as well as reactive. They expect you to alert them to potential threats and opportunities, or serve as a sounding board. You need to understand the situation but approach problems from a different perspective, and engage in a useful, relevant, informative dialogue with the client. Again we will use the Five Cs as the analytical framework for the analysis.

Diagram 5.1: The Five Cs Company View

Focus on Clients in the Context of Their Worlds

The goal of this research is to create a 360° view of the world of your foundation clients. This means understanding both the internal world of the client and the external environment—the context—in which they operate. This 360° view is broader than a lawyer's traditional focus on what is relevant to a matter at hand. Sometimes a broader sense of the client emerges from representing the same client in a series of matters. Aggregating small pieces into a larger data set is not the same as looking for the biggest picture—the client in the context of its world.

The 360° understanding of the client is the goal whether the client is an individual, a family, a privately-held business, or a multinational public company. Because this is an intensive and ongoing research commitment, you should reserve it for only a handful of clients—typically, those key clients selected to be foundation clients. The selection could represent clients of the whole firm, a practice group, a particular rainmaker attorney, or all three practice centers. The distribution of these clients is idiosyncratic, but the reason for their selection and this research remains the same: to know the client well enough to advise him as a peer.

The problem with researching is the tendency to assemble too much information. It's important to stay focused on "need to know" rather than "nice to know." Specific research objectives include an understanding of:

> the structural characteristics of the total client
> the interpersonal relationships of the people who work for the client
> the client's world as it relates to its products, services, competition, rules and regulations
> the problems and opportunities it encounters or might encounter

You already gathered some of the basic information in the context of your firm research (Chapter 4). Here, you will want to add Internet and library research to learn about the client's world (see *Appendix 2: A Basic Free Online Research Guide*) with special emphasis on sites your clients go to for information:

> their trade or professional association resources
> opinion leaders they respect and read

> local news from any location where the client has a physical entity or a large customer base

To find out what information sources your clients trust, ask them. To stay on top of relevant news, set up an Internet news feed account and enter the key issues, laws, and words you want to track. Make sure to tie the search phrases back to the specific client, industry, or issue so you are not inundated with irrelevant material. You might also want to track the client's key competitors.

Client-focused research is not a one-time activity. You should incorporate it into your decision-making process, routinely review it, and keep it updated. Share the forms and the relevant articles, laws, regulations, and court decisions with all the others who work on the client with you.

Secondary research can be augmented by first-hand perceptions from people you know at the client and the client's other service providers such as the accountant, banker, venture capitalist, insurance agent, or broker. Using the client interview process, you can ask questions to corroborate your understanding of their world. (See Chapter 2 for interviewing guidelines.)You might also want to share interesting articles with the client. Sending such materials demonstrates your continuing interest, and underscores your ongoing understanding of the context in which the client operates.

1ST C: COMPANY—
UNDERSTAND THE CLIENT'S ORGANIZATION

Begin with the client's organization, expanding out from your contacts to the total entity. Using *Forms 5.1: Client Knowledge Matrices*, page 117, as a guide, begin to profile your two or three foundation clients. Key components of this section include organization and structure, revenue, products and services, and your relationship with the client entity.

Organization and Structure

The structure of the client is important in terms of the kinds of work the client needs and the applicable laws and regulations. For example, a start-up S corporation in New York City that manufactures medical devices for hospitals in the U.S. and China presents different opportunities for legal work than a mature C corporation that packages cereal for domestic distribution.

The medical device company may need corporate papers to set up its board of directors, employee manuals, patent protection advice, international trade contracts, government regulatory responses, and litigation to deal with product liability suits. The domestic manufacturer of consumer packaged food may have litigation needs, acquisition deals, executive compensation issues, and plant environmental issues. Either company would be an excellent foundation client, but creating a practice built around one or the other's needs would lead the firm in different growth directions.

The following outline of organization structure components is primarily keyed to business entities, but can also be used for individual or family clients by thinking about the family equivalent of the corporate characteristic. (Use *Forms 5.1–5.1D: Client Basics Matrices—for Businesses* and Forms 5.1-I–5.1D-I, designed for individual or family clients.)

Structure includes not only the legal form such as corporation, S corporation, LLC, LLP, or not-for-profit or government entity. Is it a public company or a private company? If private, is it family-owned? Where a client is part of a complex structure, try to find a corporate family tree diagram to indicate the relationships.

In today's global world, geographic reach—physical and virtual—is another key indicator of potential legal issues. Physical locations include headquarters and the location of divisions, joint ventures, and other parts of the entity. There are also the physical locations where products and services are bought and sold. For example, a company like Amazon has to charge state sales tax in all states where it has a physical presence such as call centers, warehouses, or its company headquarters. Virtual reach via the Web is another important geographic component because Web-conducted business is subject to a variety of national and international regulations.

The year the entity was created is a baseline indicator of its growth cycle position. Growth cycle stages include start-up, growth, mature, decline, and exit. Where a business is on this cycle is a key determinant of its legal issues and concerns. For example, a corporate parent may be a mature company with an established position, while its newest acquisition may be a start-up in need of developmental assistance and funding.

If you represent individuals, they too have a structure—the family, which may have analogous sub-structures created by siblings, relatives, generational divisions, divorce, or remarriages. Similarly, individuals have growth cycles moving them from childhood to young adult to mature to senior citizen. As with businesses, it is important to know how long people have been in one family structure or another and their geographic location. For example, snowbirds who change their legal residence from New York to Florida, maintain a small piece of New York property, but do not come into New York State more than 184 days, pay only New York real estate and estate taxes—not income tax. If time spent in New York is more than 184 days they are taxed as residents in both states.

Revenue

Revenue figures are a major indicator of potential individual and family problems arising from revenue sources or allocations. For complicated family structures, you may want total revenue and also a breakdown by major segments.

Products and Services

Products and services are the guts of businesses and the third leg of a basic company data stool: structure, revenue, and products and services. Use *Forms 5.1A: Company Products/Services and 5.1B Company Geography,* pages 118, 119, to identify not only each major source of business but also the primary customer or market for each product or service. In a large diversified business, you may want to focus only on the major products or services. You also need to research these answers for the products and services sold by the segment of the company you work with.

Each product or service should be identified by its common name and its government industry classification number known as a SIC (Standard Industrial Classification) or NAIC (National American Industry Classification System). Usually the major products or services are listed in order of importance (size) on company data sheets. This SIC/NAIC number makes it easier to pinpoint business development locales such as trade and industry associations, trade shows, and mailing lists. People are also included in these classifications under their occupations such as lawyer offices NAIC 541110 and doctors NAIC 621111.

The markets for and buyers of services are relevant because the need for legal services, such as product liability litigation, often arises when products create consumer injuries. Similarly, geographic location is a key factor in the selection of available legal options. If your clients are individuals and families, use this section to look at their business relationships.

Relationships within the Client Entity

Decision-making is usually a group endeavor with people participating according to their responsibilities, authority, and personal influence. In order to understand how your client makes decisions, you should be familiar with their macro- and micro-decision-making environments:

> *Macro*: The traditional behavior in the client's culture. For example, does the company encourage broad-based, team decision-making, or does each segment operate independently with its own set of decision-makers?
> *Micro*: Who participates in which decisions and what is their role? For example, who participates in the hiring of outside lawyers for routine activities as compared to bet-the-company lawsuits?

One way to determine culture and leadership style is to look at the overall company hierarchy:

> Are people organized by product, expertise, geography?
> Are reporting lines rigid or diffused?
> Do people work in interdepartmental groups or alone?
> Do the lawyers participate in business decisions?

To keep the research scope manageable, analyze relationships in the context of specific decisions. Using *Form 5.1D: Decision-Making Relationships*, page 121, begin with the people who participated in the law firm hiring decisions when you were selected to work with the client. Add the decision-makers involved in the growth areas you selected in Chapter 4. In each situation, be sure to include the following:

> > *Gatekeepers*: those between you and the person you want to know.
> > *Influencers*: those who affect the content of a decision but lack expenditure sign-off authority.
> > *Decision-makers*: those who acknowledge that there is a problem to be resolved, see the need for resolution, and have the authority to spend the money.

Similar patterns exist within families and in terms of individuals' relationships with whoever led them to seek a lawyer's advice. Using *Form 5.1D-I for Individuals*, page 122, diagram the power dynamics among those directly involved in the legal issue and with their relationship with "influencers."

Now that you have a basic sense of the client, you can move on to key parts of their external world: competitors and collaborators, and the channels they use to communicate with their customers.

2ND C: CUSTOMERS/CLIENTS—UNDERSTAND YOUR CLIENT'S CUSTOMERS, CLIENTS, MARKETS

Customers are the lifeblood of your clients' businesses, the focus of their efforts, and the reason they hire you to begin with. For example, if a contract disagreement threatens to disrupt relationships with their customers, their lawyer may be called upon to straighten "the kink." As a client advisor, you may be able to fix the immediate situation and suggest an approach to prevent future kinks. Use *Form 5.2: Characteristics of Customers and Markets*, page 124, to describe the clientele for major products and services. Company Web sites and advertisements are usually good sources for this information.

3RD C: COLLABORATORS/CHANNELS— UNDERSTAND HOW YOUR CLIENT COMMUNICATES WITH ITS CUSTOMERS AND MARKETS

This research looks at the media and outreach channels the client uses to communicate with customers in its various markets. These relationships are held together with contracts, agreements, and other forms of negotiated arrangements that have to be created and enforced. Distrust and disagreement create litigation opportunities. Improper working relationships can lead to situations such as the financial ties behind the home mortgage meltdown. Use *Form 5.3: Communication Collaborators and Channels, by Market*, page 124, to identify these relationships and outreach channels.

4TH C: COMPETITORS—UNDERSTAND THE CLIENT'S COMPETITIVE ENVIRONMENT

Use *Form 5.4: Client's Competitors*, page 125, to identify each foundation client's key competitors for their major products or services. This is useful in the broad sense of anticipating situations. For example, a competitor may sue the client for infringing on a patent or pursuing a merger that raises anti-trust issues because it threatens to create an uncompetitive marketplace, or significant financial problems may arise when a competitor enters the client's major market or area of geographic strength.

5TH C: CONTEXT—UNDERSTAND THE FORCES THAT IMPACT YOUR CLIENTS' DECISIONS

When you begin to talk with your clients about their worlds, it is important to know the details and substance of factors that are affecting and will affect their future. This means tracking trends, legislation, court decisions, and any other economic, political, or legal action that affects the context in which they operate. Sample questions related to context issues include:

> How have the recently implemented [insert a category] regulations affected your business?
> Are there any changes on the international scene that will impact your business?
> How do you think passage of [insert specific piece of legislation] will affect your business?
> What trends may cause problems for you?
> Where do you see opportunities for growth in the next six to ten months?

Use *Form 5.5: Trends Tracker*, page 125, to track the important trends that create the context in which the client operates. Also see the following on the *Dodd-Frank Act* and the opportunities it created for lawyers.

Case in Point: Legal Opportunities after Passage of the *Dodd-Frank* Wall Street Reform and Consumer Protection Act

Several *New York Times* articles[1] in August–September 2011 highlighted the role of several of the largest U.S. law firms in helping financial clients modify, eliminate, or adapt to the new requirements imposed on the financial industry by the *Dodd-Frank Act* in the wake of the 2008–2009 financial meltdown. These firms stand out among law firms in terms of the client-centric nature of their response to the situation.

> A July 2011 federal appeals court decision struck down the "proxy access rule" that would have made it easier for shareholders to nominate company directors. Eugene Scalia, a partner at Gibson Dunn, won the case on behalf of the Chamber of Commerce, representing its member banks and corporations. Many lawyers see this case as a signal that other rules can be similarly challenged based on the 1996 law requiring the SEC to promote "efficiency, competition and capital formation."

> Other potential suits include challenges to the SEC's new corporate whistleblower office and program, the ban on manufactured goods using "conflict minerals" such as gold mined in the Congo, and the Commodity Futures Trading Commission's plan to restrain speculative commodities trading.

> Davis Polk & Wardwell provides a stream of communications including a corporate governance blog, reports such as the *Dodd-Frank* Progress Report, and client news-flash alerts as to rulemaking progress and challenges, all based on data generated by their proprietary Regulatory Tracker program. Thirty companies have signed up for a $7500 monthly subscription to a Davis Polk Web site that tracks the progress of every *Dodd-Frank* requirement.

> Debevoise & Plimpton has a dedicated team working on the new regulations. The firm received $100,000 for writing a seventeen-page comment letter on a new banking rule. The team has written more than thirty such letters since January 2011.

---

1. Articles from the *New York Times* "Court Ruling Offers Path to Challenge *Dodd-Frank*," August 17, 2011; "Unlike Banks, This Wall St. Group Embraces *Dodd-Frank*," August 29, 2011; "*Dodd-Frank* Inches Along," September 6, 2011; "Feasting on Paperwork," September 8, 2011; "Is *Dodd-Frank* the Original 'Jobs Bill?'," September 9, 2011; "The *Dodd-Frank* Act: A 'gold mine' for law firms?," September 12, 2011.

> A *Dodd-Frank* requirement that companies establish emergency plans in the event of a collapse ("living wills") is providing work for international law firms such as Clifford Chance, and Sullivan & Cromwell. Barclays Bank said it spent forty-eight million dollars to draft its living will.

> Derivatives lawyers are working with regulators drafting the new rules for the new highly-regulated derivatives trading platforms.

Anticipating the impact of such major legislation, these firms created client teams and client-focused expertise, and brought technological resources and communication vehicles to bear to provide proactive advice to their clients.

Seldom does a bonanza like the *Dodd-Frank* Act comes along, but alert lawyers, well versed in their client's resources and competitive environment, can position themselves similarly on a smaller scale. For example, mass firings create employment and compensation work, company divestitures need a firm's mergers and acquisitions group, and challenges to inhibiting rules create opportunities for litigators.

THE IMPORTANCE OF LAW AS AN ACTION DRIVER

Lawyers have an action advantage in that once a law goes into effect, companies and individuals are subject to it. The advisor-lawyer can help clients prepare for new requirements. Possible actions include the following:

> Draft or review their comments proffered during the comment period to shape regulations.

> Provide anticipatory advice as to what the client needs to do to comply once the law takes effect.

> Draft, amend, and edit necessary documents for compliance with the law.

> Sue to block implementation of the law.

Use *Form 5.6: Regulatory/Legal Tracker*, page 125, to track relevant government legislation, rules, and regulations as they move from op-ed columns through legislative hearings to law, implemented in regulations, and challenged in courts.

Compile Profiles for Foundation Clients

You now have the results of your research and some thoughts as to your relationship with the client. Now it's time to transfer the data from the separate forms to the summary form, *Form 5.7: Foundation Client Profile Form: Part 1—Client Characteristics and Relationships*, page 126. This long form is designed to put all the data concerning one client in one place. On the template form, one side covers specifics related to business clients, the other side covers specifics related to individuals. Use whichever data set you need. Once these forms are completed you will have a complete 360° view of each client.

Several sections of the long form require information researched in Chapter 4. In the relationships segment of the form add information concerning all *relationships* between yourself, your firm, and the client. Note not only who knows whom, but how the relationship came about and how strong it is. Jot down personal relationships with client personnel, i.e., attended the same college, support the same charities, live in the same town, etc. This 360° look at your contacts highlights your areas of support and vulnerability when overlaid with key decision-makers for specific services. Relationship data includes

> the referral source from whom the client came
> your map of who knows whom
>> in the C-suite (those executives with decision-making roles)
>> in the legal department
> your own key contacts (make note of relevant sections of their bios)

Another data segment provides information related to *business development*: what services they currently use, what additional ones you want them to use, and how you plan to show the features, benefits, and value related to these new services.

If you work with individuals regarding their personal situations rather than their business issues this list of characteristics still applies. The data categories are the same; some of the content is different.

> Instead of company details, use family details including an "org chart" of the family members and relationships.
> Instead of company financials, substitute family financials, including business revenues that are relevant to the situation.
> Instead of industry trends, think demographics: What are the defining characteristics of other people in this situation? What are they thinking and doing?

> What trends, government activities, and geographic factors impinge on this demographic?
> Personal relationship mapping is the same as for business clients.

Move from Research to Action

Use Data in an Actionable Way

Moving from data to information to actionable recommendations begins with a restatement of the reason for the research: to develop an understanding of your most important clients. This understanding will be used to build an advisor relationship and create client-centric service processes and procedures that make your firm their comfortable, trusted ally.

When presenting recommendations drawn from the research, organize your presentation point by point—one finding and its implications per page. Use visuals such as charts to highlight strengths, weaknesses, opportunities, and threats. Your content should answer three questions:

> What difference does this information make to the client?
> How can we use our resources and expertise to be more valuable to the client?
> How will our action recommendation enable us to create greater depth in our client relationship?

These presentations and discussions should occur not only when the unusual happens, but rather on a regular schedule to keep everyone abreast of new developments in the client's world.

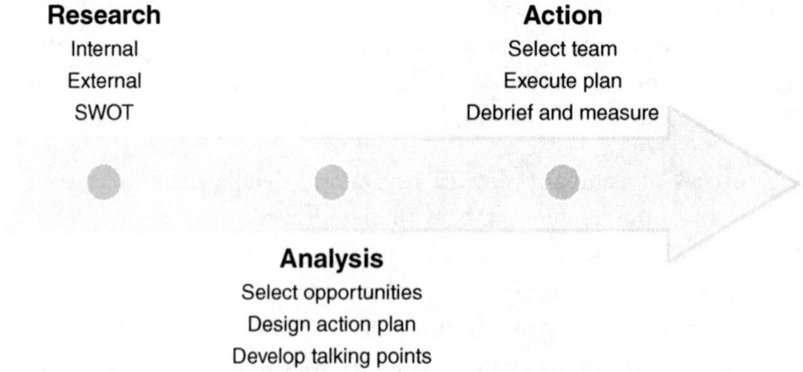

Research

Internal
External
SWOT

Action

Select team
Execute plan
Debrief and measure

Analysis

Select opportunities
Design action plan
Develop talking points

Diagram 5.2: Three Step Process from Research to Analysis to Action

Create an Action Plan

The next step is to create an action plan. Use *Form 5.8: Opportunities Work-sheet*, page 128, to highlight specific opportunities. Then use *Form 5.9: Foundation Client Profile Form: Part 2—Opportunities and Approaches*, page 129, to decide the people you need to approach at the client, the products and services you want to offer, and the benefits and value the client will be interested in.

Once you know who is important in terms of the client's decision-making you can form your own decision-making team and craft your approach. Use *Form 5.10: New Initiative Selling Points Worksheet*, page 130, to develop your specific selling points and action plan complete with assignments, due dates, and measurement metrics. Use a calendar program to chart the course of the initiative.

This cycle, in which you move from research to client-focused information, and then to action possibilities to sell to the client, should occur more frequently as you create greater "depth of client." Looking at the world through client's eyes is a mindset as well as a research process. As you continue to monitor their world, your advisor role will expand, and more opportunities will arise.

Keep it Fresh and Relevant

Client portraits age quickly. Ideally, you should work with your IT person to store the data online and to develop a process for updating and circulating new information on a regular basis. There are many tools that can help you to organize the process. Adopt tools that fit with your other office processes. If your firm has a librarian, knowledge management professional, or competitive intelligence researcher, you will want to integrate your approach with theirs. If you practice as a solo or in a small firm consider hiring a law student to create an online data repository and help you keep the research results fresh.

Form 5.1: Client Knowledge Matrices

These forms are designed to help you think about the client's world from their perspective. This is about them in their world—what is important to them in terms of their industry, key trends, and current and forthcoming regulations; and how can you use your understanding of their world to be more proactive, supportive, and effective.

Forms

For Business Entities

5.1: Client Basics—Businesses

Structure	• Legal form: • Year founded: • State founded: • Public or private:
Geographic research	• Number of entities: • HQ location: • US only or global: • If global, where?
Revenue	• Revenue current year: • Revenue past year: • Major changes in past 12 months? • Anticipated changes in next 12 months?

5.1A: Company Products/Services

This chart can be expanded to include both the major product/service line you currently work with, and those you would like to work with.

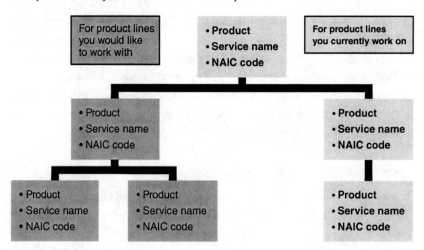

5.1B: Company Geography: National

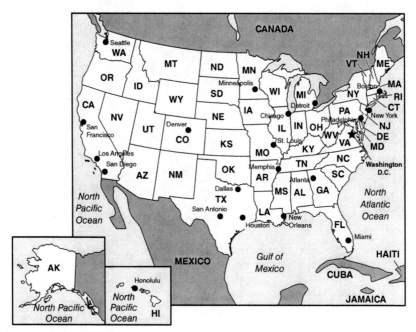

Location of:
>   Headquarters
>   Plants
>   Warehouses
>   Shipping locations
>   Offices
> Product customers
>   Sell [product] in [location]
>   Sell [product] in [location]
>   Sell [product] in [location]

Company Geography: International

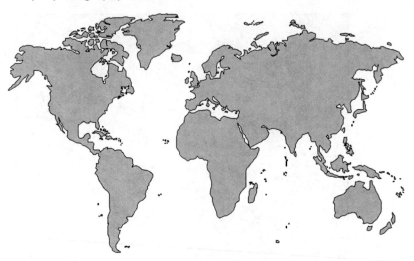

Location of:
    Headquarters
    Plants
    Warehouses
    Shipping locations
    Offices
Product customers
    Sell [product] in [location]
    Sell [product] in [location]
    Sell [product] in [location]

5.1C: Company Hierarchy

Use this chart (which can be expanded as necessary) to understand your client's organizational structure, and diagram the legal and executive reporting relationships.

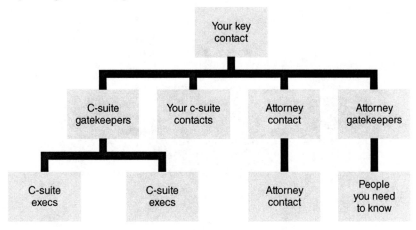

5.1D: Decision-Making Relationships

Diagram how decisions are made to hire law firms for specific kinds of work.

Hierarchical Decision-Making

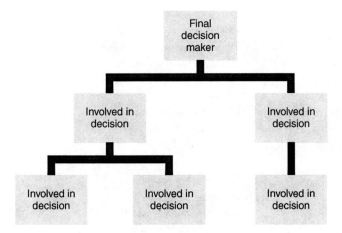

Group Decision-Making

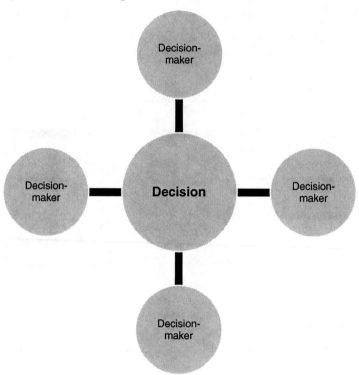

For Individuals

Form 5.1–I: Client Basics—Individuals

Structure	• Legal status: • Key dates: • Extended family components: • Relevant business interests:
Geographic rearch	• Where live now: • Extended family locations: • Business locations: • Where want to live:
Revenue	• Revenue current year: • Revenue past year: • Major changes in past 12 months? • Anticipated changes in next 12 months?

Form 5.1A–I: Current Issues Matrix

This form lays out the important aspects of current issues—internal problems related to compensation, succession planning, new markets, and such. The first box describes the issue. The second box explains what is happening that makes the issue ripe for discussion. The third box outlines the consequences of various actions or no action at all.

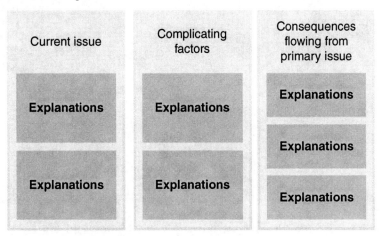

Forms 5.1B: Geography and 5.1C: Heirarchy

These forms (above) can be used for individual clients as well as business clients

Form 5.1D–I: Influencers

Use this chart to show decision-making dynamics involving the individual, the family, and outsider influencers.

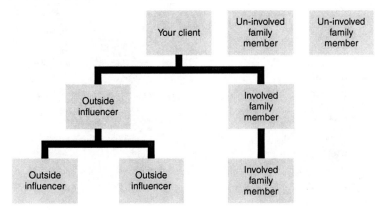

Form 5.2: Characteristics of Customers and Markets

For each major product or service line and for each product or service related to matters you handle for the client, label the product or service by its common name and its NAIC/SIC number. In the attached columns, describe the characteristics of the customers or clients that use it; the locations of the major markets in which it is produced, distributed, and sold; and major competitors in these markets.

Product or service Common name + NAIC/SIC		
Characteristics of the customers/clients	Geographic locations: Produced Distributed Sold	Competitors

Form 5.3: Communication Collaborators and Channels by Market

For each major market, identify the companies the client works with and the means used to reach the customers in that market. This becomes important for legal advisors because each communications approach has its own range of legal issues, which get further complicated by the markets involved. For example, connecting with customers in the European Union raises privacy issues not relevant to U.S. marketing communications.

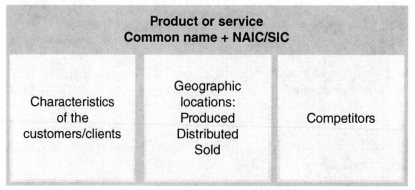

Collaborators	**Traditional channels**
PR and ad agencies	Print media
Web designers, SEO	Self-published materials
Videographers	Television ads
Photographers	Direct mail
Internet channels	**Mobile channels**
Website	Podcasts, texting
Blogs, video, email	Video
Social media	Advertising
Advertising	????

(Center: **Product/ service**)

Form 5.4: Client's Competitors

In the following table, note the major competitors along the rows and the major products/services along the columns. Place a check mark in each product/service column where the competitors (in the rows) challenge the client for customer or market share of the product/service.

Competitor Names	Product/ service name	Product/ service name	Product/ service name	Product/ service name	Product/ service name	Product/ service name
Continue to add competitor names as needed						

Form 5.5: Trends Tracker

Use this form to track current industry, economic, product-specific, and customer trends that affect the client. For impact on the client column, note the clients affected and the way in which it affects them. Under opportunity for the law firm, address how you plan to take advantage of the opportunity. Include specifics regarding what you plan to do, who will be involved in the firm, who at the client, the timing, the message, etc.

Trends	Impact on client	Opportunity for law firm
Continue to add and update at least monthly		

Form 5.6: Regulatory/Legal Tracker

Use this form to track current laws, legislation, court decisions, and rule-making activities that currently impact the client. Also identify potential legislation or rules coming down within the next twelve to eighteen months.

The decision/activities column should include legislation, statute, ordinance, regulation, rule, and court decision. The involved locales include federal, state and/or local governments or the relevant court.

Decision/ activity that affects the client	Levels of government involved	Impact on client immediately	Impact on client In 12–18 months	Opportunity for you
Continue to add and update weekly				

Form 5.7: Foundation Client Profile—Part 1 Client Characteristics and Relationships

This chart summarizes all you know about your two or three foundation clients. It includes information gathered in Chapter 4, such as relationships between yourself, your firm, and each foundation client whether the client is a business entity or a person. These include

> the referral source from which the client came
> other professionals that work for this client, including other law firms
> personal relationships with client personnel, i.e., children go to the same school, same charities

Working with Individuals Rather Than Businesses:

The data categories are the same—only the content changes.

> Instead of company details, use family details including an "org chart" of the family members and relationships
> Instead of company financials, substitute family financials, including business revenues that are relevant to the situation

> Instead of industry trends, think demographics: What are other people in this situation thinking and doing? What trends, government activities, and geographic factors impinge on everyone in this demographic?

Corporate Client Characteristics	NAME OF FOUNDATION CLIENT	Individual Client Characteristics	NAME OF FOUNDATION CLIENT
The Basics		**The Basics**	
Web site		Web site	
Legal form		Sex	
Geographic reach		Geographic reach	
Headquarters location		Client's location	
Number of years in business		Age	
Primary product(s)[2]		Religion or race (if relevant)	
Primary service(s)		Occupation/client's title	
Major markets for products/services: Geographic		Major markets for products/services: demographics	
Revenues for last fiscal year		Financial status	
Ownership arrangements		Marital status	
Number of employees		Children: sex/ages	
Growth cycle stage		Socio-economic level	
Key market trends impacting the client's products/services		Key market trends impacting the client's demographic category	
Current gossip about them		Current gossip about them	

---

2. Use the general product line name and then the NAIC/SIC classification which is more precise. Use this web site to translate product names into NAICS/SICS: http://www.naics.com/search.htm, accessed December 22, 2011.

Corporate Client Characteristics	NAME OF FOUNDATION CLIENT	Individual Client Characteristics	NAME OF FOUNDATION CLIENT
Industry (SIC/NAIC)		Demographic cohort	
Industry trends		Demographic trends	
Major trade associations/groups		Major trade associations/groups	
Key media resources –print –online		Key media resources –print –online	
Relevant federal/ state/local laws		Relevant federal/ state/local laws	
Relevant govern- ment actions		Relevant govern- ment actions	
New legislation to track		New legislation to track	
Client's sources of information about the business		Client's sources of information about the problem	
Online		Online	
Print		Print	
Associations/groups		Associations/groups	

Form 5.8: Opportunities Worksheet

How does all this collected data translate into opportunities and challenges for you and your firm?

> The *specific happening or event* column should include information such as the repercussions of the trend, relevant court decisions, legislative activities, or new laws.

> The *opportunity for you* column deals with questions such as: What is it? What aspects of your work/the firm does it relate to? Which practice areas and attorneys will be involved? Which clients does it apply to?

> The *action* column includes decisions about: Who is responsible? What are the plan details? How will it be implemented? What is the timeline—due dates? What are the measurements?

Specific Happening or Event	Opportunity for You	Action
		·
Continue to add new items and eliminate completed ones		

Form 5.9: Foundation Client Profile: Part 2 Opportunities and Approaches

These data will help you to identify the people you need to approach to discuss additional work, the specifics related to the services you want to offer, and the features, benefits and value you need to present to the client.

Corporate Client Characteristics	NAME OF FOUNDATION CLIENT	Individual Client Characteristics	NAME OF FOUNDATION CLIENT
Relationships and culture		**Relationships and culture**	
Key characteristics of their culture		Key family relationships	
Who do you know on the business side?		Who do you know in the immediate family?	
Which lawyers do you know?		Among the influencers?	
Your preferred point of contact		Your preferred point of contact	
Who do you need to know to get more work?		Who do you need to know to get more work?	
Strength of your relationship with the client: Use 1, 2, 3 1 = great, 2 = OK, 3 = weak spots		Strength of your relationship with the client: Use 1, 2, 3 1 = great, 2 = OK, 3 = weak spots	
Sales Process		**Sales Process**	
Legal work needed?		Legal work needed?	

Who gives out the work?		Who gives out the work?	
Buying decision influencers: Names/ titles Decision-makers: names/ titles		Buying decision influencers: names/ relationship to client Decision-makers: names/ relationship to client	
Your reputation in this area		Your reputation in this area	
Features/benefits/value		**Features/benefits/value**	
Features of what you do		Features of what you do	
Benefits to client		Benefits to client	
Which benefits does the client value?		Which benefits does the client value?	

Form 5.10: New Initiative Selling Points Worksheet

Describe initiative	Anticipated client action/ reaction	Client personnel involved & your relationship with them	Your sales team: Names Roles	Content of the selling proposition ("pitch")	Timeline from action decision through implementation and debriefing

CHAPTER 6

Build a Client-Centric Firm

Previous chapters have discussed communicating value that reflects clients' perceptions, and structuring communication into a 360° environment focused on the whole client. This chapter begins with a short discussion of client expectations, which set the context for the evolution of a client-centric firm. After a review of the purposes of a client-centric firm, four key components of a client-centric firm will be reviewed:

> firm culture, cross-selling, and compensation
> project management of daily work processes
> client teams
> alternatives to the billable hour

The goal of client-centricity is simple: to transform legal practices into smoothly-working systems focused on the needs and preferences of key clients.

Examine Client Expectations

What do clients want? They want concrete outcomes—results, savings in terms of time or money, and initiatives that minimize risk and maximize opportunities. Risk, from the client's point of view, pertains not only to losing the case but also to lawyer unknowns such as being surprised with a large legal bill and not being able to afford it, as well as not being able to fire your lawyer and move on to another one in the middle of the case. To minimize the risk of wayward bills, clients want their law firms to use business processes that will create efficiencies, increase staff productivity, and require the law firm to keep to a budget providing predictable costs.

On a personal level, clients are looking for safety, control, financial security, and a map to the future. They want their lawyers to treat them with respect, provide personalized top-quality service, show business smarts, solve problems quickly when necessary, and demonstrate that they value their business.[1]

These seem to be logical, obvious demands, yet when clients and law firm partners were asked "Which of the following attributes do you consider to be most important for a healthy relationship between client and advisor?" some sharp disconnects appeared between what law firm partners believed their clients were looking for and what clients said they were looking for.

> Over half of the clients said "The ability to solve a problem quickly" was the most important characteristic of a healthy relationship, compared to only one-third of the attorneys interviewed.

> Clients thought "transparency and openness," "strong relationships between board-level executives," and "relationships across the entire law firm" were more important than law firm attorneys thought they were.[2]

> Similar percentages of clients and attorneys felt that "knowledge and understanding of the client's business needs" were second in importance for a healthy relationship, with "trust" a close third.

> Law firm attorneys felt that "frequent communication," "consistency in meeting client's expectations," and "the ability to anticipate client needs" were more important than clients felt they were.

An emphasis on speed grows out of the changing composition of legal departments which are hiring more lawyers to handle normal transactions. They turn to outside firms when they don't have the time or resources to do the work in-house. Rachel Davidson, General Counsel at Airwave Solutions,[3] said, "We'll need [an external firm] to act very quickly and treat us as a significant client. I can appreciate that we expect law firms to turn on a dime and turn things around in a time-frame that we ourselves would not do, but then that's what we pay them for."[4] Simi-

---

1. *Financial Times Report: A New Dawn: Lessons for Law Firm Management in the Post-Crisis World*, 2011 [hereinafter Financial Times Report]; Thomas Clay and Eric Seeger, *Law Firms in Transition: An Altman Weil Flash Survey*, 2011.
2. *Financial Times Report, supra* note 1, at p. 18.
3. This is a London-based company that "designed, built and operates the largest public safety radio communications network in the world, delivering critical voice and data communications to organisations that provide vital public services. This includes the police, fire and ambulance services as well as local authorities, utilities and transport providers" (https://www.airwavesolutions.co.uk/, accessed December 22, 2011).
4. *Financial Times Report, supra* note 1, at. p. 19

larly in-house counsel are being asked to serve more as consigliere, participating in C-suite executives' strategic assessments of risks and opportunities. They want their outside attorneys to be familiar enough with their company and its leaders to add value to these discussions.

Reconfigure for Client-Centricity

To meet these demands, law firms need to reconfigure their firm's culture, work processes, and attorney reward systems to clearly focus on their clients. We call this a client-centric firm, created by *"Aligning the resources of [your firm] to effectively respond to the ever-changing needs of the [client], while building mutually profitable relationships."*[5] This focus has several key elements:

> ❯ alignment of lawyer and law firm resources with the client's agenda— their needs, circumstances, wishes, and perceptions
> ❯ responsiveness to changing needs
> ❯ evolution of a mutually rewarding relationship which brings clients into the lawyering process through education and teamwork

The essence of client-centricity is a mind-set that tries to understand the client's needs, wishes, and expectations and then go more than halfway to meet them. At one level, client-tuned attorneys try to think this way about every client. Client-centricity requires more time and concentration of effort because it presumes that the attorney will study not only the parts of the client that he is currently working with, but the whole entity. In order to be *that* knowledgeable about clients, their industry, their needs, wants and desires, and the context within which these play out, attorneys and firms have to prioritize to which clients they will devote their time and resources. Hence, the focus on key—or foundation—clients.

Client-centricity assumes shared knowledge. Most individual lawyers build close relationships with their clients. A deliberate client-centric firm-wide approach builds on these relationships, taking this concept to a larger arena—one in which lawyers, practice areas, offices, colleagues, and contacts work together in teams, sharing knowledge to create a seamless, information-rich platform from which to offer services. In a client-centric firm,

---

5. *Becoming Customer Centric: Finding the Voice of the Customer*, Customer Centricity, Inc., March 2006.

every point of contact that the firm has with a client is tailored and unique to that client; making it a valued client experience. . . . A valued client experience entails close collaboration where the firm knows the people, understands their business, understands the particular problem—and constantly asks for feedback about their level of understanding. And most importantly, this level of understanding must pervade the firm.[6]

Growth in a client-centric firm reflects the reality that it is cheaper and faster to get more business from current clients than to attract new clients. A marketing rule of thumb states that, eighty-five percent of next year's business is likely to come from your firm's current foundation clients.[7] "Research shows that a ten percent increase in customer retention levels result in a thirty percent increase in the value of the company."[8]

Client retention goes back to the axiom that enthusiastic, loyal clients usually don't take their business somewhere else. Customer "engagement is the emotional connection or attachment that a customer develops during the [sic] repeated and ongoing interactions."[9] A survey of business executives showed that over three-quarters of them believed that engagement would translate into more loyalty, an increase in revenue, and an increase in profits.[10]

Creating strong connections requires going beyond an individual's personal efforts and reorienting the culture of the firm to plan, promote, implement, and reward this focus.

> Ensuring the greatest possible return over the lifetime of the client relationship is dependent upon effectively expanding the scope of services delivered to a client, and providing seamless communication and client delivery across practices and geographies.[11]

To make the mindset operational, everything your firm does and everyone who works there need to be grounded in a 360° understanding of key clients. *Diagram 6.1* shows the three components of legal practice that come together in a robust client-centric firm:

---

6. Hildebrandt International, whitepaper, *Relationship Intelligence in a Competitive Market*, 2002, p. 5.
7. The Remsen Group Newsletter, "Enhancing Relationships with Existing Clients," 1998, p. 1.
8. Attributed to McKinsey, in James Digby, "50 Facts about Customer Experience," *Return on Behavior Magazine*, October 2010.
9. Kyle LaMalfa, whitepaper, *The Positive Economics of Customer Engagement*, Allegiance, Inc., 2011, p. 1.
10. *Id.*, p. 1–2.
11. Hildebrandt International, *supra* note 6, at p. 2.

> The firm—management, people, compensation system, geographic reach, technology
> Client-centric mindset—value proposition, communication standards, client feedback processes, knowledge sharing mechanisms
> Client-centric processes—client teams, project management, budgeting and metrics, billable hour alternatives, knowledge management

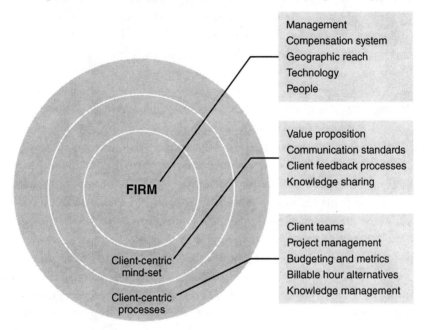

Management
Compensation system
Geographic reach
Technology
People

Value proposition
Communication standards
Client feedback processes
Knowledge sharing

Client teams
Project management
Budgeting and metrics
Billable hour alternatives
Knowledge management

FIRM

Client-centric mind-set

Client-centric processes

Diagram 6.1: Components of a Client-Centric Firm

Manage Firm Culture

For most clients, their legal experience is built around one person—their lawyer. A litigator captured the symbiotic nature of the relationship thusly:

> As lawyers we work intimately with our clients. We lay together with them under their spreadsheets. We pick up their dirty laundry. We work very closely with their management and employees on complicated matters, sometimes literally rolling up our sleeves and working all night side by side with them. We are the translators of their message to the outside world to judges, shareholders, clients, employees and their clients. We are counseling them sometimes at the worst times in their company's history. Our "bedside manner" is as important in our client's

decision to hire us and keep us as our legal intellect and experience. Any doctor can take a pulse; it's her bedside manner that keeps patients returning for care rather than moving on to find another doctor.

The narrow focus of this kind of intensity raises the question as to why a client would notice or care about the culture of the lawyer's firm? The answer is that the context within which a lawyer works influences his choices and priorities, just as the context within which the client exists influences its choices. The lawyer works within the rules—both stated and implied—set by the firm. So when a client is looking for a lawyer, the culture of the firm becomes an important differentiator among firms.

Firm culture is a "collection of shared beliefs, attitudes, practices and customs that make a business organization unique. These are the principles that guide everyday work, as well as relationships with clients and colleagues."[12] Culture underscores a firm's distinctive personality, encompasses its features, benefits, and values, and describes what its clients or customers can expect from it in terms of attitude, service, expertise, and results.

In law firms, culture is initially a by-product of the founding partners' personalities and preferences. As a firm grows, the culture changes to reflect the goals and values of new attorneys, success rates at winning/ losing cases, new practice areas, and new clients. Many law firms are content to allow these changes to evolve organically, adapting subtly over time to changes in personnel and circumstances. Usually a more directed approach is needed to move from a traditional firm organization and culture to one focused on aligning the firm's interests more closely with those of its best clients.

There are several reasons to want to manage the process of cultural change:

> keep your best clients
> meet or exceed client expectations regarding cost, service, and results
> establish better lines of communication with foundation clients
> reduce fees while simultaneously maintaining firm profitability
> expand into new geographic regions
> realize merger aspirations

---

12. David T. Brown, "Creating a Service-Driven Culture: A Strategy for Consistently Meeting Clients' Needs and Building a Strong, Enduring Firm," *Bloomberg Law Reports*, 2010, p. 1.

> reorganize management to take into account the departure of firm founders, leaders, or other important cultural influencers
> decrease firm reliance on a small number of rainmakers and increase reliance (and billing realization) on the firm's total partnership

Some of these initiatives overlap, so implementing cultural change to achieve one objective may lead to achieving some of the others. For example, establishing better communication will almost certainly result in stronger ability to meet or exceed client expectations.

Your firm already has a reputation in its markets and within its offices—every company does. Think for a minute about the different images conjured up when you talk about Wachtell, Boies, or Skadden. Before you can change the culture you'll need to take a hard look at what you are known for and known as. To pinpoint aspects of your culture that you want to change, you can begin by revisiting some of the previous research and thinking you did for Chapters 2, 4, and 5.

> Reviewing the "features" list that you created in Chapter 2 provides a guide to how you want to be perceived in the marketplace.
> Looking at what your foundation clients rely on you for provides sharper focus.
> Examining the people your firm hires and why, as well as how long they tend to stay and why they leave will give you still more insights into your firm's culture.
> Analyzing what your firm rewards—what types of behaviors and achievements lead to increases in status and/or compensation—will provide a well-rounded understanding of your firm's current culture.

Your current firm culture may only need tweaking or you may need major changes to meet the needs of your foundation clients. Use *Form 6.1: Firm Culture Congruence with Foundation Clients' Cultures*, page 156, to highlight the key components of your firm's culture and your own perspective on practicing law and then compare those characteristics to your foundation clients.

Many firms describe their cultures on their Web sites. For example, Minneapolis-based Gray Plant Moody describes itself as national, enduring (it was established in 1866), non-egotistical, collaborative, innovative, community-oriented, generous, and respectful. Reading the firm's employee-oriented culture statement, the reader gets the sense of a firm with a warm, supportive, roll-up-your-sleeves mentality. The firm also makes several statements about awards it has received for being a friendly working environment for women.[13]

Vancouver-based Farris, Vaughan, Wills & Murphy LLP delineates its culture under three headings: "a blend of tradition and innovation," "people," and "structure." The text under the first heading talks about the firm's commitment to doing great work for its clients, how it works to honor that commitment, and the environment within which it works to honor it. Under the second heading, the firm discusses its approach to balancing the individual with the team. Under the third heading, the firm presents itself as nimble and collegial, but also hints at the standards it uses for promotion and compensation.[14]

The *Financial Times' US Innovative Lawyer's Report 2011* highlights twenty-five U.S. firms that, based on client reviews, were "consistently found to be creating transformative solutions for clients."[15] No two firms have the same culture, but all consider culture to be an essential component in the promotion of innovative lawyering. The *Financial Times* also created a list of the *Business of Law Top US Innovators*[16] all of which were using business models, technology, alternative fees, or client-centric practices to provide better service at lower cost. Because the list looks at separate initiatives, firms such as Seyfarth Shaw are included in more than one category.

> Stand-out firms: Seyfarth Shaw, Bryan Cave, Axiom, Cleary Gottlieb & Hamilton, Crowell & Moring, Orrick, Herrington & Sutcliffe.
> Highly recommended: Fenwick & West, Paul Hastings, Seyfarth Shaw, WilmerHale.
> Commended: Davis Polk & Wardwell, Dechert, Dewey & LeBoeuf, Freshfields Bruckhaus Deringer, Kenyon & Kenyon, Latham & Watkins, Seyfarth Shaw, Allen & Overy, Cadwalader Wickersham & Taft, Shook Hardy & Bacon.

---

13. http://gpmlaw.com/who-we-are/culture.aspx, accessed December 22, 2011.
14. http://www.farris.com/about-farris-law/our-culture/, accessed December 22, 2011.
15. Reena SenGupta, "A Culture of Creativity," *The Financial Times*, November 3, 2011.
16. Caroline Binham, "Business of Law: forced to innovate," *The Financial Times*, November 3, 2011.

Case in Point: Transforming a Firm Culture to Meet Client Needs

Seyfarth Shaw, based in Chicago with ten other offices in the United States and one in London, is also one of the highest grossing U.S. law firms. Its Web site lists twenty categories of service offerings, ranging from securities and financial litigation to health law. Its publicly-acknowledged clients include a number of financial service firms and industrial giants such as DuPont, Motorola, and Caterpillar.

In the mid-2000s some of Seyfarth's clients made clear that they were uncomfortable continuing with the billable hour model.[17] So the firm set out to see if there was a better way to drive value for its clients than the traditional model of delivering legal services. Seyfarth wanted to provide its clients with what they were asking for: timely and efficient delivery of legal services; lower, more predictable costs; quality work that did not become commoditized; and greater transparency.[18]

Working with consultants, the firm began to look at everything it did, why it did it, and how. The result is "SeyfarthLean," a customized approach to process management and performance evaluation that starts with mapping each step of a process.[19] "SeyfarthLean" has transformed the culture from one based on traditional hierarchies and "we've always done it that way" to one where dynamic teams come together on a regular basis to ask why things need to be done a particular way and whether there is a better way to do it.

As part of its cultural transformation, Seyfarth has

> ❯　reduced client legal bills by between fifteen percent (for mergers and acquisitions, and real estate matters) and fifty percent (for a single plaintiff litigation)[20]
> ❯　deepened relationships with current clients and attracted new companies that might not otherwise have contacted the firm to retain it[21] and

---

17. Elaine Schmidt, "Law and Order: 64-year-old law firm Seyfarth Shaw adapts Six Sigma to the delivery and billing of legal services," *iSixSigma Magazine*, November/December 2009.

18. http://www.seyfarth .com has a substantial amount of information about the firm's culture conversion, including direct links to many of the articles cited here.

19. SeyfarthLean is a combination of two established process management systems, Six Sigma and Lean. Six Sigma is a data-driven approach to business process improvement in which the "product" can fail to meet customer expectations only 3.4 times per million opportunities. Lean is a process-driven approach made famous (but not originated) by Toyota in which every aspect of manufacturing a product or delivering a service is examined for potential efficiencies. Typically, those responsible for each manufacturing or delivery step are also responsible for evaluating its effectiveness. Basic information about both can be found on www.wikipedia.org. Seyfarth adapted both of these processes to meet its particular needs, streamlining them to have less reliance on data tools and less emphasis on statistical work, which its attorneys had found cumbersome (Schmidt, *supra* note 42.).

20. Schmidt, *supra* note 42.

21. *American Lawyer* interview, April 1, 2010. The interview is available in video format at http://www .seyfarth.com. As of the date of the interview, feedback mechanisms and hard measures were still pending.

❭   mapped over 110 processes, which allow attorneys to look for efficiencies across the range of its practice[22]

The process has solidified the sense of teamwork between inside and outside lawyers. Clients have become fully engaged with the firm in managing their own matters. They can see at a glance how their failure to deliver a document or piece of information on time will have a ripple effect on the entire process, according to the firm's director of strategic management.[23]

Seyfarth has received significant accolades from the legal industry. It was praised by the Association of Corporate Counsel as "five years ahead of every other *AmLaw 200* firm."[24] The firm was also mentioned three times on the *Financial Times' 2011 List of Top U.S. Innovators* in the business of law.[25]

The Seyfarths of the world are not the only ones who can institute change. At the solo level, change may be easier and faster to implement due to the absence of office politics. A solo practitioner can decided to implement the client-centric approach and in a matter of hours or days draw up the guidelines of the new processes. It may take many months of transition for the solo lawyer to become skilled in the various aspects of client-focus, but it takes years for large firms to begin to turn around even one-quarter of their practice. It is the turning radius of a sailboat compared to that of the Queen Mary. The same agility resides in small firms, once the partners agree on the new direction.

Overview of Legal Project Management

Legal project management has been defined as "a proactive, disciplined approach to the management of legal matters using tools, skills, knowledge, and systems to enhance efficiency and meet client expectations."[26] The approach, adapted from the business world,

---

22. Binham, *supra* note 16.

23. Schmidt, *supra* note 42.

24. This accolade is cited in every partner biography on the Seyfarth Shaw Web site and in nearly every article about Seyfarth's adaptation of project management.

25. The firm made it into the top tier of so-called "stand out" firms for its client service model. It was the only firm to receive a top rating of eight across all three criteria: originality, rationale, and impact. The summary states: "Using the Six Sigma management process to revamp the firm's business model in a way that is unique to the profession. In some cases, the firm has been able to reduce fees by 30 per cent." The authors of this book would argue that "business model" and "culture" are interchangeable in this context. Additionally, Seyfarth was highly commended for facilitating a multinational transaction for Royal Bank of Canada, which also involves its Six Sigma process, and commended for its cross-border business model for employment law services.

26. Susan Raridon Lambreth and Carla Landry, whitepaper, "Can Lawyers Be Trained as Project Managers," Hildebrandt Baker Robbins, 2010, p. 1.

looks at the parts of a process then reconfigures it to be more efficient and effective. Innovative leaders can "apply business process re-engineering principles to reduce inefficiencies in the delivery of legal services, which can increase quality while decreasing delivery time, eliminate redundant or unnecessary steps, and allow for the use of prior work product."[27]

Project management tools facilitate deeper client engagement, rapid evaluation of strategic approaches, and a shared focus on objectives. As *Diagram 6.2: Project Constraints* shows, every legal project is affected or constrained by four elements:[28]

> *Scope*—Objectives and work product—what the client wants to accomplish and how the attorney is going to help him accomplish it.
> *People*—The team assigned to the project on both the firm side and the client side.
> *Time*—Elapsed time from beginning to end, hours of active effort, external time constraints.
> *Cost*—The amount of money the project is likely to require—both time and expenses.

Changes in any one of these elements impact the others. For example, if in a whistleblower case the lawyer determines that more discovery is required than originally estimated, then the scope, time involved, and costs will also increase.

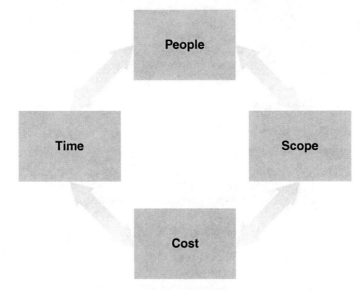

Diagram 6.2: Project Constraints

27. Anne Urda, "Rio Tinto Outsourcing Signals New Threat to Biglaw," *After the Crisis Management Lessons for Law Firms* (Law 360, 2009), p. 46.
28. *ACC Primer—Legal Project Management*, 2010, p. 5.

Project management procedures enable law firms and their clients to work together in full awareness of these constraints, making adjustments as needed. The approach also provides protocols for keeping clients informed about progress, unexpected obstacles, and a need for additional resources. The process fosters the transparency clients want because it enables the client to check in at any time at any personnel level to keep tabs on what's happening.

Using project management techniques, attorneys and clients can be fully collaborative partners in achieving client objectives. Rather than postponing unpleasant surprises until the conclusion of the matter, project management facilitates ongoing communication, work efficiencies, and cost-consciousness on both sides.

Diagram 6.3 provides a high-level overview of stages in the project management process.[29]

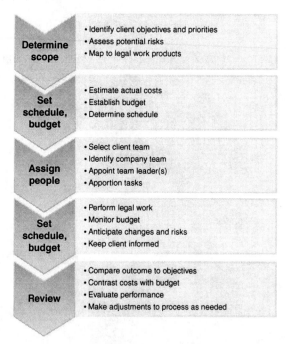

Determine scope
• Identify client objectives and priorities
• Assess potential risks
• Map to legal work products

Set schedule, budget
• Estimate actual costs
• Establish budget
• Determine schedule

Assign people
• Select client team
• Identify company team
• Appoint team leader(s)
• Apportion tasks

Set schedule, budget
• Perform legal work
• Monitor budget
• Anticipate changes and risks
• Keep client informed

Review
• Compare outcome to objectives
• Contrast costs with budget
• Evaluate performance
• Make adjustments to process as needed

Diagram 6.3: Steps in Legal Project Management

29. Different experts in legal project management take slightly different approaches. For example, Hassett's approach is organized according to eight key issues: set objectives and identify scope; identify and schedule activities; assign tasks and manage the team; plan and manage the budget; assess risks; manage quality; manage client communications and expectations; and negotiate changes of scope (*Legal Project Management Quick Reference Guide*). The ACC Value Challenge establishes four steps: scope, schedule/people/budget, conduct of legal matter, and review. Regardless of how you choose to parse the process, the essential elements are the same.

There are many ways to implement project management, from the very basic approach outlined here to the highly-structured and highly-specific blend of Six Sigma and Lean performance improvement processes adapted by Seyfarth Shaw. The right approach for your firm or practice depends on your work style and firm culture. Ideally, the firm will employ technology platforms and protocols that enable attorneys to collaborate and communicate with clients, and readily access knowledge across the firm.[30] In smaller firms and solo practices, attorneys can use cloud technology and smartphone apps to create a similarly integrated system.

Change like this can be personally disconcerting and financially expensive. The dislocation can be minimized if you begin with one practice area, one set of clients such as your foundation clients, and develop processes that coordinate with theirs and meet their goals. You can use your initial client matter meetings to establish project scope, potential risks, timeline, budget, and project team. After the client signs-off on the plan, this becomes the guide to monitor what is happening as the matter progresses. As work proceeds, both the relationship partner and the client can continually compare real-time activity to the plan.

The process specifies ongoing communication that effectively makes the client a part of the law firm's business. It also is a key way to set and refine expectations. When something in the project changes, the partner and client will review the precise nature of the change and discuss options for responding to it in order to achieve an acceptable outcome. The partner will rework the budget, timeframe, and other elements of the project plan; get client buy-in; and proceed. This is the client-centric firm approach that keeps the client at the center of your practice, demonstrates your trustworthiness, and decreases the likelihood that you will have to take a significant write-off on a particular matter.

Compensation

Two aspects of the culture are particularly important in terms of client-centricity. The first is compensation. It is a truism that people do what is rewarded. When a firm focuses financial rewards on origination of new clients rather than expansion of current clients, it will be harder to create the client-centric foundation piece: depth of client. When individuals "own"

---

30. There are many collaboration tools that allow clients to check on the progress of work and provide information. These include "cloud computing" solutions specifically adapted to the security needs of law firms. There are also knowledge and process management tools that can help firms capture raw information, innovative thinking and solutions, prior work, and best practices across the firm. See http://www.technolawyer.com for continuing updates on trends and technology applications geared toward small and solo firm practices.

their clients, it is harder to cross-sell services. When compensation is tied to billable hours, attorneys have little short-term incentive to spend non-billable hours on business development—even with their own clients.

> While firms put plenty of energy into financial metrics like revenue per lawyer and profits per partner, metrics associated with lawyer efficiency, quality of work, client satisfaction and suitability of results are completely lacking at most firms. But aren't they the elements that most accurately measure the long-term worth of a firm's client relationships—the true asset that the firm possesses? . . .[31]

Many of the largest firms are developing these types of measurements, but fewer are implementing them in a rigorous way. In smaller firms, the stumbling block to measurement may be partly an assumption that everyone is doing their best, but more likely relates to a wish to avoid uncomfortable management decisions. How do you tell a long time employee that he is not pulling his weight? How do you fire a family member in a small firm?

Compensation systems that reward expansion of services will encourage attorneys to seek client depth, by identifying new areas where their firm can offer value and then working with those colleagues to introduce their clients to them. Firms that offer soft rewards such as public recognition of client service excellence, or small gift "thank yous" for high client satisfaction marks may find that being appreciated and recognized are more consistent motivators than more money.

Cross-Selling

Practice group silos and tightly-controlled one-on-one relationships sometimes favor the well-being of a few attorneys over that of the firm as a whole and, more importantly, of clients. Hoarding discourages cross-selling, limiting the potential for what should be a slam-dunk: developing additional business from people who already know and trust you.

It is sometimes difficult to institute knowledge-sharing mechanisms in firms in where attorneys practice as "lone rangers." Attorneys are reluctant to share their most valuable asset—their clients—with others when they are not sure exactly what they do or how well they do it. To counter

---

31. Patrick McKenna and Edwin Reeser, "Low Return," The *American Lawyer*, November 2011.

this kind of isolation, firms can organize knowledge-sharing activities such as retreats, practice group or industry group meetings, and internal publicity about shared successes on the firm's communication system. Once people have a better understanding of what their colleagues are doing and a sense of pride in how well they do it, cross-selling becomes a more comfortable option.

The Successful Cross-Sale

Two examples of successful cross-selling programs demonstrate the wide variety of approaches.

At Goulston & Storrs, the marketing director spearheaded the effort which began by bringing all the partners together. Each partner filled in a one piece sheet of paper with three columns: client name, what we do for the client now, and what other legal needs the client might have. The marketing director put the data on a spreadsheet that was circulated to all the partners. The rainmaker partners began to act immediately. Others needed training, but with continued marketing assistance, cross-selling began to happen.[32]

Winston & Strawn used industry-specific roundtables as a cross-selling platform. Roundtable participants included high-level executives and selected Winston & Strawn lawyers. Questions related to major industry trends were circulated in advance. The lawyers demonstrated their expertise whenever legal issues became the topic of conversation. The cumulative effect of these meetings was more business.[33]

Cross-selling in a client-centric firm begins by thinking about what is best for the client. Will inviting one of your partners to help your client actually benefit the client? Do you know enough about the client's legal needs to assess the value to the client?

By cross-selling services, your law practice both affirms and builds client relationships. Research has shown that the longer a client has a relationship with a firm and the more of its services it uses, the less likely the client is to leave that firm.[34] Each time you perform an additional service

---

32. Jim Hassett, "Cross-Selling Strategies: Cultivating New Business from Current Clients," *Legal Management*, November-December, 2007, p. 58.
33. Jim Hassett, "Legal Business Development: Best Practices: Cross-Selling," Part 2 of 5, December 26, 2007 (http://adverselling.typepad.com/how_law_firms_sell/2007/12/draft.html, accessed December 22, 2011).
34. "Seventy-three percent of marketing managers of various large companies credit 'repeat purchase behavior' as integral to the definition of successful customer engagement." Attributed to *Forbes Magazine* [no date] in James Digby, *supra* note 8.

well for your foundation clients you are creating stronger ties between you, your firm, and the client. Use *Form 6.2: Cross-Selling Opportunities Grid*, page 157, to tie events to cross-selling opportunities to action plans.

Lawyers in solo or small firm practices can use the same client-centric focus to cross-sell services by creating their own affinity groups of like-minded colleagues and friends in different practice areas. Having already put their trust in an attorney, clients are likely to turn to her for recommendations when they need additional professional services, rather than doing the vetting themselves. Assembling virtual teams of advisors demonstrates client-centricity—and helps practices develop deeper, more lasting relationships with clients. Technology facilitates the integration of work from multiple providers. Just as in larger firms, small firm, and solo attorneys can cultivate client confidence by sharing stories about their work and advice on when clients need their services.

Enter the 21st Century: Legal Project Management

Legal project management (LPM) is a ground-breaking trend whose time has come. Paired with effective use of technology, it can jump the practice of law from the nineteenth-century world of individually crafted work product to the twenty-first–century world where best practices can be instantly replicated. At the same time, it is scary to contemplate its impact on a profession still tied to the billable hour. Thus the paradox that ninety-four percent of managing partners said that the "focus on improved practice efficiency" is a permanent trend, yet it was a 2011 top investment priority for only twenty-seven percent of them.[35]

LPM practices are not reserved for the law firms that can afford project management software. Project management applies equally, if not more significantly, to the sole practitioner and small firm who have fewer resources to do more tasks. Some lawyers in small firms and solo practices see it as a career canceller because it will do away with many repetitive legal tasks that build up billable hours. This may be true, but at the same time, it will enable lawyers to charge for their value instead

---

35. Thomas Clay and Eric Seeger, *supra* note 1; The three investments that managing partners believed would "yield the greatest expected returns" were: business development (focused on new clients), adding new lawyers, client relationships (focused on building relationships with current clients).

of their time. It can free them to be advisors and creative problem solvers, adding value by seeing business problems through a legal lens.

Certainly for small firms, project management makes sense as an investment priority because implementation of these practices harnesses technology so lawyers can work more efficiently, take advantage of "best practices" anywhere in the firm, and avoid "reinventing the wheel" syndrome.[36] "The benefits of LPM, however, are just as applicable to small firms and solo practitioners. . . . Already, the small-firm attorney has more hands-on practice-management experience than his or her big-law counterpart. . . . Attorneys in smaller firms have to fill more roles and are involved in more aspects of managing a matter than attorneys at larger firms."[37]

Small law firms can begin with training in the role of project manager and how to integrate that with the role of lawyer. Begin by considering how to use current techniques in a process management framework. "A well-designed client-intake form, for example, can help you and your client begin formulating the theory of the case, manage client expectations, and provide an outline for an initial consultation. Similarly, project charters, work-breakdown structures, communication plans, budgeting spreadsheets, and scheduling tools can help you focus on project-management considerations."[38]

Traditional firm structure and processes, such as hourly billing, are focused on the law firm and its attorneys rather than on the clients the work is supposed to benefit. The introduction of legal project management tools is one way to modernize law firm management practices and move the workplace focus more toward the client. The trend is driven by clients—particularly general counsel who want their outside lawyers to use the same business processes they use.

> At the root of this experimentation [with business-based legal service delivery systems] is the need for both large and small firms to assess the services they provide, define the value proposition they offer their

---

36. This was the fourth of eight findings in *Financial Times Report, supra* note 1, at p. 3). Also note that the same study showed clients placing a much higher priority than attorneys on the ability to solve problems quickly (p. 18).
37. Paul Easton, Small Firm Legal Project Management Challenges, October 28, 2010 at http://adverselling.typepad.com/
38. Id.

clients and communicate both of these. . . . Legal competence alone . . . no longer guarantees professional or economic success.[39]

"Already some progressive law firms are beginning to offer clients customized project pricing and unbundled services and to increase their use of offshore partners and contract lawyers."[40] In firms that adopt business-process techniques, the "lone ranger" work schedule and personal time management system are replaced by processes that:

> define the roles and functions of everyone who works on a matter
> enable the client to review staffing patterns and communicate directly with those doing the work
> create budgets and schedules which avoid the "surprise" factor of missed deadlines and cost overruns
> increase efficiency by focusing on workflow
> reinforce the client's interest in the best job accomplished within his time parameters rather than the perfect job that runs over them

See the overview of legal project management on page 140 for more detail.

Consider Client Teams

Client teams have increasingly become the vehicle for implementing practice management. In a 2011 Thomson Reuters survey of law firm leaders, twenty-nine percent said that they are planning to increase the use of teams to manage matters.[41]

Client teams typically include the relationship attorney, all other personnel who work on the client's matters (including paraprofessionals, librarians, and support staff), and lawyers from practice areas that might be of value to the client. Teams can range in size from three to thirty-three people. Regardless of size, the purpose is to ensure that everyone working for a client knows what everyone else is doing so efforts are coordinated.

39. NYSBA Report of the Task Force on the Future of the Legal Profession, April 2, 2011, p. 31.
40. Julie Zeveloff, "Recession Gives Law Firms Chance for Change," *Law 360: After the Crisis: Management Lessons for Law Firms* (Portfolio Media, Inc., 2009).
41. "Insights," *Hildebrandt Headlines*, June 3, 2011 (http://hildebrandt.staged.hubbardone.com/June-3-2011-06-03-2011, accessed December 22, 2011).

Teams become the focal point and conduit for the research collected in Chapters 4 and 5 about what the client needs and what the firm can do to address—even anticipate—those needs. Team objectives reflect the client-centric firm's commitment to client value. The team format maximizes the potential that your foundation clients represent to you, and at the same time, provides a vehicle for enhancing the client's perception of received value. Bryan Cave and WilmerHale were cited on the *FT Business of Law Innovative Lawyers* 2011 list for their teams.[42]

Client teams are also important at Latham & Watkins, where they have four objectives—all client focused:

> optimize client relationships by providing a high level of service for the total client in their global environment
> give clients a team of consistent personnel, and use the team situation to deepen relationships among firm members and within the client
> identify and resolve any client satisfaction issues
> institutionalize the client within the firm by expanding their use of the firm across practice areas, departments, and offices[43]

In an era where laterals often follow the highest bidder for their book of business, client service teams protect a firm's major assets—its clients—by building multiple relationships within and between client and law firm.

The "voice of the client" as reflected in client interview feedback (see Chapter 2) and individual matter process plans should guide client teams' strategies. Teams meet on a regular basis to:

> share information about client happenings and current events of relevance to the client
> strategize on ways to increase the firm's relevance and value for the client

---

42. Binham, *supra* note 16. See more about the firms at http://www.bryancave.com/bryancave/overview/ and http://www.wilmerhale.com/.
43. Despina Kartson, CMO, Latham & Watkins, Slides at New York Bar Association CLE, "Running a Client-Centric Practice—the Why & How," October 26, 2011; Larry Bodine, "Thompson & Knight Builds 50 Client Teams in a Year," *Law Marketing Portal*, December 12, 2002 (since removed); Jim Rishwain, "Commentary: Making Client Teams Work," May 18, 2007 (http://www.law.com/jsp/article .jsp?id=900005555250, accessed December 22, 2011, subscription required) discussing Pillsbury Winthrop's teams. He quotes a BTI survey that in 2007 seventy percent of the AmLaw 200 were using client teams.

> review service delivery status and deal with any quality issues
> plan specific initiatives and assign responsibilities
> coordinate and replicate best practices

Client teams began in the largest firms, but smaller firms can also apply the concept, which is less about size and more about a unified, strategic, proactive, results-oriented approach to clients' issues. The size of the team is less important than its function as a staging ground for integrated client attention and care. In a small firm, lawyers can create teams including themselves, paralegals, administrative staff who work with the client plus law school interns and others who do client research. Solos can create teams within their referral attorney groups. Once you create teams, use *Form 6.3: Client Team Action Grid*, page 158, to record progress and plan for next steps.

Successful teams foster firm growth in three ways:

> protection—the client-team relationship cements relationships
> penetration—client teams increase the ability to anticipate ways to work with the client, which leads to expanded use of firm services
> profitability—teams focus firm growth on firms' capabilities to increase their depth of client and identify and win business from similar new clients

Where teams contribute to the stability and profitability of the firm, there is always the support of top management and a reward system that compensates team members for participation and performance. The firm also invests in the infrastructure needed for the team to learn, anticipate, and deliver on client's needs before a crisis occurs. Large firms are investing in technology-based knowledge management systems; a robust research process to find, update, compile, analyze, and distribute relevant information; and a communication system that facilitate the team's role. In smaller firms, cloud-based technology can be used in a similar fashion.

Deliver a Better Value: Alternative Fee Arrangements

There is no disputing the fact that alternative fee arrangements (AFAs) are on the rise. Increased competition, decreased or zero leverage, and client demands for less costly and more predictable fees all point in the direction of less reliance on the straight billable hour. In a 2011 survey of law firm management trends, eighty-eight percent of the managing partners and chairs who responded said that "more price competition" will be a permanent trend going forward.[44]

The term "alternative fee arrangements" generally means all fees not based strictly on quoted rates for billable hours. Some versions like contingency fees and flat rates have always been around; with newer hybrid arrangements both client and law firm share the risk and reward of process efficiencies and success. *Form 6.4: Alternative Fee Arrangements Overview*, page 158, reviews the advantages and disadvantages of some of the major versions.

Firms are responding to both marketplace and client demands for pricing discount predictability. According to Altman Weil's 2011 *Lawyers in Transition Flash Survey*, ninety-five percent of all firms, regardless of size, were using AFAs in 2011.[45] One hundred percent of the respondent firms with more than 250 lawyers reported using AFAs.[46] Data in *Fulbright's Litigation Trends Survey Report* corroborates this trend: They report an increase in the use of AFAs for litigation matters from forty-five percent in 2009 to sixty-two percent in 2011.[47]

Law firms are not racing to embrace the AFA concept, however. Managing partners in the Altman Weil survey by two to one said that their use of AFAs was reactive—in response to clients' requests, not proactive. Forty percent of the firms with a reactive stance felt AFAs were less profitable, while sixty percent of the proactive firms felt AFAs were either more profitable than or as profitable as the billable hour formula.[48] Reactive or proactive, three-quarters of the respondents know non-hourly billing is here to stay.

Alternative fees reflect both the nature of the work and the value assigned to the matter by the client. Thus, commodity work is price sensitive, while bet-the-company or highly-specialized work is price insensitive. In between is the whole range of services where price depends on the qualifications and brand power of the provider and the importance of the solution to the client. Services can move between categories; for example,

---

44. Thomas Clay and Eric Seeger, *supra* note 1.
45. Thomas Clay and Eric Seeger, *supra* note 1, at p. 3. The survey was distributed to managing partners and chairs at 805 U.S. firms with fifty or more lawyers; 240 responded.
46. Id.
47. Fulbright & Jaworski LLP, *8th Annual Litigation Trends Report*, 2011.
48. Thomas Clay and Eric Seeger, *supra* note 1, at p. 3.

patent prosecutions once price insensitive are now becoming viewed as a commodity and priced at a correspondingly lower level flat rate.

The point of an alternative fee arrangement is to provide your clients maximum value (as defined by them) while simultaneously achieving profitability for your firm. Initiating discussions about alternative fee arrangements with your current and potential foundation clients *before they ask* demonstrates your commitment to identifying and delivering what they value. The downside risk is fairly low because you already have some understanding of these clients and the demands they might place on your firm. The upside reward is potentially great because these clients will recognize that the AFA offer reflects the fact that you are making an investment in your relationship.

Three U.S. firms made the *Financial Times Business of Law Innovative Firms,* 2011 list for their approach to alternative fee arrangements:[49]

> Crowell & Moring embraced the concept of AFAs and uses them with twenty-five of their top clients; the fees represented one-third of revenue in 2010.

> WilmerHale was one of the first firms to go to market with a comprehensive AFA program as part of a full revamping of the firm to focus on client relationships, strategy, and team management as well as billing arrangements. Fifteen percent of the firm's fees are under AFAs.[50]

> Shook, Hardy & Bacon worked with Tyco to control litigation costs using AFAs. The firm now uses AFAs in other practice areas and with other clients. A key biography on the Shook, Hardy & Bacon Web site, states: "Since 2004, Paul has managed the firm's role as Tyco International's National Counsel of Product Liability Litigation, leading a team of SHB lawyers in a flat-fee partnership with the company. Together, he and the company have reduced Tyco's overall inventory of product liability cases by more than half and its level of new matters filed has been decreased by nearly sixty percent. In 2010, Tyco International expanded its relationship

---

49. Binham, *supra* note 16.
50. See http://www.wilmerhale.com/about/alternative_fee_arrangements/ (accessed December 22, 2011).

with SHB, naming the firm National Counsel of Automotive and General Liability Litigation."[51]

AFAs have not arrived without pushback from both in-house attorneys and law firms who feel that the use of success sweeteners requires a lawyer to promise outcomes and that incentives to shave costs imply lower quality work. In fact, creating AFAs requires no absolute outcome promises, and if structured properly, incentivizes law firms to use business processes and technology to create efficiencies that are rewarded by the client under the terms of the agreement.

What AFAs *do* require is a closer understanding of where, when, and how a lawyer makes money. AFAs and project management go hand in hand: project management segments work flow into tasks and budgets dollars and staff to each segment. AFAs use that breakdown to set fee ranges for matters, projects, or segments of a process such as the early case assessment or deposition phase in litigation. Both AFAs and project management require three preconditions:

> trust among firm members and with the client
> attorney knowledge as to how much it costs to do what you do, and how important the matter is to your client
> empowered and rewarded law firm participants

In order to set alternative fees at levels that allow you to make money, you need to know your cost of doing business. Numerous matter management, e-billing, and budgeting programs facilitate data collection. Many firms use the ABA's LEDES (Legal Electronic Data Exchange Standard) billing codes to track time and expenses at the task level.[52]

To establish the firm's average cost for specific types of work, you should track at least six months and analyze your matters by type of activity, staffing level, and realization. Segmenting costs by task allows you to break down litigation and long transactions into component parts

---

51. See Paul Williams' biography at http://www.shb.com/attorney_detail.aspx?id=273 (accessed December 22, 2011).
52. "Law firms that use e-billing create computerized invoices that conform in their arrangement of entries and their data file format to a preset model, most often LEDES. . . . Information on the standard is at www.ledes.org. Into this standard LEDES format the firm enters numeric codes that describe actions taken on behalf of clients. These codes also conform to a preset format, usually UTBMS, which stands for Uniform Task-Based Management System. Details on those codes can be found at the American Bar Association Section of Litigation's site at www.abanet.org/litigation/_litnews/practice/uniform.html."—"Catching the E-Billing Wave: Feature with Phillip M. Perry," *Law Practice Management*, September, 2003.

and price each according to the activity and level of risk. These data can then be analyzed for median and mean averages to discern guidelines for pricing component parts of a matter. Add this time and money data to time and expertise level projections that reflect the jurisdiction, number of parties, size of transaction, and other variables. You might also want to follow the lead of other businesses and insert an amount for fixed costs including overhead, salaries, and ordinary office expenses such as faxes, copying, etc. Finally, you want to add in a profit percentage.[53]

Law firms are under increasing pressure to not only understand their clients' businesses, but also to function more like them. Performance measurements will become more common, and these will need alternative fee arrangements in order to be meaningful. Creativity in developing legal solutions for clients will be fueled by strategic reuse and adaptation of prior processes and work, which lends itself to alternative fee arrangements. The growing number of options for obtaining routine legal work will also put demands on law firms to answer "How much does it cost?" before proceeding with many standard legal matters. The good news is that clients are nearly as concerned with transparency of pricing as they are with competitive pricing.[54] This gives firms a tremendous opportunity to demonstrate client-centricity by adjusting fees so they are driven by client needs, rather than billable hours.

Keep Your Foundation Clients Front and Center

Client-centric plans for individual clients are a natural outgrowth of a firm that seeks, as its raison d'être, to create value for clients. It is important to begin with foundation clients because the learning curve about clients' worlds can be steep. Attorneys can maximize their knowledge investment by focusing on the clients and industries or demographic cohorts that represent the foundation clients.

---

53. See ACC Value Challenge (http://www.acc.com/valuechallenge, accessed December 2011) for a variety of approaches to all the topics discussed in this chapter. There is no standard formula for determining profit margins for law firms. According to a *2010 Bloomberg Businessweek* study (Joel Stonington, *Most and Least Profitable Business Types: Tracking 2010 Profit Margins in 97 Industries*), legal services were ranked third in terms of profitability, with a net profit margin of 16.75 percent. A whitepaper on alternative fee arrangements for law firms from accounting firm Marks Paneth & Shron (*Law Firm Solutions: Strategies and Solutions for Continuing to Grow Your Firm*, March 2011), suggests that law firms seeking to offer clients fixed fees should, after doing a thorough cost accounting analysis to determine actual costs, add twenty-five to thirty-three percent for profits.
54. *Financial Times Report, supra* note 1, at pp. 13, 15, 16.

Client teams, project management techniques, alternative fees, and other client-focused initiatives can be designed keeping the needs of these core clients in mind.

Create a Client-Focused Action Plan for Your Foundation Clients

Drawing on what you know about your firm and your foundation clients from your research in Chapters 4 and 5, use *Form 6.5: Foundation Client Outreach Form*, page 161, to outline a goal-driven client care plan to increase your depth of client. This may mean work for additional practice areas or expansion into different kinds of work within one practice area. For example, a litigator could create a plan to expand the number of practice areas a foundation client uses by introducing attorneys from the employment and corporate practice areas, or he could decide to expand the breadth of litigation services with the client by adding directors and officers liability and employment cases to complement the product liability work the group does already. To get the most out of each client program include a client feedback plan, metrics to track progress, and a series of in-person relationship strengthening initiatives.

Include Metrics from the Beginning

The first step is to benchmark where you are at the point where you initiate client-centric changes. As you plan programs, think about how you can measure the success of the activity. There are many analytical programs that can track each segment of your plan. You don't need computer programs to begin benchmarking, though.

> How many matters have we completed with _____ client since the beginning of the client-centric program?
> How many practice areas do these clients use now compared to during the benchmark period?
> How has the relationship expanded within the firm and at the client since the benchmark date?
> How many referrals have people at the client organization made to you and others on the client team? How many referrals have been made to and for client contacts?
> Looking at your "80/20," assess the number of new clients in this group, and review reasons clients dropped down.

> Are you less dependent on a handful of key clients for the majority of your revenue?
> How many clients in your "80/20" are also in the "80/20" for key practice areas and geographic areas?

Expand Client-Centricity in Your Firm

It's incredible to think that in a recent survey of marketing professionals fewer than twenty percent of marketers include client-focused initiatives among their top three strategic initiatives for 2011.[55] By contrast, the client-centric firm will focus on client retention and growth—delighting clients by exceeding their expectations, and growing the firm by creating expanded relationships with key clients. Of course, foundation clients are not the end of a client-centric program: they are the beginning point. As you create communications programs, modernize your work processes, and support the collaborative elements in your culture you will want to expand what works to other clients.

Forms

Form 6.1: Firm Culture Congruence with Foundation Clients' Cultures

This worksheet is intended to help you assess the degree of congruence between the cultural characteristics of your firm and the cultural characteristics you've identified as important for each of your foundation clients.

> In the left-hand column, write down the eight to twelve key characteristics of your culture—what is rewarded and how it feels to work at the firm. Then circle a number between one and five to indicate which characteristic is closer to the culture of the firm.
> In the middle column, circle the number that comes closest to showing the degree of congruence between your culture and that of each foundation client. Use five to represent a strong similarity and one to show a disconnect.

---

55. "Is Customer Retention Really Marketing's Lowest Priority?" *Go-To-Market Strategies*, 9/12/11 (http://www.gtms-inc.com/Is-Customer-Retention-Really-Marketings-Lowest-Priority_ep_179.html, accessed December 22, 2011).

> In the right-hand column, define any actions you may want to take to strengthen the areas of similarity and make changes in the areas that show a disconnect.

Major Culture Characteristics	Degree of Congruence with Foundation Clients low high	Initiatives to Align Cultures
Style 1 2 3 4 5 Substance	Insert foundation client name 1 2 3 4 5	
Casual 1 2 3 4 5 Formal	Insert foundation client name 1 2 3 4 5	
Highly Leveraged 1 2 3 4 5 Low Leverage	Insert foundation client name 1 2 3 4 5	
Top-down Leadership 1 2 3 4 5 Collaborative Work style	Insert foundation client name 1 2 3 4 5	
Innovative 1 2 3 4 5 Traditional	Insert foundation client name 1 2 3 4 5	
Reward Acquisitions 1 2 3 4 5 Reward depth of client	Insert foundation client name 1 2 3 4 5	
Add others to reflect your firm	*Add additional clients as appropriate*	

Form 6.2: Cross-Selling Opportunities Grid

Use this to tie specific context opportunities or changes at the client to services you offer, and then draft the action plan to introduce those resources to your client.

Specific Happening or Event	Services to Offer and Reasons Why	Action Plan
Continue to add new items and eliminate completed ones		

Form 6.3: Client Team Action Grid

In each team meeting, use this form to document progress to date, individuals involved at both the client and in the firm, and anticipated next steps with assigned responsibilities, time line, due dates, and measurement metrics.

Client _____ Date _____

Existing Business Update	New Business Update	Cross-Selling Update
Continue to add new items and eliminate completed ones		

Form 6.4: Alternative Fee Arrangements Overview

Alternatives to Straight Billable Hour Basis for Fees[56]	Advantages	Disadvantages	When Used
Usually a Version of Billable Hour Rates			
Fixed/Flat fees - per deliverable - per matter	• Fee known from the beginning • Leverages firm's expertise and efficiency • Requires specificity regarding work to be done because sets "all-in" price • Creates some shared risk • Clients can compare prices of firms, so over time will drive down price	• Still based on billable hours • When unforeseen events arise: –Firm assumes cost overruns risk –Client assumes risk of bad outcome	• High volume, routine, commodity work where costs are easy to predict and surprises rare • *Per deliverable*: Use for distinct, measurable component pieces of work—e.g., draft and argue summary motion, per deposition, produce initial draft of specific contract • *Per matter*: e.g., specific type of commercial RE transaction, defense of a single plaintiff employment lawsuit up to trial

---

56. Adapted from James Durham and Deborah McMurray (eds), *The Lawyer's Guide to Marketing Your Practice*, (ABA Law Practice Management Section, 2d ed, 2004), Chapter 9, and Association of Corporate Counsel, *ACC Value-Based Fee Primer*, July 2010, pp. 6–8, 31–32. The advantages and disadvantages in this table are as perceived by the client.

Alternatives to Straight Billable Hour Basis for Fees	Advantages	Disadvantages	When Used
Blended hourly rates	• Easy to negotiate and administer • Encourages delegation of work • Clients pay low hourly rates	• Based on billable hour • May use less experienced lawyers and compromise work product • Can threaten profitability of firm unless attorneys have figured their costs well OR client may overpay	• Routine matters • Low level of expertise required • Can predict required tasks and skill level needed to perform them
Volume discounts discounted fees **Exclusivity in exchange for a deep discount**	• Guaranteed work for firm • Client incentive to give firm more of the work • Can be used to encourage specific results when combined with rewards for achievement of client goals • Can compare prices of firms, so over time will drive down price	• Still based on billable hour • Incentive for lawyers is to bill more hours, discourages efficiency • Can threaten profitability of firm unless they have figured their costs well OR client may overpay • Firms risk offending other clients who don't have this arrangement	• For high volume, routine matters where cost is the client's primary concern
Usually a Version of Billable Hour Rates			
Retainers Flat fee per period of time	• Clients more likely to seek help - can budget for legal work • Firm gets paid up front • Can compare prices of firms, so over time will drive down price	• May be keyed to billable hours • Client must pay up front—it's a deposit against future work • May cost firm money if it does not accurately reflect the costs of providing services • Potential disagreements over what is included in retainer	• When firm needs positive cash flow • When client wants known financial outlay • Requires a trust relationship because clients may fear firm will use junior lawyers to save money • Per period of time: e.g., per diem fee for trial representation, monthly fee for regulatory advice, quarterly fee for set volume of commercial agreements

Alternatives to Straight Billable Hour Basis for Fees	Advantages	Disadvantages	When Used
Your version of these fees			
Shared Risk Alternatives			

Capped fees	• Rewards firms that leverage efficiencies and expertise
	• Fee predictability for clients – sets ceiling on fees
	• Shifts some financial responsibility to law firm
	• Accommodates uncertainty in future scope of work by pricing in units
		• Firm assumes risk of cost overruns – problem if misjudge costs
		• Quality of work product may decline if the firm underbid
		• Client assumes risk of bad outcome
		• Requires client time and effort to track; for some, time investment to assess historical parameters and costs
			• High volume, routine, commodity work
			  - Costs easy to predict
			  - Surprises rare
			• When client-firm relationship is strong
			• e.g., legal fees for a matter in set calendar year, drafting and arguing an appeal, handle a specific transaction

Retainer **'Concierge plan'/ portfolio** **Fixed fee** **Flat fee per period**	• Predictability • Savings if the dollar amount is correct • Usually for several years • Law firm incentive to be efficient • Reduced admin burdens for client • Law firm gains deeper working knowledge of client's operations • Increases incentives to reduce fees and liabilities	• Requires time and effort to properly assess portfolio, select firm, implement terms • Client may overpay • Locks client in to one firm • Firm may use as training for associates • When does change in volume of work warrant change in fee?	• Group of matters is similar enough, recurring, predictable— consistent pattern • High volume work requiring expertise and judgment • e.g., patent/trademarks, routine contracts, routine arbitrations, security portfolio filings, all "x" category of litigation
Hybrid arrangements **"Litigation by the bucket"**	• True risk sharing • Key to achieving firm profitability and client satisfaction because shares risk and rewards • Litigation by the bucket gives set amount to law firm and then firm runs the litigation • True risk sharing—incentives and fees linked to outcomes, work quality	• Can be cumbersome to keep revising to meet current conditions • May lead to decline in quality of the work • May lead to discounts for lesser outcomes	• When client and firm know each other well • When can calculate value to client of results achieved • Requires great trust between firm and client

Retrospective fee based on value Performance-based holdback	• Shifts focus from time to value of results—firm compensation tied to value delivered (outcomes) • Client defines amount of fee and value of results • Aligns incentives • Rewards efficiency • Flexible enough to adjust along the way	• Need contract worked out in great detail • Requires time and effort to define value • May disagree on value • Lawyers are often uncomfortable with decision tree analysis and calculating expected value	• When client and firm know each other well • When can calculate value to client of results achieved • Requires great trust between firm and client
Pure contingency Results-based fees	• Stronger correlation between law firm fees and value generated • Lots of potential upside • Clients pay when successful results are achieved • Allows economically challenged clients to secure representation	• Lots of potential downside • Harder to craft effective terms outside the context of recovery-type work • Firm has all the risk • Fee may be capped by court	• When firm feels they can be successful • When represent clients with valid claim who cannot pay any other way
Your version of these fees			

Form 6.5: Foundation Client Outreach Form

Use this form to create goal-oriented growth plans for each foundation client based on the research initiatives in Chapters 4 and 5. This plan is not a tablet engraved in stone. It is a living document to be amended, revised, and updated as you learn more about your clients or in response to context changes.

Client Name _____ Plan date _____

Responsible partners _____

Plan Specifics	Strategy 1	Strategy 2	Strategy 3
Purpose			
Definition of success			
Builds on which strengths			
Areas to build up			
Practice areas involved			
Relevant relationships in your firm			

Plan Specifics	Strategy 1	Strategy 2	Strategy 3
Relevant relationships at the client			
–Who do we know?			
–Who do we need to know?			
–How will we meet the people we need to meet?			
Pitch components			
–key features			
–key benefits			
–overall value			
Team for this initiative?			
–assignments?			
–timeline?			
–due dates?			
Metrics			
Other factors?			

CHAPTER 7

Replicate Your Foundation Clients

The previous chapters discuss how to build a client-centric practice geared to the attitudes, wishes, and needs of your foundation clients. This chapter addresses the need not only to grow current client relationships but also to add new clients. Typically, firms lose approximately ten percent of their clients annually due to no fault of their own—merger, bankruptcy, relocation, change of personnel, or non-recurring "one-off" engagements. Just to stay even, attorneys need to obtain new clients every year.[1]

Once you have invested the time and resources in creating a client-centric firm, it makes sense to use this differentiation as the pivot for finding, wooing, and winning new clients who resemble your foundation clients in terms of their needs, the services they use, and their definition of high-value service. This chapter will show you how to use the research you have already completed, and the programs and guidelines you have put into effect, to attract new clients with legal needs similar to those of your foundation clients.

Understand How Prospects Choose

As important as it is to understand a client's decision-making process, it is also important to understand what potential clients are looking for in an attorney and how they handle the buying situation. Armed with this knowledge, a client-centric attorney can apply the same mental approach he uses with his current foundation clients to find new clients like them.

Seventy-nine percent of buyers of any professional service said they initially identified potential providers by asking colleagues; seventy-five percent sought referrals from other service providers; and seventy-three percent identified people they already knew. Approximately two-thirds

---

1. Attributed to McKinsey in James Digby, "50 Facts about Customer Experience," *Return on Behavior Magazine*, October 2010.

said they identified and learned about service providers from seminars, conferences, or events where the provider was a speaker.[2] In the legal world, the same preference for introductions comes into play: among corporate counsel survey respondents, over half (fifty-five percent) turned to informal networks or peer referrals for provider suggestions.[3]

Corporate counsel's reasons for recommending or hiring a law firm follow the preferences laid out in previous chapters:

> When general counsel were asked why they recommend firms to their colleagues, thirty-four percent said exceptional client focus, fifteen percent said the firm delivers value for the dollar.[4]
> The top three responses as to why they hire a specific firm reinforce the reasons to recommend: "understand my business" (twenty-one percent), "understand my company needs" (twenty-one percent), "responsive" (nineteen percent).[5]

These findings suggest two effective strategies for targeted prospecting:

> Seek connections to potential clients who will value your knowledge of their industry, their company characteristics, and their preferred business strategies.
> Encourage referrals from your colleagues and clients.

Follow the Client Acquisition Process

A targeted client acquisition process applies the client-centric approach outlined in the previous chapters to non-clients who are similar to the attorney's foundation clients. All the communication techniques that reinforce the advisor-client connection come into play in the selling process: a thorough understanding of the whole client, active listening skills, and proactive, results-based legal advice.[6]

---

2. Promotional excerpt from Mike Schultz and John Doerr, *How Clients Buy: 2009 Benchmark Report on Professional Services Marketing and Selling from the Client Perspective* (RainGroup, 2009).
3. Despina Kartson, Quoting BTI data in a CLE Presentation, New York City Bar Association, October 26, 2011.
4. *Id.*
5. *Id.* There was no consensus regarding other reasons for hiring a firm, but the next four reasons were "deliver value for the dollar" (fifteen percent), "thought leadership" (eleven percent), valued counselor (eleven percent), and specific expertise (nine percent).
6. Prospecting and selling fall under the ethics prohibitions related to advertising. Every state has different rules, which the prudent attorney will review before sending out any materials.

When the client acquisition process is designed around the best characteristics of the law firm's foundation clients, the new client acquisition process itself becomes more efficient. Instead of beginning from square one, the attorney begins midway in the process because he already knows a great deal about the target market from his work with his foundation clients. The process begins at the "warm" stage because it begins with a referral from a client or someone in your network who knows the prospect and knows the attorney's talents.

This targeted selling process, shown in *Diagram 7.1*, has three steps:

1. Define the ideal prospect's attributes selected from foundation clients' characteristics.
2. Create a strategy to generate interest in the target market and mine your relationships in this market to identify connections to prospects.
3. Plan the conversation with prospects so that it focuses on the kind of benefits you can deliver and highlights your track record of value to clients like them.

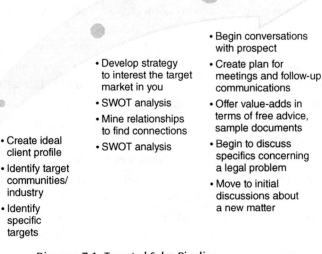

Diagram 7.1: Targeted Sales Pipeline

Target Your Ideal Prospects

Let's assume that you have created a client "sweet spot" for your firm with service guidelines and legal services attuned to that certain set of clients. It makes sense to find new clients that will benefit from your expertise. A focus on acquiring more clients like your foundation clients begins with a profile of an ideal prospect. A prospect is a potential client, someone who is deciding whom to hire and has been introduced to you through mutual acquaintances.

Use *Form 7.1: Ideal Prospect Profile* to create an ideal prospect profile based on the characteristics of your "80/20", page 177, and your A and B clients. (You may want to review *Form 5.7: Foundation Client Profile Part 1 Client Characteristics and Relationship*, page 126.)

Questions to consider as you define the ideal prospect:

> What is it about foundation clients that you want to replicate in new clients?
> Why do your best clients hire you?
> What kind of value do you provide for them?
> What services do they use?

Foundation clients have identifiable common characteristics, problems, and service needs. You may choose to focus your prospect search on only one or two aspects of their total profile. For example, if you have a strong corporate department you may look for companies that will be affected by the *Dodd-Frank Act*'s provisions that focus on corporate governance issues. Or you may want to move your matrimonial practice away from litigated divorces toward collaborative law, so you will focus on clients that might be amenable to this negotiation process. Or a litigator might review the kinds of cases handled for foundation clients and decide to focus on one subset.

A well thought out ideal prospect profile is the key step in developing high quality new business based on a strong track record with current clients. The ideal prospect profile will focus your business development effort. You can target your new client recruitment efforts toward finding and vetting prospects that resemble the ideal client.

Because you are targeting prospects similar to current key clients, you already know a great deal about the world in which these clients operate, you belong to their organizations, and you actively exchange relevant information with them. To understand how to use knowledge to attract new clients, it's important to understand why people buy legal services. Use *Form 7.2: Target Group Worksheet,* page 178, to identify why members of the target market would buy your services. You may want to include your research on the firm and foundation clients from Chapters 4 and 5.

Understand Why Prospects Buy Legal Services

As the managing partner of a business and tax-focused law firm explained, "Coming to a lawyer is a 'have-to.' How can I make it a 'want-to?' A want-to is created when you say to a businessman, 'How would you like to save an additional $50,000 on your staff pension plan?' Or offer to reduce a businessman's estate taxes or provide a doctor with asset protection."

People buy legal services to find a solution to a problem or take advantage of an opportunity. If confronted with a problem, often they wait until the last minute when they are faced with an alternative worse than making an immediate decision. The attorney needs to understand the buyer's dilemma in order to tailor his services to the specific situation. At the same time, he wants to highlight the benefits that will accrue from a decision to take legal action. One way to begin this conversation is with the "three Fs" of sales:

> *Feel*—I understand how you feel.
> *Felt*—Many of my clients have felt the same way.
> *Found*—Many clients found that by doing "x" the problem was resolved.

In making the decision to hire, buyers are looking for "a simple, clear, and compelling buying preference. A reason to choose one over the other."[7] The person trying to create a working relationship needs to key in to the buyer's personal decision-making behavior, the upside and downside risks related to the buyer's issue, and the importance of the matter to the buyer's personal future well being, not just the issue at hand.

---

7. Jimmy Vee and Travis Miller, "Exposed: Your Customers' Most Secret Desires," January 19, 2006 (http://chiefmarketer.com/customers_secret_desires_01142006/, accessed December 22, 2011).

Lawyers often think they are hired for their legal pedigree and track record. However, when the lawyer selection process begins with a referral, legal acumen tends to be assumed. Buyers assess legal expertise as fungible and key in on the intangible service aspects of the transaction—how they imagine it will be to work with you.

> There is not so much a moment of truth when someone decides to buy your services as there is a series of decisions in which less acceptable alternatives are discarded and the highest value is ultimately placed on the most desirable one.[8]

PROSPECTS' MINDSET

The best way to understand the buyer's mindset is to think about your own experience as a buyer of professional services—perhaps a doctor or accountant—in a situation that presents unknowns, is necessary but risky, and requires you to make a major decision based more on your gut feeling than your intellect. You may not be able to second-guess the doctor on the need for surgery or the accountant on the meaning of an arcane IRS ruling, but you can use the selection interview as an indication of what it would be like to work with this professional.

David Maister sets out the classic roadmap of feelings and questions that swirl within the buyer of professional services.[9] Your potential clients may feel:

> uncomfortable about taking a personal risk and giving up some degree of control
> insecure because the decision will be based on imperfect, incomplete information—the result isn't guaranteed
> skeptical about being burned by professionals—again
> concerned that the matter isn't large enough to warrant priority attention
> afraid that the attorney will not include the buyer in the decision-making

---

8. Mike McCaffrey, "The Personal Marketing of Professional Services," *Practicing CPA*, August 1987, p.5. See also, Ann Lee Gibson, "IN-House Counsel: The Search for a Few Good Reasons to Buy," *Strategies*, October 2003, p.5.
9. David Maister, "How Clients Choose," chap. 10 in *Managing the Professional Service Firm* (Free Press, 1993).

Everyone has such feelings to one degree or another. They are present when a general counsel hires a firm to take his company through bankruptcy or to handle a major product catastrophe. They are present when family members struggle with divorce, special needs litigation, guardianships, or estate planning. They are also present when an employee has to negotiate a buy-out, feels slighted because of her race, or is retaliated against because she becomes a whistle-blower. The combination of uncertainty, an important stake in the outcome, and personal emotions creates an illogical context for decision-making.

Logic and rationality are subsumed in the anxieties. Influenced by their feelings, buyers look for criteria that offer clues to future behavior. The attorney's behavior in the interview becomes a stand-in for future behavior vis-à-vis the buyer, just as an unprofessional-looking work environment may become a symbol of an attorney's capacity to organize. Some examples from the buying process:[10]

> attorney asks a very general question about the company—buyer assumes lack of preparation, laziness, and no special interest in him
> attorney talks a lot about his firm and his accomplishments—buyer sees it as a spiel[11] that shows a lack of interest in him and is not relevant to the situation that led to this meeting
> attorney asserts expertise and tells buyer about the best solution—buyer sees this as patronizing, pompous, and arrogant

"Give me some *new* information. . . . Give me an education. . . . The key talent in good selling is being good at getting me, the client, to reveal my problems, needs, wants, and concerns. . . . Ask good questions and listen. . . . The key is empathy."[12] Adding new clients similar to your foundation clients just adds another forum for good communication skills—the counselor-advisor approach that is the key to a client-centric practice.

---

10. *Id.*
11. "Spiel" means "a glib plausible style of talk, associated especially with salesmen" according to the Microsoft Word Dictionary.
12. David Maister, *Managing the Professional Service Firm, supra* note 9 (emphasis in original).

"IF IT AIN'T BROKE, DON'T FIX IT."

The most common reason prospects don't become clients is inertia. For example, the sidewalk is uneven but no one has fallen lately; a business fails to take precautions against fraud; or an executive fails to read the fine print in his employment agreement. They need the seller to educate them as to the consequences if a problem goes unresolved or an opportunity is missed. This becomes the basis of the selling conversation.

The attorney needs to understand the prospect's situation enough to be able to provide relevant information that encourages the hiring decision. He can discuss the nature, magnitude, consequences, organizational, and personal impacts of possible actions by painting scenarios. Leading the buyer through a "what if" conversation will help him increase his understanding of the situation from the attorney's point of view, acknowledge the importance of the situation, and realize the need to take action.

In any buying decision, there are three kinds of participants:

> ultimate decision-maker—the person with the authority to buy and the money to pay for it
> influencers—those who are part of the decision-making process, but lack the ultimate buying authority
> gatekeepers—the people who control access to influencers and the ultimate decision-maker

The well-prepared attorney can control the direction of the selling process by creating an open conversation process that allows all the stakeholders to recognize and articulate their perceptions of the problem and their own stake in the outcome of any decision. The process replicates the client-focused approach to explaining steps in the legal process relevant to the matter at hand. In both cases, the conversation itself leads to buy-in, a discussion of next steps, and agreement.

The hiring decision boils down to an assessment of the relevance of the legal skills, and trust that the attorney can deliver on his promises. The attorney's role is to use his knowledge to show a prospect how the law can improve a situation and why an action should occur sooner rather than later. This requires an understanding of the emotional context of rational decisions, discussed above, and the use of a counselor approach to conversation, discussed in Chapters 2 and 3.

Understand What You Sell

Attorneys sell not only specific results that demonstrate their legal expertise, but also, the intangible service-based relationship that exists between attorney and client. The prospect hires you because she believes you can help her reach a goal. Beginning in the hiring interview and continuing in the initial client meeting, the attorney sets certain expectations as to how the legal process will unfold. The intangible service element only becomes evident to the buyer as it is happens. The buyer sees the attorney at first as a technical expert hired to remove an impediment or take advantage of an opportunity. Hopefully, as the emotional connections in the service relationship evolve, the buyer's trust level rises and the attorney becomes an advisor as well as a legal technician.

Interestingly, if you ask lawyers what they sell they may divide their legal work into two catagories:

> products—work product such as briefs, pleadings, contracts, and wills
> services—legal activities such as appearing before judges in hearings, conducting real estate closings, and orchestrating settlements

Traditionally, lawyers have sold their services as the time it takes to produce the work product, and the time it takes to prepare for and conduct the activities. Yet few, if any, would go into a prospect's office and show a PowerPoint presentation of their most persuasively written twenty-two page "motion to dismiss" in order to show the prospect their work product. Prospects, like clients, are not interested in legal process. They are interested in the benefits that accrue to them from those processes. Benefits begin as intangibles, identified and embodied in the client service process. They only become tangible when the legal process ends.

Engage in Relationship Marketing

A marketing rule of thumb states that to move from an introduction to a new client requires eight to twelve "touches"—relevant interactions with a prospect. You can shortcut the path to appropriate prospect introductions by asking for introductions from mutual acquaintances. Think about professionals you've come to know or met at clients' industry events who also work with your clients and could introduce you to specific prospects. Look for connections on social media sites such as Facebook and LinkedIn or do a search engine query to see if your contacts know people you want to meet. When you find a friend or colleague has relevant connections, set up a meeting to discuss whom among their contacts you want to meet, why you want to meet them, and how you think you can help them.

Another approach is to request referrals from your contacts at foundation clients. Often clients make connections to their colleagues just as client-focused attorneys introduce their clients to investors, advisors, and vendors when they see a need. As one partner said, "Good referrals solve a need, help others to do their job, and make a client happy."

One rainmaker asks for referrals by saying, "If you have any friends with similar needs, please share our success story with them, as we will for you." Loyal clients are usually more than willing to make introductions when you can share specifics about what you are looking for or ask for introductions to specific prospects. Referrers can also help you be relevant to prospects by sharing some of their similar concerns and issues.

MARKETING MATERIALS

Although the services buying process is essentially person-to-person, marketing materials offer useful assists if they are relevant. In a client-centric firm, the attorneys already create and share material of interest to their foundation clients. This material can also be used as follow-up or value-added "touches" that reinforce aspects of the attorney's conversation with a prospect. Such materials can include

> case studies
> whitepapers commenting on specific legal trends, new laws or regulations, or the implications of a recent court decision
> clippings from magazines, newspapers, or Web sites

Marketing is nothing more than an invitation to conversation. All marketing materials, including online and printed materials, should be designed to begin or supplement that conversation. This means emphasizing value first, benefits second, and the features of your practice last.

Because materials need to be relevant to the recipient, it helps to visualize the issues of importance to the target:

> What are their main concerns and hot-button issues?
> What threats are they facing right now?
> What are the opportunities they might encounter down the road?

In general, when preparing materials, first address your prospects' concerns and interests, then weave in your services as problem solvers. See the following on marketing materials for further discussion.

Marketing Materials Content Suggestions

Firms need to have both a Web presence and some print materials. The Web has become essential for credibility. As soon as someone hears about you or is introduced to you, they are almost certain to look you up on the Web to find out more. The print pieces have a slightly different purpose. Print material serves as a kind of ambassador for your firm to keep the conversation moving. Ideally, you would send a relevant piece after your preliminary meeting with a prospect. If it's well-designed, engaging, and follows the value-driven approach, it is likely to sit on your prospect's desk as a reminder of your conversation and reinforcement of what you have to offer.

The most effective legal marketing materials begin from the client's perspective. Try to visualize the people you want to reach with your marketing materials—people who are very much like your current foundation clients:

> What are their main concerns and hot-button issues?
> What threats are they facing right now?
> What are the opportunities they might encounter down the road?

These questions are relevant regardless of the size of your firm—or of your clients'.

Your marketing materials should always lead with answers directed toward one of these items. It can be posed as a question or as a statement of fact, as appropriate. Following from that, you can discuss the benefits clients receive from working with you, but talk about it in their terms. Some examples that might be appropriate in a firm brochure or Web site:

> Every year, copyright infringement costs companies in [industry x] millions of dollars. Here's what you can do about that.

> The typical in-house legal department spends x percent of its time managing out-side counsel. Here's why outside counsel are typically so hard to manage—and what you can do about it.

> In 2010, our international reach saved our clients $x and x time. Here's how we did it.

Only after you address your prospects' concerns and interests should you put forward your own services, achievements, and credentials (i.e., features). In the model above, you would weave the most relevant features into the storyline about how you address each problem. Once you have engaged prospects in conversation and demonstrated your keen understanding of their issues, you can wrap up the entire piece by presenting your firm's story and credentials. On your Web site, a link would direct prospects to the relevant features.

Essentially, effective marketing materials provide corroboration for your client-centric approach.

Move From Introduction to New Client

Once you have an introduction to someone at the prospect's organization you need to research both the company and the person you plan to meet in order to understand how they are similar to and different from your foundation clients. Preparation for your initial meeting includes seeking answers to key questions such as:

> What will this client need?
> What stories can I use to show my experience in resolving this need?
> What aspects of my practice will be most relevant to them?
> What benefits can I offer?
> How will I illustrate the value they will get from my services?
> What value-added services can I offer in the introductory stages?

In addition, you will want to create a list of specific, research-based questions to ask during the meeting. The research forms in Chapter 5 may be useful in this regard because the approach in both instances is the same—360° communication based on understanding as much about the whole client as you can. After you complete your research, turn to *Form 7.3: Target Market SWOT Analysis*, page 180, to prepare a summary analysis that brings together all your research and lays the foundation for your campaign to turn prospects into clients.

This kind of preparation encourages the advisor-style approach to selling. Instead of pitching your capabilities, you can go to the prospect-meeting armed with good ideas about them—where they might be incurring grave risks, a legal strategy they might employ to prepare for new regulations, the impact of a recent court decision on their growth strategy. This kind of discussion answers the buyer's need to assess the person because it demonstrates not only your legal acumen but also your approach to client relationships.

As with your marketing materials, you should remain keenly aware that the marketing conversations are not about you; they are about your prospective client. If you are doing more of the talking than your prospect, you are diminishing your chances of a conversion to satisfied—and ultimately loyal—client. You are also missing the opportunity to gather the types of information that you will need to deliver value. In the earlier conversations, you will want to use open-ended questions. The idea is to get the prospect talking—and you listening. There are many angles from which to approach this. Perhaps the most logical place to start is with the SWOT questions (see the related worksheet from Chapter 2). Find out what your prospect sees as strengths, weaknesses, opportunities, and threats on both enterprise and personal levels. During subsequent conversations you can follow up on what you learned, at first inviting status updates, and later, venturing to offer advice.

When you offer advice, as discussed in Chapter 3, it is often a good idea to broach it initially as a question. This is especially critical when you are trying to convert a prospect to a client. Instead of offering an immediate solution, say "I wonder whether you would consider [solution]?" or "Does it make any sense to pursue [solution]?" This more indirect approach has four significant benefits:

1. You convey your respect for the prospect and acknowledge that the decision-making power rests with him or her.
2. You create a framework for open conversation, suggesting with this behavior the kind of dialogue you have with clients.
3. You encourage the prospect to tell you more about the situation.

4. You move ever closer to the ultimate question of when you can start work on the matter. On this last point, you will be able to tell from the prospect's candor, depth of response, and reactions to your questions whether there is really an opportunity here.

Before your first meeting with a prospect, develop your strategy using *Form 7.4: Prospect Checklist*, page 181. Use the form for each meeting in the chain leading from introduction to new client. It's often difficult to identify the transition between the marketing/sales stage and the engagement stage, particularly where a professional service is concerned. The dialog can continue over a fairly long period of time, often with the professional being asked to provide informal legal advice at no charge. To a point, this is acceptable; the prospective client will have an opportunity to test your mettle and you will be able to demonstrate your value. You may be able to broaden the scope of the potential engagement and deepen your relationship. Of course, if you do a conflict check and find a problem you need to end the process.

Follow-up depends on the nature of the conversation and what requests or promises were made:

> If the meeting was "hot" and you were getting along like gangbusters, most likely the potential client and you charted out the next steps— "Send me an engagement letter," "Send me an estimate." Of course, you may want to make sure those requests indicate a genuine interest. Sometimes prospects will make requests simply to postpone making a real decision (and receive the benefit of thought devoted to their projects at no cost to them).

> If the meeting was "warm" and friendly but not yet engaged—"I've got to ask my boss," "Get back to me in three months," "I'm not ready to get divorced yet"—there is more work to do. You would want to add her to your mailing list, making sure she receives only appropriately-targeted materials, and calendar in a time for your next "touch point."

> If the meeting was a "cold" non-starter, be polite but cut your losses. Perhaps he said, "I don't have any money to pay you." This is a typically American way of saying "no thanks." Unless there are other reasons to continue to pursue the prospect, you should send a thank you note and categorize him in your database as no longer an active

prospect. You might want to add him to the firm mailing list if he is friends with many members of your referral circle.

Write up meeting notes immediately after the meeting and then meet with your team (either in your firm, or colleagues who are helping you) to determine next steps. These are relationship building-blocks that show the prospect how you would value him as a client, the kind of service posture you practice, and the relevance of your legal knowledge and experience to his situation.

After a "warm" meeting, your choice of next steps is very important because you want to remind the prospect of the best parts of the meeting, and at the same time, illustrate the service attributes she most admires. For example, after a discussion about the implications of a recent court decision, you could send a whitepaper or article analyzing the implications, volunteer to come to the prospect's office for a complimentary seminar on the topic, or suggest you go together to a CLE on the topic. These are three variations on the same theme, but one will usually stand out as the best next step.

Use Appendix 3, the client-centric initiatives list, as a jumping off point for selecting appropriate next steps.

The progression continues with each step moving the relationship forward by allowing the prospect to visualize how it would be to work with you until the process ends with a decision to proceed on a specific matter.

Forms

Form 7.1: Ideal Prospect Profile

Corporate/ Organization Foundation Client Characteristics	Characteristics to Replicate in New Clients	Individual Foundation Client Characteristics	Characteristics to Replicate in New Clients
Legal form		Sex	
Geographical dispersion		Geographic location	
Number of years in business		Age	
Primary product(s)		Religion or race (if relevant)	

Corporate/ Organization Foundation Client Characteristics	Characteristics to Replicate in New Clients	Individual Foundation Client Characteristics	Characteristics to Replicate in New Clients
Primary service(s)		Occupation	
Revenues for last fiscal year		Financial status	
Industry (SIC/NAIC)		Demographic group (e.g., age, religion, illness)	
Ownership arrangements		Marital status	
Growth stage		Lifestyle	
Number of employees		Children: sex/ages	
In-house lawyer (yes/no)		Socio-economic level	
Other important defining characteristics		Other important defining characteristics	
Where to look for information about the target		**Where to look for information about the target**	
Online		Online	
Print		Print	
Associations/ groups		Associations/ groups	
Other?		Other?	

Form 7.2: Target Group Worksheet

Use this planning form to help you think through your approach to target groups/specific markets or geographic areas.

Prospecting worksheet	Target group #1	Target group #2
Key characteristics you want to replicate		
Why you want this target		
New laws or regulations that are appropriate to this group		

Your foundation clients in this target group (names)		
What are the target's most important needs—today?		
What will be some important upcoming needs?		
Services you can provide		
Benefits/value you offer		
How is your practice keyed to their needs and preferences		
Specific prospect names		
1.		
2.		
3.		
Services/benefits/value		
Services to pitch		
Problems/opportunities to address		
Benefits to the potential client		
Other professionals with contacts in your target market (names)		
Colleagues in your firm Other lawyers in other firms Accountants Bankers Insurance brokers Financial professionals		
Competition		
Competitors for the kind of clients you want to target		
Competitors for the kind of services you want to promote		
Your team		
Attorneys		
Non-legal staff		
Referral sources to talk to		

Form 7.3: Target Market SWOT Analysis
(SWOT = Strengths, Weaknesses, Opportunities, Threats)

The purpose of a target market focused SWOT analysis is to lay out on one page all your experience vis-à-vis this market, including your key relationships. The very process of creating a SWOT should force thoughtful, strategic, creative thinking about the what, why, where, and how of your approach to this group of prospects.

Purpose of this SWOT analysis _____

_____

_____

Participants _____ Date _____

STRENGTHS	WEAKNESSES
What do you know about this market?	*Where can you improve?*
What advantages does your firm have?	*What resources do you need to compete*
Why do these clients hire you?	*more effectively?*
In what ways is your firm/practice keyed	*What mistakes have you made that create*
to these kinds of clients?	*buying obstacles?*
Consider also:	Consider also:
Firm resources—people, geography, technology	Gaps in your/your firm's expertise/ experience
Financial stability	Gaps in your product/service offerings
Reputation—of firm and individual attorneys	Gaps in your client service implementation
Unique selling proposition	Financial area weaknesses
Practice area strengths	Leadership/personnel/leverage issues
Leadership commitment	Resource inadequacies
Work flow/staffing procedures promoting efficiency	Technology inadequacies
Leverage	
Client service style	
Foundation clients [names] in this market	
Successes/track record	
STRATEGIES for capitalizing on strengths	*STRATEGIES for minimizing or remediating weaknesses.*

OPPORTUNITIES	THREATS
What trends lend support to your strengths?	*What challenges do you face?*
	Who are your competitors?
What are the current problems created by economic or political conditions or new laws or regulations?	*What are your competitors doing?*
	What trends hurt your selling proposition?
Market trends	Market trends
Size of market share	Demand curve for the service
Client needs	Size of market share
Context trends, e.g. Economic, Political, Legal	Fee pressures
	Context trends, e.g.: Economic, Political, Legal
Globalization, Lifestyle changes/ consumer tastes	Globalization, Lifestyle changes/ consumer tastes
Role of the internet/social media, Environmental issues	Role of the internet/social media, Environmental issues
Pace of technological change	Pace of technological change
STRATEGIES for leveraging opportunities	*STRATEGIES for eliminating or minimizing threats*

Form 7.4: Prospect Checklist

This checklist will help you assess the most important aspects of each prospect, and create a selling campaign just for them.

Prospect's Characteristics	What you know about these points What you plan to do	Assignment/Assigned to/due date
Name of company		
Key characteristics		
Similar to which current clients—names		
How are they similar?		
Most useful information sources		
What they need		
Why they need it		
Services to offer immediately		
Services to offer later in the relationship		

Prospect's Characteristics	What you know about these points What you plan to do	Assignment/Assigned to/due date
Benefits of your services		
Ultimate value of your services		
Decision-makers		
Influencers		
Gatekeepers		
Whom do you know at the prospect?		
Whom do you need to meet?		
Contacts who know people at the prospect		
Members of your team		
Steps in the plan		
1.		
2.		
3. etc.		

CHAPTER 8

Pick the Low-Hanging Fruit—Summary

The environment for practicing law has changed substantially over the past few years and will continue to do so. Clients have become increasingly demanding, asking for lower fees, more transparent pricing structures, greater responsiveness, and increased involvement in managing their own matters. It now seemingly takes more effort than ever to keep a legal client happy—and to derive satisfaction and appropriate compensation from the practice of law.

Using this low-hanging fruit system will help attorneys tend to what is most rewarding in their practices, while reducing the squeeze that the changing environment for the purchase and use of legal services creates. It also demonstrates how focus on the firm's best clients can lead to a more profitable and satisfying practice.

This chapter reviews the system's main points.

Focus on Clients to Build Your Firm

Law firms are built around delivering legal services to clients, but they are not always focused on the right clients. The Pareto principle, also known as the law of the vital few, states that eighty percent of effects come from twenty percent of causes. In business terms, this means that eighty percent of a firm's income will be derived from just twenty percent of its clients. Largely overlapping with that critical twenty percent are the clients who provide the firm's most intellectually-stimulating work and are most stylistically compatible with the firm's attorneys. Those key clients are the firm's *foundation clients*.

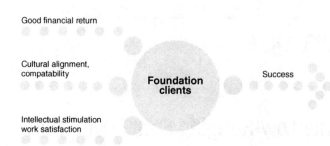

Diagram 8.1: Foundation Clients

Centering a law firm on foundation clients can lead to greater depth of relationship with those clients (with attendant financial rewards), open opportunities with clients who share similar characteristics, and make the practice of law more personally rewarding for attorneys.

Use Value to Create a Foundation of Loyalty

Professionals by and large tend to do a very good job of satisfying clients, but there is a profound difference between a satisfied client and a loyal one. The former may hire you again; the latter would not think of hiring anyone else. Value is at the heart of any loyal client relationship.

Value is based on perspective. Attorneys may value one thing, while clients may value something different. In building a client-centric practice, it is only the client's perception that matters. To understand the value a firm provides, it is essential to enumerate the features (just about anything that can be said about the firm and its attorneys) and appreciate the benefits that clients will acknowledge receiving.

Diagram 8.2: The Value Continuum

To put it differently:

$$\frac{\text{Features + Benefits}}{\text{Time}} = \text{Value}$$

Diagram 8.3: The Value Equation

In addition to performing a self-assessment of features, benefits, and value, as described in Chapter 2, firms may also wish to use the ACC Value Challenge to create benchmarks for delivering value. It is also essential to conduct interviews with clients to get direct feedback. The interview process is reviewed below.

Once an attorney or firm begins to understand the value clients might receive, the process of becoming a trusted advisor can begin. While most professionals believe that they are trusted advisors, the truth is that everyone who is paid to provide a product or service starts a relationship as a vendor. Vendors are retained for their technical expertise and ability to perform specific tasks. At the other end of the spectrum, trusted advisors are called upon for advice on a plethora of business and personal issues. The continuum of professional relationship development usually looks something like this:

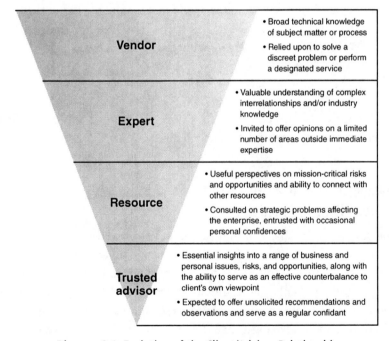

Diagram 8.4: Evolution of the Client/Advisor Relationship

Client interviews are an essential catalyst for moving along this continuum. These are structured conversations that involve advance research, skillful posing of questions, disciplined listening, and follow-up.

Interviews are preferably conducted by the lead attorney who works with the client, but there may be a reason to assign this task to designated staff or an outside consultant. Clients are not billed for any time associated with interviews. The point of interviews is threefold:

> to gain the client's direct feedback on the firm's work and what clients value in it
> to demonstrate willingness to invest in the relationship—and in the client
> to probe for potential opportunities to do more business with the client by providing more value—or by expanding the areas in which value is provided

The interview process is critical for building loyalty because it is often the only reliable checkpoint to review results achieved, solicit feedback on service, and gain a firsthand view of what is valuable to the client.

$$\text{Quality (service} \times \text{results)} + \frac{\text{Value}}{\text{Time}} = \text{Loyalty}$$

Diagram 8.5: The Loyalty Equation

Loyal clients will return to a firm time and again, gladly pay its fees, provide stimulating work, and make requests rather than demands.

Master Communication Techniques to Build a Client-Centric Practice

The practice of law has communication at its core. From the initial consultation, through the preparation of legal documents, through representation in court, attorneys are constantly communicating with, and on behalf of, their clients. Successful attorneys are highly adept at communication in the delivery of legal services. Communication in the course of building and managing a client relationship is not always treated with the same level of attention. Communication-related issues are the single biggest reason clients cite in leaving a law firm. These include

> lack of understanding of the client
> failure to do what the client wanted

> delay in returning phone calls and responding to inquiry

As with value, perception rules in communication—and again the important perception here is the client's, rather than the attorney's. The client's perception of communication is also frequently a stand-in for how he perceives the service. In many instances, this means that quality of service is more important (or at least more evident) to the client than the quality of work. A strong interpersonal relationship with the attorney, supported by effective communication, is essential.

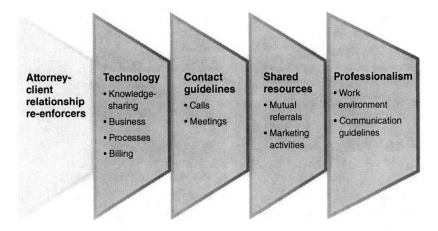

Diagram 8.6: Aspects of 360° Communication

This goes far beyond responsiveness. Effective communication between attorney and client is characterized by equality within the relationship, open lines of communication, an emotional connection, and the ability to think ahead. It is facilitated by attorneys understanding client communication preferences (method, timing, etc.), involving the client appropriately in matter management, and being responsive to client inquiries. It is supported by strict adherence to professional ethics; the ability to present items in clear English without legal terms of art; and clear management of expectations, including desired results, roles, and responsibilities in relation to the matter, process, and budget.

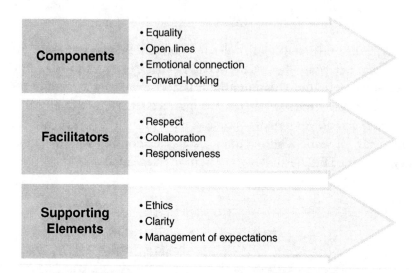

Diagram 8.7: Effective Communication in Attorney/Client Relationships

There are several opportunities for communication. During the course of a matter, they occur naturally; between matters, it is essential for the attorney to actively seek out opportunities to communicate through casual face-to-face encounters, participation in client charitable activities, and strategic offers of complimentary assistance.

It is also important to remember that everything communicates. A cluttered conference room or unhelpful paraprofessional introduces tremendous risk of communication failure. A bill that lists hours spent without showing progress toward the client's desired outcome or value delivered is also a potential communication failure. Technology can help attorneys and firms communicate more successfully with clients. Mobile technologies facilitate staying in touch, cloud technologies allow for shared workspaces between attorney and client—or even within the firm, and knowledge management tools help the firm access its own expertise across disciplines (similar tools allow for cross-firm collaboration or the creation of virtual firms).

Shared communication activities can be profoundly useful in building an attorney/client relationship and can even contribute to both the attorney's and the client's financial well-being. Attorneys, like professionals in other fields, can thrive by becoming thought leaders, intellectual resources whose ideas and opinions are widely quoted. Communication vehicles such as articles, newsletters, blogs, and podcasts can help establish an attorney as a thought leader, starting with the firm's client base. Joint marketing efforts or attorney contributions to client marketing efforts can also prove valuable.

Effective communication is a process with many intersecting elements. The more of them a firm can employ strategically with foundation clients, the greater its likelihood of making a smooth transition from vendor to trusted advisor.

Research to Understand Your Current Practice

Most attorneys can readily list at least some of their best clients. Simply making the list does not provide the information needed to deepen—and replicate—foundation client relationships. The circumstances of both the client's world and the attorney's world need to be taken into account and the nexus between the two identified.

"The Five Cs" are an old marketing mnemonic used to provide insight into what a business needs and why. To perform a "Five C" analysis of any business from the inside, work from what is closest to the business itself to what is furthest away.

Diagram 8.8: The Five Cs, Firm View

The company/firm analysis looks at the firm's competitive position in the marketplace for similar legal services. The competitor analysis looks at any firm—law firm or not—that offers similar services. The collaborator analysis examines client service delivery from a broad view of opportunities to work with other service providers, such as financial advisors or even other attorneys. The client/customer analysis is a detailed view of the client within the context of the firm, and then in their own world. Finally, the context analysis explores the climate within which both the firm and its clients operate.

An important part of the company/firm analysis is identifying the clients on which the firm should focus—its foundation clients. Some clients are a good fit for a particular firm, and offer opportunities to expand the relationship, while some are not. Firm analysis helps to clearly recognize the twenty percent of clients who provide eighty percent of the firm's revenues. Another way to examine the firm's client base is to segment it into A, B, C, and D categories, with "A" clients being the most profitable and easiest to work with and "D" being the least profitable and most difficult to work with.

Another component of the comprehensive firm analysis is the SWOT (Strengths, Weaknesses, Opportunities, and Threats) analysis, which lays out all the firm's advantages and disadvantages on a single sheet of paper.

Research to Understand Your Foundation Clients' Worlds

Once the firm's foundation clients and candidates (the twenty percent of clients that contribute eighty percent of the revenue or the "A" and "B" segment clients) have been identified, similar analysis is performed on their businesses or life circumstances.

The company—or family—analysis involves understanding many aspects of the client's circumstances. Some information—too much in some circumstances—will be available online or through the corporate client's publications. This information should be gathered first. Next, a macro-level understanding should be achieved through a client interview.

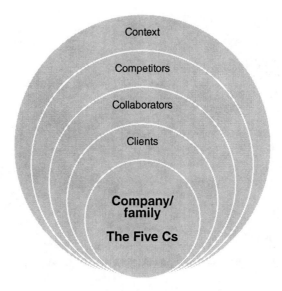

Diagram 8.9: The Five Cs Company View

For businesses:

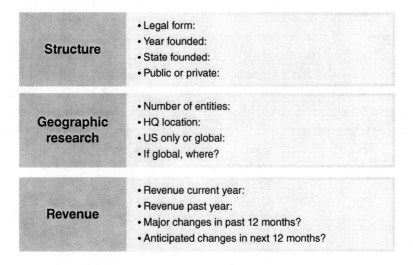

Structure	• Legal form: • Year founded: • State founded: • Public or private:
Geographic research	• Number of entities: • HQ location: • US only or global: • If global, where?
Revenue	• Revenue current year: • Revenue past year: • Major changes in past 12 months? • Anticipated changes in next 12 months?

Diagram 8.10: Client Basics - Businesses

And for individuals:

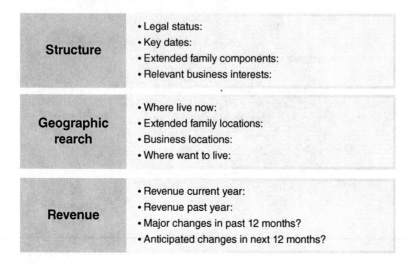

Structure	• Legal status: • Key dates: • Extended family components: • Relevant business interests:
Geographic rearch	• Where live now: • Extended family locations: • Business locations: • Where want to live:
Revenue	• Revenue current year: • Revenue past year: • Major changes in past 12 months? • Anticipated changes in next 12 months?

Diagram 8.11: Client Basics - Individuals

The firm will also want to understand the decision-making structure in place for each client. For companies, this is usually somewhat formal; for families, it can be quite informal, and include both involved family members and outside influencers.

When the "Five C" analysis is complete, a SWOT analysis is performed just as it was for the law firm. One further step is taken for a client-side SWOT analysis: an examination of the law as an action driver (for example, compliance with *Dodd-Frank* regulations). With all of the data aggregated into a "client portrait," you will do some creative thinking about each client in order to define more exactly the nature of your relationship and your emotional response.

The final step is to turn all of the research into an action plan.

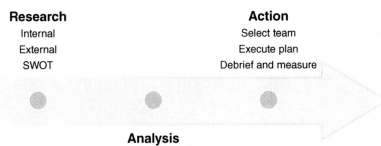

Research
Internal
External
SWOT

Action
Select team
Execute plan
Debrief and measure

Analysis
Select opportunities
Design action plan
Develop talking points

Diagram 8.12: Three-Step Process from Research to Analysis to Action

Your previous analysis will tell you which decision-makers you need to approach at the client, the products and services you want to offer, and the benefits and value the client will be interested in. Set up measurement metrics, assignments for your team and a schedule. Even if the client does not accept your recommendations and hire you for additional business, your stature as an advisor will have grown and more opportunities will arise.

Not surprisingly, client portraits age rather quickly, meaning that some opportunities will become obsolete, while others will emerge. To build a legal practice on foundation client relationships, it is essential to keep portraits up-to-date. Technology can help.

Build a Client-Centric Firm

Much of what is traditional in the practice of law was established for the comfort and convenience of attorneys, with the expectation that clients would recognize and appreciate the highly-skilled legal services provided. This is no longer so. As stated previously, in the current competitive environment for legal services, clients are demanding more concrete outcomes from their attorneys, greater responsiveness, more involvement as matters progress, and more predictable fees. This means that successful firms of all sizes will need to shift their focus to what matters to clients.

A client-centric firm is one where attorneys' technical skills and service focus and the firm's processes and procedures are deliberately aligned with foundation clients' agendas.

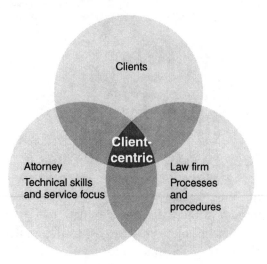

Diagram 8.13: Anatomy of a Client-Centric Firm

Successfully doing this will build a mutually-profitable relationship between the law firm and its foundation clients, allowing the firm to respond to changing client needs while simultaneously bringing clients appropriately into the lawyering process through education and teamwork.

Almost every element that makes a law firm function can also help it function in a more client centric manner.

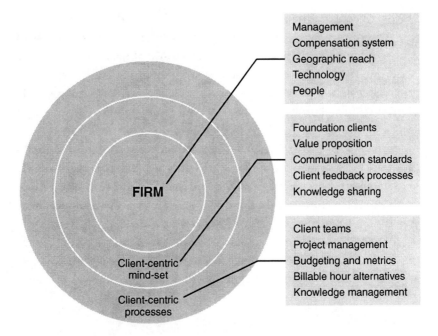

Diagram 8.14: Components of a Client-Centric Firm

Cultural alignment with foundation clients is critical to becoming client-centric. Culture is one of those "soft-focus" concepts that can nevertheless have a tremendous impact on a firm's relationships with its key clients. Culture is roughly equivalent to a physician's bedside manner. Attorneys are often called upon to counsel clients at the worst times in their company—or personal—history. People want to work with professionals who treat them in the way they would like to be treated, who understand both their business-driven and personal wishes, and who listen attentively to their concerns before considering courses of action.

This has broad implications for the way law is practiced and law firms constituted. The behaviors law firms reward reveal a great deal about their underlying cultures. Traditional compensation structures are skewed toward a few senior attorneys who bring in new business. Little or no recognition is given to the work that goes into developing longevity in client relationships. Furthermore, because archetypal firms operate as loose associations of practice areas, there is little encouragement to build breadth of client across practice areas.

Client-centric firms use flexible compensation and recognition structures that reward personnel for contributing to the long-term success of a client relationship. They also create cross-disciplinary teams to move client ownership from a single senior attorney to the entire firm. Over time, the firm benefits by being able to cross-sell services from a variety of practice areas, while clients benefit from receiving full-spectrum legal service, where nothing is done in a vacuum. In some ways, this mirrors the primary care model that has been applied so successfully to medical practice. There will always be a lead attorney, but in a client-centric model that attorney has the freedom and the incentive to draw on other expertise. This can be within the firm, or in the case of solos and other small-scale practices, through carefully-chosen alliances.

Project management is another critical differentiator of the client-centric firm. Four elements impact any legal matter: people, time, scope, and cost. Changes in any one of these will impact the others.

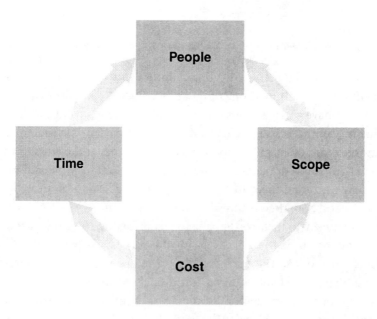

Diagram 8.15: Project Constraints

The traditional practice of law needed no mechanisms to take this into account. Changes in the legal team, time spent, or scope simply resulted in additional billable hours, which was good for the short-term interests of the law firm. This is not, however, necessarily good for client interests, as clients are under pressure to control costs and have become increasingly intolerant of surprises. Project management processes support close collaboration between attorney and client, allow for joint decision-making when appropriate, and help the attorney manage client expectations.

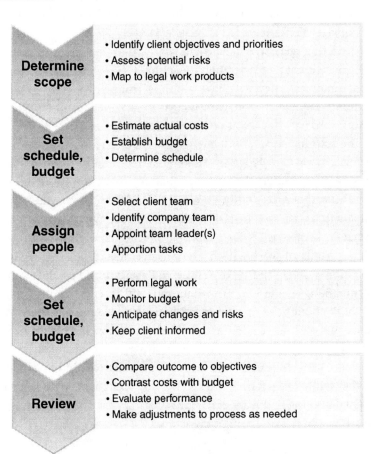

Determine scope
- Identify client objectives and priorities
- Assess potential risks
- Map to legal work products

Set schedule, budget
- Estimate actual costs
- Establish budget
- Determine schedule

Assign people
- Select client team
- Identify company team
- Appoint team leader(s)
- Apportion tasks

Set schedule, budget
- Perform legal work
- Monitor budget
- Anticipate changes and risks
- Keep client informed

Review
- Compare outcome to objectives
- Contrast costs with budget
- Evaluate performance
- Make adjustments to process as needed

Diagram 8.16: Steps in Legal Project Management

Larger firms use project management software, but the process can be readily scaled to fit the resources at hand.

The final critical element of creating a client-centric firm is the alternative fee arrangement (AFA). The legal profession's long-established reliance on the billable hour shifts all the risk to clients, while reserving all the reward for the attorney. Several models of alternative fee arrangement have been successfully developed and deployed, often leading to reduction in legal costs for clients while not having a deleterious impact on the law firm's bottom line. Combined with project management practices, carefully crafted AFAs can help attorneys work more efficiently and manage client expectations more effectively.

Firms that develop robust client-centric practices are more attractive to clients, current and new, than those that follow established attorney-centric practices. They will have a strong competitive edge in what is becoming a global market with increasing avenues for obtaining legal services, some of which will not involve attorneys.

The learning curve about clients' worlds can be steep; attorneys can maximize their knowledge investment by focusing on the clients, and industries or demographic cohorts that represent the foundation clients. To do this successfully, take what you know about your foundation clients and create an action plan to increase your depth of client. This could involve work for additional practice areas or expansion into different kinds of work within one practice area. From the beginning, this action plan should be driven by goals and fueled by data. Start by benchmarking where you are when you initiate client-centric changes and think about how you can measure the success of the activity. While you can use software to do this, straightforward benchmarks include the number of matters you complete with a particular client, the number of practice areas they use, ways in which the relationship has expanded, and the number of referrals you receive from the client. With a carefully designed and meticulously executed set of client-centric initiatives, you will see steady growth in all of these areas.

Replicate Your Foundation Clients

Approximately ten percent of every firm's clients leave each year, often for reasons beyond the firm's control. This creates a need for firms to be continually prospecting for new clients. Foundation clients are the key to successful prospecting. You already have a deep understanding of their values and needs—and you have configured your firm to accommodate them. Rather than accepting any client who happens to walk through the door, it makes far more sense to actively search for the kind of client you know you can work with successfully.

Your foundation clients provide a blueprint for an ideal client profile. Once you have created this, you can begin to target prospects by identifying where the people who match those characteristics can be found, whether they are individuals or representatives of organizations. Keep in mind, though, that it will likely require eight to twelve relevant interactions with a prospect before he decides to hire you. The reason for this is twofold: you are seeking to initiate a relationship, not sell a product or even a stand-alone service; your prospect has a particular reference point when it comes to buying professional services.

Buyers of professional services tend to act only when they feel a need—either a problem to be resolved or an opportunity to be captured. Sometimes this need exists and is urgent, sometimes addressing it has been put off, and sometimes the prospect is not even aware of it. The precise circumstances will become evident as you interact with the prospect and ask relevant questions.

In addition to the fact that professional services are typically purchased on a need-driven basis, prospective buyers often feel some level of uncertainty about the problem or opportunity they face. They are uncomfortable about the risk involved in taking action, they are skeptical because they have been treated poorly by other professionals, they are insecure in making a decision based on incomplete information, and they are concerned that you will not give their matter priority. Note that most of this is unquantifiable and emotional. Most buying decisions are made at the emotional level and only confirmed at the rational level. During the relationship marketing process, it is important to build personal and emotional connections with the prospect, just as you do when you try to deepen a client relationship from vendor to trusted advisor status.

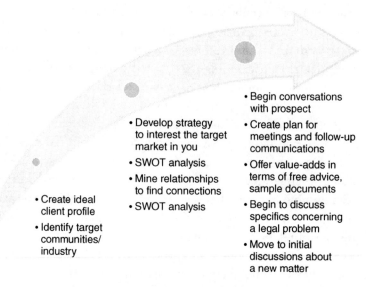

- Create ideal client profile
- Identify target communities/ industry

- Develop strategy to interest the target market in you
- SWOT analysis
- Mine relationships to find connections
- SWOT analysis

- Begin conversations with prospect
- Create plan for meetings and follow-up communications
- Offer value-adds in terms of free advice, sample documents
- Begin to discuss specifics concerning a legal problem
- Move to initial discussions about a new matter

Diagram 8.17: Targeted Sales Pipeline

Marketing materials can support coaxing a prospect through the sales pipeline, but they, too, must keep the prospect's state of mind at the forefront. Materials that emphasize firm or attorney credentials are ineffective at best. Materials that present problems or opportunities similar to those the prospect is facing and provide information about how the firm addresses such situations are far more powerful, and build on the personal connection you are trying to create.

Seeking referrals is an effective way to shorten the marketing/sales process. Your foundation clients are likely well-positioned to help you identify people or organizations with needs and situations similar to their own. This can help you overcome some of the initial objections and move quickly to more substantial interactions.

Before your first meeting with a prospect, develop a strategy. Be prepared to ask insightful questions about the prospect's world—just as you would with a client. It is often difficult to identify the precise transition point between the marketing/sales stage and the engagement stage. The dialog can continue over a long period of time and many contacts. You may be asked to provide informal legal advice. This is acceptable up to a point, as it will give both you and the prospect an opportunity to see if you are a good fit for each other.

The progression continues with each step, moving the relationship forward by allowing the prospect to visualize how it would be to work with you until the process ends with a decision to proceed on a specific matter.

Follow the Process for a More Profitable, Enjoyable Practice

This system shows you how to create a more profitable—and enjoyable—law practice by focusing on three core elements. Foremost, there are your clients. Identifying those that are the best fit for your firm, understanding who they really are and what they genuinely value about the work you do for them is a critical first step. Next, there is you, the attorney. Aligning your technical skills, business knowledge, and service practices with foundation clients' desires is the second step. Finally, there are the processes, technologies, and procedures that support your work. Reconfiguring them to support managing client expectations, meeting client requirements, and cultivating appropriate client collaboration is the third step. Taking the time now to follow the processes outlined in this book will yield only dividends as the market for legal services becomes ever more competitive and commoditized.

APPENDIX 1

Model Rules of Professional Responsibility

Links to Selected Portions

ABA list of the forty-six jurisdictions that have adopted the *Model Rules*, with the date of adoption: http://www.americanbar.org/groups/professional_responsibility/publications/model_rules_of_professional_conduct/alpha_list_state_adopting_model_rules.html

ABA Ethics Review Status Chart—Status of state review of professional conduct rules showing state changes to *Rules* and status of proposed changes: http://www.americanbar.org/content/dam/aba/migrated/cpr/pic/ethics_2000_status_chart.authcheckdam.pdf

ABA links to state legal ethics rules: http://www.americanbar.org/groups/professional_responsibility/resources/links_of_interest.html

ABA list of professionalism codes adopted by local and state bar associations and state court systems: http://www.americanbar.org/groups/professional_responsibility/resources/professionalism/professionalism_codes.html

ABA list of professionalism commissions: http://www.americanbar.org/groups/professional_responsibility/resources/professionalism/profcommissions.html

Pertinent Excerpts from the Model Rules
Rule 1.0 Terminology

(b) "Confirmed in writing," when used in reference to the informed consent of a person, denotes informed consent that is given in writing by the person or a writing that a lawyer promptly transmits to the person confirming an oral informed consent. . . .

(e) "Informed consent" denotes the agreement by a person to a proposed course of conduct after the lawyer has communicated adequate information and explanation about the material risks of and reasonably available alternatives to the proposed course of conduct.

(n) "Writing" or "written" denotes a tangible or electronic record of a communication or representation, including handwriting, typewriting, printing, photostating, photography, audio or videorecording, and email. A "signed" writing includes an electronic sound, symbol, or process attached to or logically associated with a writing and executed or adopted by a person with the intent to sign the writing.

Client-Lawyer Relationship

Rule 1.1 Competence

A lawyer shall provide competent representation to a client. Competent representation requires the legal knowledge, skill, thoroughness, and preparation reasonably necessary for the representation.

Rule 1.1(6) Informed Consent Comment

[6] Many of the Rules of Professional Conduct require the lawyer to obtain the informed consent of a client or other person (e.g., a former client or, under certain circumstances, a prospective client) before accepting or continuing representation or pursuing a course of conduct. See, e.g., Rules 1.2(c), 1.6(a) and 1.7(b). The communication necessary to obtain such consent will vary according to the Rule involved and the circumstances giving rise to the need to obtain informed consent. The lawyer must make reasonable efforts to ensure that the client or other person possesses information reasonably adequate to make an informed decision. Ordinarily, this will require communication that includes a disclosure of the facts and circumstances giving rise to the situation, any explanation reasonably necessary to inform the client or other person of the material advantages and disadvantages of the proposed course of conduct and a discussion of the client's or other person's options and alternatives. In some circumstances it may be appropriate for a lawyer to advise a client or other person to seek the advice of other counsel. A lawyer need not inform a client or other person of facts or implications already known to the client or other person; nevertheless, a lawyer who does not personally inform the client or other person assumes the risk that

the client or other person is inadequately informed and the consent is invalid. In determining whether the information and explanation provided are reasonably adequate, relevant factors include whether the client or other person is experienced in legal matters generally and in making decisions of the type involved, and whether the client or other person is independently represented by other counsel in giving the consent. Normally, such persons need less information and explanation than others, and generally a client or other person who is independently represented by other counsel in giving the consent should be assumed to have given informed consent.

[7] Obtaining informed consent will usually require an affirmative response by the client or other person. In general, a lawyer may not assume consent from a client's or other person's silence. Consent may be inferred, however, from the conduct of a client or other person who has reasonably adequate information about the matter. A number of Rules require that a person's consent be confirmed in writing. See Rules 1.7(b) and 1.9(a). For a definition of "writing" and "confirmed in writing," see paragraphs (n) and (b). Other Rules require that a client's consent be obtained in a writing signed by the client. See, e.g., Rules 1.8(a) and (g). For a definition of "signed," see paragraph (n).

Client-Lawyer Relationship

Rule 1.2 Scope of Representation and Allocation of Authority Between Client and Lawyer

(a) Subject to paragraphs (c) and (d), a lawyer shall abide by a client's decisions concerning the objectives of representation and, as required by Rule 1.4, shall consult with the client as to the means by which they are to be pursued. A lawyer may take such action on behalf of the client as is impliedly authorized to carry out the representation. A lawyer shall abide by a client's decision whether to settle a matter. In a criminal case, the lawyer shall abide by the client's decision, after consultation with the lawyer, as to a plea to be entered, whether to waive jury trial, and whether the client will testify.

(b) A lawyer's representation of a client, including representation by appointment, does not constitute an endorsement of the client's political, economic, social or moral views or activities.

(c) A lawyer may limit the scope of the representation if the limitation is reasonable under the circumstances and the client gives informed consent.

(d) A lawyer shall not counsel a client to engage, or assist a client, in conduct that the lawyer knows is criminal or fraudulent, but a lawyer may discuss the legal consequences of any proposed course of conduct with a client and may counsel or assist a client to make a good faith effort to determine the validity, scope, meaning, or application of the law.

Rule 1.2 Scope of Representation and Allocation of Authority between Client and Lawyer Comment

[1] Paragraph (a) confers upon the client the ultimate authority to determine the purposes to be served by legal representation, within the limits imposed by law and the lawyer's professional obligations. The decisions specified in paragraph (a), such as whether to settle a civil matter, must also be made by the client. See Rule 1.4(a)(1) for the lawyer's duty to communicate with the client about such decisions. With respect to the means by which the client's objectives are to be pursued, the lawyer shall consult with the client as required by Rule 1.4(a)(2) and may take such action as is impliedly authorized to carry out the representation.

[2] On occasion, however, a lawyer and a client may disagree about the means to be used to accomplish the client's objectives. Clients normally defer to the special knowledge and skill of their lawyer with respect to the means to be used to accomplish their objectives, particularly with respect to technical, legal, and tactical matters. Conversely, lawyers usually defer to the client regarding such questions as the expense to be incurred and concern for third persons who might be adversely affected. Because of the varied nature of the matters about which a lawyer and client might disagree and because the actions in question may implicate the interests of a tribunal or other persons, this Rule does not prescribe how such disagreements are to be resolved. Other law, however, may be applicable and should be consulted by the lawyer. The lawyer should also consult with the client and seek a mutually acceptable resolution of the disagreement. If such efforts are unavailing and the lawyer has a fundamental disagreement with the client, the lawyer may withdraw from the representation. See Rule 1.16(b)(4). Conversely, the client may resolve the disagreement by discharging the lawyer. See Rule 1.16(a)(3).

[3] At the outset of a representation, the client may authorize the lawyer to take specific action on the client's behalf without further consultation. Absent a material change in circumstances and subject to Rule 1.4, a lawyer may rely on

such an advance authorization. The client may, however, revoke such authority at any time.

[4] In a case in which the client appears to be suffering diminished capacity, the lawyer's duty to abide by the client's decisions is to be guided by reference to Rule 1.14.

Independence from Client's Views or Activities

[5] Legal representation should not be denied to people who are unable to afford legal services, or whose cause is controversial or the subject of popular disapproval. By the same token, representing a client does not constitute approval of the client's views or activities.

Agreements Limiting Scope of Representation

[6] The scope of services to be provided by a lawyer may be limited by agreement with the client or by the terms under which the lawyer's services are made available to the client. When a lawyer has been retained by an insurer to represent an insured, for example, the representation may be limited to matters related to the insurance coverage. A limited representation may be appropriate because the client has limited objectives for the representation. In addition, the terms upon which representation is undertaken may exclude specific means that might otherwise be used to accomplish the client's objectives. Such limitations may exclude actions that the client thinks are too costly or that the lawyer regards as repugnant or imprudent.

[7] Although this Rule affords the lawyer and client substantial latitude to limit the representation, the limitation must be reasonable under the circumstances. If, for example, a client's objective is limited to securing general information about the law the client needs in order to handle a common and typically uncomplicated legal problem, the lawyer and client may agree that the lawyer's services will be limited to a brief telephone consultation. Such a limitation, however, would not be reasonable if the time allotted was not sufficient to yield advice upon which the client could rely. Although an agreement for a limited representation does not exempt a lawyer from the duty to provide competent representation, the limitation is a factor to be considered when determining the legal knowledge, skill, thoroughness, and preparation reasonably necessary for the representation. See Rule 1.1.

[8] All agreements concerning a lawyer's representation of a client must accord with the Rules of Professional Conduct and other law. See, e.g., Rules 1.1, 1.8, and 5.6.

Criminal, Fraudulent, and Prohibited Transactions

[9] Paragraph (d) prohibits a lawyer from knowingly counseling or assisting a client to commit a crime or fraud. This prohibition, however, does not preclude the lawyer from giving an honest opinion about the actual consequences that appear likely to result from a client's conduct. Nor does the fact that a client uses advice in a course of action that is criminal or fraudulent of itself make a lawyer a party to the course of action. There is a critical distinction between presenting an analysis of legal aspects of questionable conduct and recommending the means by which a crime or fraud might be committed with impunity.

[10] When the client's course of action has already begun and is continuing, the lawyer's responsibility is especially delicate. The lawyer is required to avoid assisting the client, for example, by drafting or delivering documents that the lawyer knows are fraudulent or by suggesting how the wrongdoing might be concealed. A lawyer may not continue assisting a client in conduct that the lawyer originally supposed was legally proper but then discovers is criminal or fraudulent. The lawyer must, therefore, withdraw from the representation of the client in the matter. See Rule 1.16(a). In some cases, withdrawal alone might be insufficient. It may be necessary for the lawyer to give notice of the fact of withdrawal and to disaffirm any opinion, document, affirmation, or the like. See Rule 4.1.

[11] Where the client is a fiduciary, the lawyer may be charged with special obligations in dealings with a beneficiary.

[12] Paragraph (d) applies whether or not the defrauded party is a party to the transaction. Hence, a lawyer must not participate in a transaction to effectuate criminal or fraudulent avoidance of tax liability. Paragraph (d) does not preclude undertaking a criminal defense incident to a general retainer for legal services to a lawful enterprise. The last clause of paragraph (d) recognizes that determining the validity or interpretation of a statute or regulation may require a course of action involving disobedience of the statute or regulation or of the interpretation placed upon it by governmental authorities.

[13] If a lawyer comes to know or reasonably should know that a client expects assistance not permitted by the Rules of Professional Conduct or other law or if the lawyer intends to act contrary to the client's instructions, the lawyer

must consult with the client regarding the limitations on the lawyer's conduct. See Rule 1.4(a)(5).

Client-Lawyer Relationship
Rule 1.3 Diligence

A lawyer shall act with reasonable diligence and promptness in representing a client.

Rule 1.3 Diligence Comment

[1] A lawyer should pursue a matter on behalf of a client despite opposition, obstruction, or personal inconvenience to the lawyer, and take whatever lawful and ethical measures are required to vindicate a client's cause or endeavor. A lawyer must also act with commitment and dedication to the interests of the client and with zeal in advocacy upon the client's behalf. A lawyer is not bound, however, to press for every advantage that might be realized for a client. For example, a lawyer may have authority to exercise professional discretion in determining the means by which a matter should be pursued. See Rule 1.2. The lawyer's duty to act with reasonable diligence does not require the use of offensive tactics or preclude the treating of all persons involved in the legal process with courtesy and respect.

[2] A lawyer's work load must be controlled so that each matter can be handled competently.

[3] Perhaps no professional shortcoming is more widely resented than procrastination. A client's interests often can be adversely affected by the passage of time or the change of conditions; in extreme instances, as when a lawyer overlooks a statute of limitations, the client's legal position may be destroyed. Even when the client's interests are not affected in substance, however, unreasonable delay can cause a client needless anxiety and undermine confidence in the lawyer's trustworthiness. A lawyer's duty to act with reasonable promptness, however, does not preclude the lawyer from agreeing to a reasonable request for a postponement that will not prejudice the lawyer's client.

[4] Unless the relationship is terminated as provided in Rule 1.16, a lawyer should carry through to conclusion all matters undertaken for a client. If a lawyer's employment is limited to a specific matter, the relationship terminates

when the matter has been resolved. If a lawyer has served a client over a substantial period in a variety of matters, the client sometimes may assume that the lawyer will continue to serve on a continuing basis unless the lawyer gives notice of withdrawal. Doubt about whether a client-lawyer relationship still exists should be clarified by the lawyer, preferably in writing, so that the client will not mistakenly suppose the lawyer is looking after the client's affairs when the lawyer has ceased to do so. For example, if a lawyer has handled a judicial or administrative proceeding that produced a result adverse to the client and the lawyer and the client have not agreed that the lawyer will handle the matter on appeal, the lawyer must consult with the client about the possibility of appeal before relinquishing responsibility for the matter. See Rule 1.4(a)(2). Whether the lawyer is obligated to prosecute the appeal for the client depends on the scope of the representation the lawyer has agreed to provide to the client. See Rule 1.2.

[5] To prevent neglect of client matters in the event of a sole practitioner's death or disability, the duty of diligence may require that each sole practitioner prepare a plan, in conformity with applicable rules, that designates another competent lawyer to review client files, notify each client of the lawyer's death or disability, and determine whether there is a need for immediate protective action. *Cf.* Rule 28 of the American Bar Association Model Rules for Lawyer Disciplinary Enforcement (providing for court appointment of a lawyer to inventory files and take other protective action in absence of a plan providing for another lawyer to protect the interests of the clients of a deceased or disabled lawyer).

Client-Lawyer Relationship

Rule 1.4 Communication

(a) A lawyer shall:

(1) promptly inform the client of any decision or circumstance with respect to which the client's informed consent, as defined in Rule 1.0(e), is required by these Rules;

(2) reasonably consult with the client about the means by which the client's objectives are to be accomplished;

(3) keep the client reasonably informed about the status of the matter;

(4) promptly comply with reasonable requests for information; and

(5) consult with the client about any relevant limitation on the lawyer's conduct when the lawyer knows that the client expects assistance not permitted by the Rules of Professional Conduct or other law.

(b) A lawyer shall explain a matter to the extent reasonably necessary to permit the client to make informed decisions regarding the representation.

Rule 1.4 Communication Comment

[1] Reasonable communication between the lawyer and the client is necessary for the client effectively to participate in the representation.

Communicating with Client

[2] If these Rules require that a particular decision about the representation be made by the client, paragraph (a)(1) requires that the lawyer promptly consult with and secure the client's consent prior to taking action unless prior discussions with the client have resolved what action the client wants the lawyer to take. For example, a lawyer who receives from opposing counsel an offer of settlement in a civil controversy or a proffered plea bargain in a criminal case must promptly inform the client of its substance unless the client has previously indicated that the proposal will be acceptable or unacceptable or has authorized the lawyer to accept or to reject the offer. See Rule 1.2(a).

[3] Paragraph (a)(2) requires the lawyer to reasonably consult with the client about the means to be used to accomplish the client's objectives. In some situations—depending on both the importance of the action under consideration and the feasibility of consulting with the client—this duty will require consultation prior to taking action. In other circumstances, such as during a trial when an immediate decision must be made, the exigency of the situation may require the lawyer to act without prior consultation. In such cases the lawyer must nonetheless act reasonably to inform the client of actions the lawyer has taken on the client's behalf. Additionally, paragraph (a)(3) requires that the lawyer keep the client reasonably informed about the status of the matter, such as significant developments affecting the timing or the substance of the representation.

[4] A lawyer's regular communication with clients will minimize the occasions on which a client will need to request information concerning the representation. When a client makes a reasonable request for information, however, paragraph (a)(4) requires prompt compliance with the request, or if a prompt response is not feasible, that the lawyer, or a member of the lawyer's staff, acknowledge receipt of the request and advise the client when a response may be expected. Client telephone calls should be promptly returned or acknowledged.

Explaining Matters

[5] The client should have sufficient information to participate intelligently in decisions concerning the objectives of the representation and the means by which they are to be pursued, to the extent the client is willing and able to do so. Adequacy of communication depends in part on the kind of advice or assistance that is involved. For example, when there is time to explain a proposal made in a negotiation, the lawyer should review all important provisions with the client before proceeding to an agreement. In litigation a lawyer should explain the general strategy and prospects of success and ordinarily should consult the client on tactics that are likely to result in significant expense or to injure or coerce others. On the other hand, a lawyer ordinarily will not be expected to describe trial or negotiation strategy in detail. The guiding principle is that the lawyer should fulfill reasonable client expectations for information consistent with the duty to act in the client's best interests, and the client's overall requirements as to the character of representation. In certain circumstances, such as when a lawyer asks a client to consent to a representation affected by a conflict of interest, the client must give informed consent, as defined in Rule 1.0(e).

[6] Ordinarily, the information to be provided is that appropriate for a client who is a comprehending and responsible adult. However, fully informing the client according to this standard may be impracticable, for example, where the client is a child or suffers from diminished capacity. See Rule 1.14. When the client is an organization or group, it is often impossible or inappropriate to inform every one of its members about its legal affairs; ordinarily, the lawyer should address communications to the appropriate officials of the organization. See Rule 1.13. Where many routine matters are involved, a system of limited or occasional reporting may be arranged with the client.

Withholding Information

[7] In some circumstances, a lawyer may be justified in delaying transmission of information when the client would be likely to react imprudently to an immediate communication. Thus, a lawyer might withhold a psychiatric diagnosis of a client when the examining psychiatrist indicates that disclosure would harm the client. A lawyer may not withhold information to serve the lawyer's own interest or convenience or the interests or convenience of another person. Rules or court orders governing litigation may provide that information supplied to a lawyer may not be disclosed to the client. Rule 3.4(c) directs compliance with such rules or orders.

Client-Lawyer Relationship

Rule 1.5 Fees

(a) A lawyer shall not make an agreement for, charge, or collect an unreasonable fee or an unreasonable amount for expenses. The factors to be considered in determining the reasonableness of a fee include the following:

(1) the time and labor required, the novelty and difficulty of the questions involved, and the skill requisite to perform the legal service properly;

(2) the likelihood, if apparent to the client, that the acceptance of the particular employment will preclude other employment by the lawyer;

(3) the fee customarily charged in the locality for similar legal services;

(4) the amount involved and the results obtained;

(5) the time limitations imposed by the client or by the circumstances;

(6) the nature and length of the professional relationship with the client;

(7) the experience, reputation, and ability of the lawyer or lawyers performing the services; and

(8) whether the fee is fixed or contingent.

(b) The scope of the representation and the basis or rate of the fee and expenses for which the client will be responsible shall be communicated to the client, preferably in writing, before or within a reasonable time after commencing the representation, except when the lawyer will charge a regularly represented client on the same basis or rate. Any changes in the basis or rate of the fee or expenses shall also be communicated to the client.

(c) A fee may be contingent on the outcome of the matter for which the service is rendered, except in a matter in which a contingent fee is prohibited by paragraph (d) or other law. A contingent fee agreement shall be in a writing signed by the client and shall state the method by which the fee is to be determined, including the percentage or percentages that shall accrue to the lawyer in the event of settlement, trial, or appeal; litigation and other expenses to be deducted from the recovery; and whether such expenses are to be deducted before or after the contingent fee is calculated. The agreement must clearly notify the client of any expenses for which the client will be liable whether or not the client is the prevailing party. Upon conclusion of a contingent fee matter, the lawyer shall provide the client with a written statement stating the outcome of the matter and, if there is a recovery, showing the remittance to the client and the method of its determination.

(d) A lawyer shall not enter into an arrangement for, charge, or collect:

(1) any fee in a domestic relations matter, the payment or amount of which is contingent upon the securing of a divorce or upon the amount of alimony or support, or property settlement in lieu thereof; or

(2) a contingent fee for representing a defendant in a criminal case.

(e) A division of a fee between lawyers who are not in the same firm may be made only if:

(1) the division is in proportion to the services performed by each lawyer or each lawyer assumes joint responsibility for the representation;

(2) the client agrees to the arrangement, including the share each lawyer will receive, and the agreement is confirmed in writing; and

(3) the total fee is reasonable.

Client-Lawyer Relationship

Rule 1.5 Fees - Comment

Reasonableness of Fee and Expenses

[1] Paragraph (a) requires that lawyers charge fees that are reasonable under the circumstances. The factors specified in (1) through (8) are not exclusive. Nor will each factor be relevant in each instance. Paragraph (a) also requires that expenses for which the client will be charged must be reasonable. A lawyer may seek reimbursement for the cost of services performed in-house, such as copying, or for other expenses incurred in-house, such as telephone charges, either by charging a reasonable amount to which the client has agreed in advance or by charging an amount that reasonably reflects the cost incurred by the lawyer.

Basis or Rate of Fee

[2] When the lawyer has regularly represented a client, they ordinarily will have evolved an understanding concerning the basis or rate of the fee and the expenses for which the client will be responsible. In a new client-lawyer rela-

tionship, however, an understanding as to fees and expenses must be promptly established. Generally, it is desirable to furnish the client with at least a simple memorandum or copy of the lawyer's customary fee arrangements that states the general nature of the legal services to be provided, the basis, rate or total amount of the fee, and whether and to what extent the client will be responsible for any costs, expenses, or disbursements in the course of the representation. A written statement concerning the terms of the engagement reduces the possibility of misunderstanding.

[3] Contingent fees, like any other fees, are subject to the reasonableness standard of paragraph (a) of this Rule. In determining whether a particular contingent fee is reasonable, or whether it is reasonable to charge any form of contingent fee, a lawyer must consider the factors that are relevant under the circumstances. Applicable law may impose limitations on contingent fees, such as a ceiling on the percentage allowable, or may require a lawyer to offer clients an alternative basis for the fee. Applicable law also may apply to situations other than a contingent fee, for example, government regulations regarding fees in certain tax matters.

Terms of Payment

[4] A lawyer may require advance payment of a fee, but is obliged to return any unearned portion. See Rule 1.16(d). A lawyer may accept property in payment for services, such as an ownership interest in an enterprise, providing this does not involve acquisition of a proprietary interest in the cause of action or subject matter of the litigation contrary to Rule 1.8 (i). However, a fee paid in property instead of money may be subject to the requirements of Rule 1.8(a) because such fees often have the essential qualities of a business transaction with the client.

[5] An agreement may not be made whose terms might induce the lawyer improperly to curtail services for the client or perform them in a way contrary to the client's interest. For example, a lawyer should not enter into an agreement whereby services are to be provided only up to a stated amount when it is foreseeable that more extensive services probably will be required, unless the situation is adequately explained to the client. Otherwise, the client might have to bargain for further assistance in the midst of a proceeding or transaction. However, it is proper to define the extent of services in light of the client's ability to pay. A lawyer should not exploit a fee arrangement based primarily on hourly charges by using wasteful procedures.

Prohibited Contingent Fees

[6] Paragraph (d) prohibits a lawyer from charging a contingent fee in a domestic relations matter when payment is contingent upon the securing of a divorce or upon the amount of alimony or support or property settlement to be obtained. This provision does not preclude a contract for a contingent fee for legal representation in connection with the recovery of post-judgment balances due under support, alimony, or other financial orders because such contracts do not implicate the same policy concerns.

Division of Fee

[7] A division of fee is a single billing to a client covering the fee of two or more lawyers who are not in the same firm. A division of fee facilitates association of more than one lawyer in a matter in which neither alone could serve the client as well, and most often is used when the fee is contingent and the division is between a referring lawyer and a trial specialist. Paragraph (e) permits the lawyers to divide a fee either on the basis of the proportion of services they render or if each lawyer assumes responsibility for the representation as a whole. In addition, the client must agree to the arrangement, including the share that each lawyer is to receive, and the agreement must be confirmed in writing. Contingent fee agreements must be in a writing signed by the client and must otherwise comply with paragraph (c) of this Rule. Joint responsibility for the representation entails financial and ethical responsibility for the representation as if the lawyers were associated in a partnership. A lawyer should only refer a matter to a lawyer whom the referring lawyer reasonably believes is competent to handle the matter. See Rule 1.1.

[8] Paragraph (e) does not prohibit or regulate division of fees to be received in the future for work done when lawyers were previously associated in a law firm.

Disputes over Fees

[9] If a procedure has been established for resolution of fee disputes, such as an arbitration or mediation procedure established by the bar, the lawyer must comply with the procedure when it is mandatory, and, even when it is voluntary, the lawyer should conscientiously consider submitting to it. Law may prescribe a procedure for determining a lawyer's fee, for example, in representation of an

executor or administrator, a class or a person entitled to a reasonable fee as part of the measure of damages. The lawyer entitled to such a fee and a lawyer representing another party concerned with the fee should comply with the prescribed procedure.

Client-Lawyer Relationship
Rule 1.6 Confidentiality of Information

(a) A lawyer shall not reveal information relating to the representation of a client unless the client gives informed consent, the disclosure is impliedly authorized in order to carry out the representation or the disclosure is permitted by paragraph (b).

(b) A lawyer may reveal information relating to the representation of a client to the extent the lawyer reasonably believes necessary:

(1) to prevent reasonably certain death or substantial bodily harm;

(2) to prevent the client from committing a crime or fraud that is reasonably certain to result in substantial injury to the financial interests or property of another and in furtherance of which the client has used or is using the lawyer's services;

(3) to prevent, mitigate, or rectify substantial injury to the financial interests or property of another that is reasonably certain to result or has resulted from the client's commission of a crime or fraud in furtherance of which the client has used the lawyer's services;

(4) to secure legal advice about the lawyer's compliance with these Rules;

(5) to establish a claim or defense on behalf of the lawyer in a controversy between the lawyer and the client, to establish a defense to a criminal charge or civil claim against the lawyer based upon conduct in which the client was involved, or to respond to allegations in any proceeding concerning the lawyer's representation of the client; or

(6) to comply with other law or a court order.

Client-Lawyer Relationship
Rule 1.6 Confidentiality of Information - Comment

[1] This Rule governs the disclosure by a lawyer of information relating to the representation of a client during the lawyer's representation of the client. See

Rule 1.18 for the lawyer's duties with respect to information provided to the lawyer by a prospective client, Rule 1.9(c)(2) for the lawyer's duty not to reveal information relating to the lawyer's prior representation of a former client and Rules 1.8(b) and 1.9(c)(1) for the lawyer's duties with respect to the use of such information to the disadvantage of clients and former clients.

[2] A fundamental principle in the client-lawyer relationship is that, in the absence of the client's informed consent, the lawyer must not reveal information relating to the representation. See Rule 1.0(e) for the definition of informed consent. This contributes to the trust that is the hallmark of the client-lawyer relationship. The client is thereby encouraged to seek legal assistance and to communicate fully and frankly with the lawyer even as to embarrassing or legally damaging subject matter. The lawyer needs this information to represent the client effectively and, if necessary, to advise the client to refrain from wrongful conduct. Almost without exception, clients come to lawyers in order to determine their rights and what is, in the complex of laws and regulations, deemed to be legal and correct. Based upon experience, lawyers know that almost all clients follow the advice given, and the law is upheld.

[3] The principle of client-lawyer confidentiality is given effect by related bodies of law: the attorney-client privilege, the work product doctrine and the rule of confidentiality established in professional ethics. The attorney-client privilege and work-product doctrine apply in judicial and other proceedings in which a lawyer may be called as a witness or otherwise required to produce evidence concerning a client. The rule of client-lawyer confidentiality applies in situations other than those where evidence is sought from the lawyer through compulsion of law. The confidentiality rule, for example, applies not only to matters communicated in confidence by the client but also to all information relating to the representation, whatever its source. A lawyer may not disclose such information except as authorized or required by the Rules of Professional Conduct or other law. See also Scope.

Paragraphs [4]–[18] not included here.

Client-Lawyer Relationship

Rule 1.7 Conflict of Interest: Current Clients

(a) Except as provided in paragraph (b), a lawyer shall not represent a client if the representation involves a concurrent conflict of interest. A concurrent conflict of interest exists if:

(1) the representation of one client will be directly adverse to another client; or

(2) there is a significant risk that the representation of one or more clients will be materially limited by the lawyer's responsibilities to another client, a former client or a third person or by a personal interest of the lawyer.

(b) Notwithstanding the existence of a concurrent conflict of interest under paragraph (a), a lawyer may represent a client if:

(1) the lawyer reasonably believes that the lawyer will be able to provide competent and diligent representation to each affected client;

(2) the representation is not prohibited by law;

(3) the representation does not involve the assertion of a claim by one client against another client represented by the lawyer in the same litigation or other proceeding before a tribunal; and

(4) each affected client gives informed consent, confirmed in writing.

Client-Lawyer Relationship
Rule 1.7 Conflict of Interest: Current Clients—Comment
General Principles

[1] Loyalty and independent judgment are essential elements in the lawyer's relationship to a client. Concurrent conflicts of interest can arise from the lawyer's responsibilities to another client, a former client or a third person or from the lawyer's own interests. For specific Rules regarding certain concurrent conflicts of interest, see Rule 1.8. For former client conflicts of interest, see Rule 1.9. For conflicts of interest involving prospective clients, see Rule 1.18. For definitions of "informed consent" and "confirmed in writing," see Rule 1.0(e) and (b).

[2] Resolution of a conflict of interest problem under this Rule requires the lawyer to: 1) clearly identify the client or clients; 2) determine whether a conflict of interest exists; 3) decide whether the representation may be undertaken despite the existence of a conflict, i.e., whether the conflict is consentable; and 4) if so, consult with the clients affected under paragraph (a) and obtain their informed consent, confirmed in writing. The clients affected under paragraph (a) include both of the clients referred to in paragraph (a)(1) and the one or more clients whose representation might be materially limited under paragraph (a)(2).

[3] A conflict of interest may exist before representation is undertaken, in which event the representation must be declined, unless the lawyer obtains the informed consent of each client under the conditions of paragraph (b). To determine whether a conflict of interest exists, a lawyer should adopt reasonable procedures, appropriate for the size and type of firm and practice, to determine in both litigation and non-litigation matters the persons and issues involved. See also Comment to Rule 5.1. Ignorance caused by a failure to institute such procedures will not excuse a lawyer's violation of this Rule. As to whether a client-lawyer relationship exists or, having once been established, is continuing, see Comment to Rule 1.3 and Scope.

Paragraphs [4]–[17] omitted

Informed Consent

[18] Informed consent requires that each affected client be aware of the relevant circumstances and of the material and reasonably foreseeable ways that the conflict could have adverse effects on the interests of that client. See Rule 1.0(e) (informed consent). The information required depends on the nature of the conflict and the nature of the risks involved. When representation of multiple clients in a single matter is undertaken, the information must include the implications of the common representation, including possible effects on loyalty, confidentiality and the attorney-client privilege, and the advantages and risks involved. See Comments [30] and [31] (effect of common representation on confidentiality).

Paragraphs [19]–[35] omitted

Rules 1.8–1.18 omitted.

Counselor

Rule 2.1 Advisor

In representing a client, a lawyer shall exercise independent professional judgment and render candid advice. In rendering advice, a lawyer may refer not only to law but to other considerations such as moral, economic, social, and political factors, that may be relevant to the client's situation.

Counselor

Rule 2.1 Advisor - Comment
Scope of Advice

[1] A client is entitled to straightforward advice expressing the lawyer's honest assessment. Legal advice often involves unpleasant facts and alternatives that a client may be disinclined to confront. In presenting advice, a lawyer endeavors to sustain the client's morale and may put advice in as acceptable a form as honesty permits. However, a lawyer should not be deterred from giving candid advice by the prospect that the advice will be unpalatable to the client.

[2] Advice couched in narrow legal terms may be of little value to a client, especially where practical considerations, such as cost or effects on other people, are predominant. Purely technical legal advice, therefore, can sometimes be inadequate. It is proper for a lawyer to refer to relevant moral and ethical considerations in giving advice. Although a lawyer is not a moral advisor as such, moral and ethical considerations impinge upon most legal questions and may decisively influence how the law will be applied.

[3] A client may expressly or impliedly ask the lawyer for purely technical advice. When such a request is made by a client experienced in legal matters, the lawyer may accept it at face value. When such a request is made by a client inexperienced in legal matters, however, the lawyer's responsibility as advisor may include indicating that more may be involved than strictly legal considerations.

[4] Matters that go beyond strictly legal questions may also be in the domain of another profession. Family matters can involve problems within the professional competence of psychiatry, clinical psychology, or social work; business matters can involve problems within the competence of the accounting profession or of financial specialists. Where consultation with a professional in another field is itself something a competent lawyer would recommend, the lawyer should make such a recommendation. At the same time, a lawyer's advice at its best often consists of recommending a course of action in the face of conflicting recommendations of experts.

Offering Advice

[5] In general, a lawyer is not expected to give advice until asked by the client. However, when a lawyer knows that a client proposes a course of action that is

likely to result in substantial adverse legal consequences to the client, the lawyer's duty to the client under Rule 1.4 may require that the lawyer offer advice if the client's course of action is related to the representation. Similarly, when a matter is likely to involve litigation, it may be necessary under Rule 1.4 to inform the client of forms of dispute resolution that might constitute reasonable alternatives to litigation. A lawyer ordinarily has no duty to initiate investigation of a client's affairs or to give advice that the client has indicated is unwanted, but a lawyer may initiate advice to a client when doing so appears to be in the client's interest.

Client-Lawyer Relationship

Rule 1.5 Fees

(a) A lawyer shall not make an agreement for, charge, or collect an unreasonable fee or an unreasonable amount for expenses. The factors to be considered in determining the reasonableness of a fee include the following:

(1) the time and labor required, the novelty and difficulty of the questions involved, and the skill requisite to perform the legal service properly;

(2) the likelihood, if apparent to the client, that the acceptance of the particular employment will preclude other employment by the lawyer;

(3) the fee customarily charged in the locality for similar legal services;

(4) the amount involved and the results obtained;

(5) the time limitations imposed by the client or by the circumstances;

(6) the nature and length of the professional relationship with the client;

(7) the experience, reputation, and ability of the lawyer or lawyers performing the services; and

(8) whether the fee is fixed or contingent.

(b) The scope of the representation and the basis or rate of the fee and expenses for which the client will be responsible shall be communicated to the client, preferably in writing, before or within a reasonable time after commencing the representation, except when the lawyer will charge a regularly represented client on the same basis or rate. Any changes in the basis or rate of the fee or expenses shall also be communicated to the client.

(c) A fee may be contingent on the outcome of the matter for which the service is rendered, except in a matter in which a contingent fee is prohibited by paragraph (d) or other law. A contingent fee agreement shall be in a writing signed by the client and shall state the method by which the fee is to be determined, including the percentage or percentages that shall accrue to the lawyer in the event of settlement, trial or appeal; litigation and other expenses to be deducted from the recovery; and whether such expenses are to be deducted before or after the contingent fee is calculated. The agreement must clearly notify the client of any expenses for which the client will be liable whether or not the client is the prevailing party. Upon conclusion of a contingent fee matter, the lawyer shall provide the client with a written statement stating the outcome of the matter and, if there is a recovery, showing the remittance to the client and the method of its determination.

Paragraphs (d) and (e) omitted

Client-Lawyer Relationship

Rule 1.5 Fees - Comment

Reasonableness of Fee and Expenses

[1] Paragraph (a) requires that lawyers charge fees that are reasonable under the circumstances. The factors specified in (1) through (8) are not exclusive. Nor will each factor be relevant in each instance. Paragraph (a) also requires that expenses for which the client will be charged must be reasonable. A lawyer may seek reimbursement for the cost of services performed in-house, such as copying, or for other expenses incurred in-house, such as telephone charges, either by charging a reasonable amount to which the client has agreed in advance or by charging an amount that reasonably reflects the cost incurred by the lawyer.

Basis or Rate of Fee

[2] When the lawyer has regularly represented a client, they ordinarily will have evolved an understanding concerning the basis or rate of the fee and the expenses for which the client will be responsible. In a new client-lawyer relationship, however, an understanding as to fees and expenses must be promptly established. Generally, it is desirable to furnish the client with at least a simple memorandum or copy of the lawyer's customary fee arrangements that states the general nature of the legal services to be provided, the basis, rate or total amount

of the fee and whether and to what extent the client will be responsible for any costs, expenses, or disbursements in the course of the representation. A written statement concerning the terms of the engagement reduces the possibility of misunderstanding.

[3] Contingent fees, like any other fees, are subject to the reasonableness standard of paragraph (a) of this Rule. In determining whether a particular contingent fee is reasonable, or whether it is reasonable to charge any form of contingent fee, a lawyer must consider the factors that are relevant under the circumstances. Applicable law may impose limitations on contingent fees, such as a ceiling on the percentage allowable, or may require a lawyer to offer clients an alternative basis for the fee. Applicable law also may apply to situations other than a contingent fee, for example, government regulations regarding fees in certain tax matters.

Terms of Payment

[4] A lawyer may require advance payment of a fee, but is obliged to return any unearned portion. See Rule 1.16(d). A lawyer may accept property in payment for services, such as an ownership interest in an enterprise, providing this does not involve acquisition of a proprietary interest in the cause of action or subject matter of the litigation contrary to Rule 1.8 (i). However, a fee paid in property instead of money may be subject to the requirements of Rule 1.8(a) because such fees often have the essential qualities of a business transaction with the client.

[5] An agreement may not be made whose terms might induce the lawyer improperly to curtail services for the client or perform them in a way contrary to the client's interest. For example, a lawyer should not enter into an agreement whereby services are to be provided only up to a stated amount when it is foreseeable that more extensive services probably will be required, unless the situation is adequately explained to the client. Otherwise, the client might have to bargain for further assistance in the midst of a proceeding or transaction. However, it is proper to define the extent of services in light of the client's ability to pay. A lawyer should not exploit a fee arrangement based primarily on hourly charges by using wasteful procedures.

APPENDIX 2

Basic Guide to Online Research

With almost infinite sites for Internet research, the trick is to make sure that you use the reputable ones. In this appendix, you'll find a listing of free sites for general research. You can also search for information at sites such as

> trade associations
> professional associations
> major university Web sites
> Lexis-Nexis, FindLaw, and other law resource sites
> LinkedIn and other social sites
> Yahoo and Google also have lists of trade associations, etc.

General Research Information

http://www.biblioscape.com/web_general.htm—portal to many libraries, research books, and online sources

http://www.britannica.com—access to the encyclopedia

http://www.worldopinion.com—international research Web site with research tips, findings from key reports, and research organization directory

http://www.refdesk.com—an encyclopedia-like reference resource

http://2010.census.gov/2010census/data/—2010 state and local census data

General Legal Sites

http://www.acc.com/valuechallenge—American Corporate Counsel value challenge resources site

http://www.americanbar.org/portals.html—American Bar Association, Resources for Lawyers section

http://lp.findlaw.com/—FindLaw for legal professionals

http://www.ilrg.com—public legal—a categorized list of four thousand legal Web sites from all over the world http://www.law-library.rutgers.edu/ilg/general.php—General legal sites

http://scholar.google.com/—Google Scholar—legal opinions and journals

http://www.oc.gov/law/index.php—Law Library of Congress

http://www.lawyerist.com—technology tips for small firm practices

Company Information: Factual

http://www.Bizweb.com—guide to 44,140 companies within 190 industry categories

http://www.Businesswire.com—corporate press releases and business articles

http://www.prnewswire.com—press releases and key business news

http://www.Companiesonline.com—Lycos business reference site with data from D&B

http://www.Freeedgar.com or http://www.edgarscan.tc.pw.com/EdgarScan—both sites make it easier to search the SEC's EDGAR database. The latter one is a free site provided by PricewaterhouseCoopers

http://www.Corpfinet.com—profiles on financial services (banks, investment banks, mutual funds, etc.); professional services firms, finance, and technology companies; news; and link to EDGAR online

http://www.Corporateinformation.com—profiles of 350,000+ public and private, U.S. and foreign companies, plus research reports and links to other research sites

http://www.Hoovers.com—descriptions of over thirteen thousand companies (but you can access more data if you subscribe), plus news, newsletters, etc. (for more complete information you need to join)

http://www.Reportgallery.com—links to over two thousand current corporate annual reports

http://www.Wsrn.com/home/companyresearch.html—information on the markets and public companies

http://www.naics.com/search.htm or gov/epcd/naics02/N02TOS87.htm—NAIC-SIC industry classification correspondence tables

Corporate Information: Softer, "Gossip"

http://www.Deja.com—searches Usenet discussion groups for mention of a particular company

http://www.Companysleuth.com—"all" information on US publicly traded companies

http://www.LinkedIn.com—and other social Web sites, some specifically for doctors, realtors, etc.

http://www.Vaultreports.com—profiles and employee message boards for over one thousand companies and law firms

Industry Information

http://www.Industrylink.com—links to industry specific and cross-industry databases and reference sites

http://valuationresources.com/IndustryReport.htm—covers four hundred industry categories

http://www.Thomasregister.com—information on 155,000 manufacturing companies

http://legacy.www.nypl.org/research/sibl/trade/index.cfm—directories within specific industries

http://www.chiff.com/business/industry.htm—a consumer-oriented listing of directories in an assortment of areas

Not for Profit Organizations

http://www.Uwnyc.org or http://www.opportunitynocs.org—information on not-for-profit organizations

http://www.irs.gov/charities/article/0,,id=96136,00.html—all charities filing with the federal government

http://charity.lovetoknow.com/—List of Nonprofit Organizations—incomplete but wide-ranging list of charities organized by subject

http://www.charitywatch.org/toprated.html—watchdog site that rates charities according to the percentage of funds spent on the charitable purpose

http://www.nonprofitlist.org/—search for nonprofits by state/locale

Trade and Professional Association Lists

http://www.weddles.com/associations/index.cfm—recruiting/human resources oriented site with profiles of over three thousand associations

http://www.inc.com/articles/2001/02/22070_Printer_Friendly.html—INC magazine article with this attached list that links by industry category to trade and professional associations

http://www.imex.com/imex/assoc/tradealpha.html—alphabetical listing of international trade associations http://dir.yahoo.com/business_and_economy/organizations/trade_assoc iations/—eclectic mixture of trade association resources

http://www.asaecenter.org/Community/Directories/associationsearch.cfm— searchable database on the American Society for Association Executives' Web site

http://www.valuationresources.com/MoreResources/TradeAssociation Directories.htm—searchable database

U.S. Government Sites

http://www.usa.gov—basic U.S. government access portal

http://www.usa.gov/Agencies/federal.shtml—U.S. agency portal

http://www.fedworld.gov/index.html—Department of Commerce site that includes links to key government agencies, court decisions, government reports, etc.

State Government websites—e.g. http://www.ny.gov

APPENDIX 3

Guide to Client-Centric Initiatives

Client-centricity is the sum of small changes—an attitude, a guideline, a process—all of which are designed to build a knowledge-based, transparent, client-responsive approach to the delivery of legal services. The goal is to create loyal clients, comfortable with you and your firm, who will give you more of their business and recommend your services to colleagues and friends. Each of the activities presented below can be part of the client-centric practice you build. Some activities will be more comfortable for rainmaker-lawyers, others will fit naturally into the practice of a shyer, more technically-focused attorney.

This list is not intended to be definitive. Consider it as you might a menu, where you can select the initiatives that work best for you and your foundation clients. Or use it as a springboard to develop initiatives customized to your firm, your style and personality, and your clients' personalities. The important thing is to deliberate on how you can make small changes to your practice that will eventually transform it into one with a solid—and well-deserved—reputation for client-centricity.

In addition to providing ideas for specific activities, the list also shows you how to use marketing tools such as Web sites, newsletters, and speaking engagements in an effective way to build a client-centric practice.

The initiatives are grouped around three client-centric goals. Some of these activities are more resource-intensive than others, but most can be adopted in smaller firms—especially if the attorneys are technologically-savvy. The firm sizes below represent the total number of firm employees, rather than number of attorneys, as many of the activities can be managed or maintained appropriately by paraprofessionals or administrative staff.

The five firm size groupings are:

1. 200+
2. 100–199
3. 11–99
4. 2–10
5. 1

The three client-centric goals are:

1. to develop a stronger relationship with the client
2. to establish regular and open communication pathways as part of the attorney/client relationship
3. to incorporate modern best business practices to make the legal processes within your firm more efficient and effective

1. To Develop a Stronger Relationship with the Client

Become More Involved in Their Company

Activity Firm size →	200+ 1	100–199 2	11–99 3	2–10 4	Solo 5
Know the client's work environment and personnel:					
• Visit the client's place of business; if appropriate, ask for a tour	X	X	X	X	X
• Ask to meet everyone you work with in the client's organization	X	X	X	X	X
• Get to know your contact's support staff	X	X	X	X	X
• Get to know your contact's colleagues on the business side	X	X	X	X	X
• Get to know the staff whose work may impact yours, including billing, procurement, and internal legal support teams	X	X	X	X	X
Support the client's business by providing complimentary value-added services:					
• Offer legal briefings for the C-suite executives	X	X	X	X	X
• Perform compliance audits for a specific segment of the business	X	X	X	X	X
• Do on-site CLE programs for in-house counsel	X	X	X	X	X
• Offer to review a manual or contract	X	X	X	X	X
• Share relevant educational materials—especially on emerging issues that pose threats or present opportunities	X	X	X	X	X

(continued)

Activity Firm size →	200+ 1	100–199 2	11–99 3	2–10 4	Solo 5
Become a familiar presence at the company:					
• Hold "office hours" at the client's office to answer work-related questions about compliance issues, e-discovery, etc.	X	X	X	X	X
• Place junior attorneys with the client for a week	X	X	X		
• Ask if you can attend their planning meetings in order to understand their goals more completely	X	X	X	X	X
• Attend key events, such as new offices openings	X	X	X	X	X
Acknowledge their pride in their accomplishments:					
• Remember company milestones	X	X	X	X	X
• Support the company's charitable activities	X	X	X	X	X
• Nominate the company and its executives for industry and community awards	X	X	X	X	X

Build Personal Relationships with Clients

Activity Firm size →	200+ 1	100–199 2	11–99 3	2–10 4	Solo 5
Socialize with them, as appropriate:					
• Include family members in activities when appropriate	X	X	X	X	X
• Invite clients to entertainment and sports events (be cognizant of the company's gift guidelines)	X	X	X	X	X
• Create a series of knowledge-themed dinners for key clients	X	X	X	X	X
• Hold special dinners for key clients	X	X	X	X	X
• Create opportunities—educational and social—to get to know both the lawyers and executive decision-makers at the client	X	X	X	X	X

(continued)

Activity Firm size →	200+ 1	100–199 2	11–99 3	2–10 4	Solo 5
Support their personal interests:					
• Attend community and charity events	X	X	X	X	X
• Make contributions, as appropriate	X	X	X	X	X
Make helpful introductions:					
• Offer to help personally when your contacts are changing jobs	X	X	X	X	X
Give suitable gifts:					
• Keep gifts within corporate guidelines	X	X	X	X	X
• Key gift to individual interests	X	X	X	X	X

Develop Joint Marketing Approaches

Activity Firm size →	200+ 1	100–199 2	11–99 3	2–10 4	Solo 5
Invite them to join a business or networking group of which you are a member	X	X	X	X	X
Collaborate on newsletters:					
• Submit an article for their newsletter or invite them to submit one to yours	X	X	X	X	X
• Join their newsletter editorial board	X	X	X	X	X
• Invite them to serve on the editorial board of your newsletter	X	X	X		
Consider a collaborative electronic marketing strategy:					
• Create guest posts for their blogs and invite them to do the same for yours	X	X	X	X	X
• Connect with them on business-focused social media pages (e.g., LinkedIn, Facebook, Twitter)	X	X	X	X	X
• Monitor their blogs and social media feeds, and comment as appropriate	X	X	X	X	X
• Invite their comments on your social media feeds and acknowledge them	X	X	X	X	X
• Link to their Web site and invite them to link to yours	X	X	X	X	X
• Post favorable news about them on your Web site, blog, and social media feeds	X	X	X	X	X

(continued)

Activity Firm size →	200+ 1	100–199 2	11–99 3	2–10 4	Solo 5
Join forces on presentations:					
• Collaborate on seminars, etc., for outside audiences	X	X	X	X	X
• Co-chair or present at one of their company seminars and invite them to do the same at yours	X	X	X	X	X
• Look for opportunities to involve them in your speaking engagements, such as panel discussions, educational cable TV programs, etc.	X	X	X	X	X

Participate in Their World

Activity Firm size →	200+ 1	100–199 2	11–99 3	2–10 4	Solo 5
Join their industry association or personal interest group:					
• Attend a meeting or conference with them	X	X	X	X	X
• Offer to participate on a panel at one of their meetings	X	X	X	X	X
• Offer to host one of their meetings at your office	X	X	X	X	X
Get to know their other professional service providers—accountant, banker, venture capitalist, insurance broker, financial broker, outside consultants	X	X	X	X	X
Use technology to keep up on—and advance—their interests:					
• Use Web alerts or news feeds to keep abreast of company and industry issues, or demographic and issue (e.g., sports, entertainment, public policy) interests for individual clients	X	X	X	X	X
• Create a client-centric blog(s) or podcast series, looking at their areas of interest from a legal angle (without offering legal advice)	X	X	X	X	X

Support Client Products/Services

Activity Firm size →	200+ 1	100–199 2	11–99 3	2–10 4	Solo 5
Whenever possible, use your client's products/services:					
• Make them visible in your office environment, if appropriate	X	X	X	X	X
• Let your client know if you are using a product/service and enjoying it	X	X	X	X	X
Make connections that support their businesses:					
• Send them work, if appropriate	X	X	X	X	X
• Make helpful introductions—ask what they are looking for	X	X	X	X	X
• Offer to help them find new hires when they are looking for employees	X	X	X	X	X

Cultivate Referral Relationships

Activity Firm size →	200+ 1	100–199 2	11–99 3	2–10 4	Solo 5
Ask for and make referrals	X	X	X	X	X
Send handwritten thank-you notes for new matters or introductions	X	X	X	X	X

2. To Establish Open Lines of Communication

Develop Systems to Keep in Contact

Activity Firm size →	200+ 1	100–199 2	11–99 3	2–10 4	Solo 5
Schedule contact—calls, emails, and in-person—routinely as part of process management plan:					
• Follow up several weeks after matter is concluded to see how things are going	X	X	X	X	X
• Make "stay in touch" calls between matters	X	X	X	X	X
• Schedule regular lunch dates with foundation clients	X	X	X	X	X
Share contact information:					
• Include mobile and home telephone numbers as you feel comfortable	X	X	X	X	X
• Provide office directories with direct dial numbers and email addresses so client has easy access to whomever they need in the firm—include staff relevant to their matters	X	X	X	X	X
Share communication preferences:					
• Understand clients' communication preferences	X	X	X	X	X
• Ask clients what contact information they would like from you	X	X	X	X	X
• Ask clients what time of day they prefer to be contacted	X	X	X	X	X
• Ask clients if they want to be called on weekends or vacations	X	X	X	X	X
• Establish contact guidelines	X	X	X	X	X
• Use preferred method of communication whenever possible	X	X	X	X	X

(continued)

Activity Firm size →	200+ 1	100–199 2	11–99 3	2–10 4	Solo 5
Prepare your staff to facilitate contacts courteously:					
• Appoint someone to cover your calls when you are out of the office or unable to take a call	X	X	X	X	X
• Make your out-of-office message reflect your current situation (rather than use the generic, "I am out of my office or away from my desk.") so that it becomes another source of contact information for your clients and colleagues	X	X	X	X	X
• Instruct others who answer your phone to always give their name when they answer, i.e. Hello, this is Richard, Carol's assistant. She is in a meeting; may I help you?"	X	X	X	X	X

Configure Your Work Processes
to Put Client Interests Front and Center

Activity Firm size →	200+ 1	100–199 2	11–99 3	2–10 4	Solo 5
Keep clients appraised of dates and times of legal deadlines and activities, and include them when possible:					
• Invite them to attend court hearings	X	X	X	X	X
• Send out scheduling orders and changes to scheduling orders	X	X	X	X	X
• Share calendar dates	X	X	X	X	X
• Be clear about matter timeline and progress	X	X	X	X	X
Follow up after each event (e.g., hearing) as appropriate:					
• Hold conference calls to review what happened	X	X	X	X	X
• Outline any changes to the matter plan as a result of the event	X	X	X	X	X

Institute a Client Feedback Program

Activity　　　　　　　　Firm size →	200+ 1	100–199 2	11–99 3	2–10 4	Solo 5
Conduct regularly-scheduled formal client interviews:					
• Create a process to support client interviews that includes pre-interview preparation and interviewer training	X	X	X	X	X
• Distribute information from the interview afterwards	X	X	X	X	X
• Make appropriate changes—and let the client know	X	X	X	X	
Use questionnaires and surveys to obtain client feedback:					
• Use periodic surveys or focus groups to get client input into proposed changes in the way you deliver services, or regarding initiatives such as a new practice area	X	X	X	X	
• Distribute "How did we do?" post-matter/engagement questionnaires/ surveys	X	X	X	X	X

Involve Clients with Your Firm's Activities

Activity　　　　　　　　Firm size →	200+ 1	100–199 2	11–99 3	2–10 4	Solo 5
Send anniversary cards on the anniversary of when they first became a client	X	X	X	X	X
Ask clients to speak to your lawyers about themselves and important issues in their world	X	X	X	X	
Invite them to participate in a special segment of a partner retreat or in firm planning meetings	X	X	X	X	
Convene ad hoc informal client roundtables to provide feedback and discussion about important trends	X	X	X	X	X

(continued)

Activity Firm size →	200+ 1	100–199 2	11–99 3	2–10 4	Solo 5
Share your ideas for planned firm investments in technology or online activities or new practice areas	X	X	X	X	X
Create a ten- to twelve-person client advisory board composed of key clients, key referral sources, relevant decision-makers in the financial, economic, and political world to serve as a sounding board and educational resource for the firm	X	X	X	X	X

3. To Ingrain Best Practices within Your Firm

Set Expectations by Using Defined Client Service Standards

Activity Firm size →	200+ 1	100–199 2	11–99 3	2–10 4	Solo 5
Develop a client service manual	X	X	X	X	X
Give a printed statement of your client service policies to clients	X	X	X	X	X
Provide client service training for everyone in the firm	X	X	X	X	

Offer Alternative Fee Arrangements Wherever Practical

Activity Firm size →	200+ 1	100–199 2	11–99 3	2–10 4	Solo 5
Offer clients the option of alternative fee arrangements such as success fees, blended rates, discounts, contingency fees	X	X	X	X	X
Consider flat fees for turnkey aspects of services, combined with billable hour-based fees for matters or tasks where the scope of work is unclear	X	X	X	X	X

(continued)

Activity Firm size →	200+ 1	100–199 2	11–99 3	2–10 4	Solo 5
Develop a method for tracking time and costs by tasks to facilitate matter budgeting and cost estimates for non-billable hour based fees	X	X	X	X	X

Establish Clear, Client-Friendly Billing Guidelines

Activity Firm size →	200+ 1	100–199 2	11–99 3	2–10 4	Solo 5
Ask clients how they prefer to receive invoices and if there are any client billing guidelines they want you to follow	X	X	X	X	X
Organize invoices by activity rather than chronological time increments: • Tie to the budget and project process established at the beginning of the matter	X	X	X	X	X
• Use clear, active language so clients see your movement toward their goals	X	X	X	X	X
• Show complimentary services on the bill	X	X	X	X	X
Establish retainer arrangements for ongoing engagements such as serving in an outside counsel role for smaller and private businesses	X	X	X	X	X
Send bills as near the conclusion of a matter as possible (data show that the greater the time between completion of an activity and billing, the less likely you are to be paid in full.)	X	X	X	X	X

Deploy Client Teams

Activity Firm size →	200+ 1	100–199 2	11–99 3	2–10 4	Solo 5
Take a comprehensive view when creating teams:					
• Involve attorneys from all legal practices relevant to client's business	X	X	X		
• Include all firm personnel who work with the client	X	X	X	X	
• Create "virtual alliances" with other firms and attorneys to provide the range of needed services				X	X
Institute structures to promote team success:					
• Ensure that team members understand client's business and concerns	X	X	X	X	X
• Train team members in their roles and responsibilities	X	X	X	X	X
• Develop a schedule for team meetings and measurement metrics for team activities	X	X	X	X	X
• Establish a reward structure that recognizes team success	X	X	X	X	
Adapt the client team concept to smaller firms:					
• Involve all staff who work on the client's matters	X	X	X	X	
• For solos and small partnerships, include attorneys with complementary skill sets from other small firms				X	X

Invest in Technology, Particularly for Customer Relationship (CRM) and Knowledge Management (KM)

Activity Firm size →	200+ 1	100–199 2	11–99 3	2–10 4	Solo 5
Evaluate the feasibility of key technologies for mobility, "cloud" storage, and collaboration, and implement those that are the best fit for your firm	X	X	X	X	X
Gather and manage knowledge within the firm:					
• Track "relationship intelligence," i.e., who knows whom, who meets with whom, stylistic affinities, and stylistic clashes	X	X	X	X	X
• Establish protocols for accessing and reusing work products (see technology entries below)	X	X	X	X	X
Share technology investments:					
• Encourage clients to use your technology investments, such as videoconferencing facilities, for their own purposes	X	X	X	X	X
• Explore the possibility of using shared technology, such as budgeting software, process management evaluation software, billing system software, etc.	X	X	X	X	X
• Develop joint training programs	X	X	X	X	
Consider using technology to facilitate closer collaboration:					
• Build online shared work venues, such as extranets and deal rooms, where you can collaborate with clients	X	X	X	X	X
• Create processes that facilitate client transparency (ability to monitor progress, review work product, etc.)	X	X	X	X	X
• Share knowledge management initiatives, from whitepapers to document repositories	X	X	X	X	X
• Develop a section(s) on your firm Web site to aggregate articles and links related to common foundation client interests	X	X	X	X	X
• Create research databases that support the work of client teams	X	X	X	X	X

Assemble Composite Service Packages

Activity Firm size →	200+ 1	100–199 2	11–99 3	2–10 4	Solo 5
Compile service packages from the client's perspective: • Coordinate use of assorted practice areas by one attorney (e.g. a corporate merger client will work primarily with the attorney managing the deal, who will also be the point person for the other services the client needs such as employment law, compensation, benefits, pension planning, intellectual property etc.)	X	X	X		
Solos and small firms can create similar packages by aligning with others who provide the needed services (e.g., a divorce attorney can establish connections with professionals in the fields of real estate, taxes, estate planning, and guardianship, etc.)				X	X

Institute a Cross-Selling Program

Activity Firm size →	200+ 1	100–199 2	11–99 3	2–10 4	Solo 5
Develop internal knowledge-sharing programs:					
• Hold meetings where one practice area or attorney shares specifics about their current practice with the goal of helping other attorneys understand when their services could be useful, and sharing stories that make the practice come alive	X	X	X	X	
• Place synopses of successes from different practices—and their relevance to clients—in firm newsletters, on intranets, etc.	X	X	X	X	
• Pair partners from complementary legal fields (e.g., the mergers and acquisitions/employment law and divorce/trusts and estates examples above) so they understand what each can offer and can work towards integrated service packages	X	X	X	X	
Create programs to measure and reward/recognize cross-selling initiatives and results	X	X	X	X	

Launch Diversity Initiatives

Activity Firm size →	200+ 1	100–199 2	11–99 3	2–10 4	Solo 5
Align values with your clients' (e.g. if diversity is important to them, consider recognizing it when you staff matters)	X	X	X	X	
Make a concerted effort to offer a workplace environment that encourages diversity in ideals, personnel, and vendor relations	X	X	X	X	

Educate Clients as to the Value Received

Activity Firm size →	200+ 1	100–199 2	11–99 3	2–10 4	Solo 5
Teach attorneys how to use initial client meetings to establish expectations and process parameters for each matter	X	X	X	X	X
Send end of matter reports with the final bill summarizing the objective, process, and results and highlighting what you were able to do that provided value to the client	X	X	X	X	X
Consider compiling these end of matter reports into a year-end executive summary for key clients, and also present your perspective on important legal happenings for them in the past year, as well as some thoughts on what to expect for the coming year	X	X	X	X	X

Add Legal Project Management Processes to Your Practice

Activity Firm size →	200+ 1	100–199 2	11–99 3	2–10 4	Solo 5
Incorporate business-style processes that coordinate with your client's business processes and enable you to anticipate, budget for, and coordinate your legal process	X	X	X	X	X
Agree on the points at which you and your client will want to reevaluate the original plans and projections	X	X	X	X	X

Create an Office Environment That Reflects
the Value of Your Profession

Activity Firm size →	200+ 1	100–199 2	11–99 3	2–10 4	Solo 5
Create a reception area that looks inviting and professional	X	X	X	X	X
Ensure that conference rooms and other public spaces are clean and clear of confidential client documents	X	X	X	X	X
Train all personnel, attorneys, and staff, in the proper attitude toward colleagues and clients	X	X	X	X	
Consider guidelines on appropriate dress and behavior	X	X	X	X	

Reward Client-Centric Behavior
(Both Compensation and Recognition)

Activity Firm size →	200+ 1	100–199 2	11–99 3	2–10 4	Solo 5
Develop standards and measurements for client service and reward those who consistently meet or exceed them	X	X	X	X	
Include client-centric attitudes and activities in annual evaluations and reviews	X	X	X	X	
Compensate for exemplary performance of client service—include quality, responsiveness, availability, ability to collaborate with the client, timeliness of task completion	X	X	X	X	
Use soft rewards, such as public recognition or small "thank you" gifts (these are often more consistent motivators than money)	X	X	X	X	

Selected Bibliography

Association of Corporate Counsel. *ACC Value Challenge*. ACC, 2007–2011. Various resources at http://www.acc.com/valuechallenge, visited Nov 26, 2011.

Asher, Joey. *Selling & Communication Skills for Lawyers*. ALM, 2005.

Aun, Michael A. *It's the Customer, Stupid*. Wiley, 2011.

Beckwith, Harry. *The Invisible Touch: The Four Keys to Modern Marketing*. Warner, 2000.

Beckwith, Harry. *Selling the Invisible: A Field Guide to Modern Marketing*. Business Plus, 1997.

Beckwith, Harry. *What Clients Love: A Field Guide to Growing Your Business*. Warner, 2003.

Cialdini, Robert B. *Influence: The Psychology of Persuasion*. Rev. ed. Collins, 2006.

Connor, Dick and Jeff Davidson. *Marketing Your Consulting and Professional Services*. 3rd ed. Wiley, 1997.

Cross, Richard and Janet Smith. *Customer Bonding: Pathway to Lasting Customer Loyalty*. NTC, 1995.

Dahut, Henry. *Marketing the Legal Mind*. LMG, 2004.

DeLong, Thomas J. *When Professionals Have to Lead: A New Model for High Performance*. Harvard, 2007.

Denney, Robert W., Carole Jordan, and Sandra Yost. *Keeping Happier Clients: How to Build and Improve Client Relations*. American Bar Association, 1991.

Derrick, John. *Boo To Billable Hours*. Podia, 2008.

Downey, Michael. *Introduction to Law Firm Practice*. American Bar Association, 2010.

Dunn, Paul and Ronald J. Baker. *The Firm of the Future*. Wiley, 2003.

Durham, James A. and Deborah McMurray, eds. *The Lawyer's Guide to Marketing Your Practice*. 2nd ed. ABA Law Practice Management Section, 2004.

Ewalt, Henry. *Through Client's Eyes: New Approaches to Get Clients to Hire You Again and Again*. 2nd ed. American Bar Association, 2002.

Fleming, Julie A. *The Reluctant Rainmaker*. Crow Creek, 2009.

Foonberg, Jay G. *How to Start and Build a Law Practice*. 5th ed. American Bar Association, 2004.

Gale, Bradley T. *Managing Customer Value*. Free Press, 1994.

Gibson, K. William, ed. *Flying Solo: A Survival Guide for the Solo and Small Firm Lawyer*. 4th ed. American Bar Association, 2005.

Gitomer, Jeffrey. *Customer Satisfaction Is Worthless, Customer Loyalty Is Priceless*. Bard, 1998.

Grella, Thomas C. and Michael L. Hudkins. *The Lawyer's Guide to Strategic Planning*. American Bar Association, 2004.

Harding, Ford. *Rain Making: The Professional's Guide to Attracting New Clients*. Adams, 1994.

Haserot, Phyllis Weiss. *The Rainmaking Machine: Marketing, Planning, Strategies, and Management for Law Firms*. CBC, 1990.

Hayden, C.J. *Get Clients NOW!* AMACOM, 1999.

Hedley, Andrew. *Developing Strategic Client Relationships*. Ark Conferences, 2008.

Iezzi, John G. *Results-Oriented Financial Management—A Step-by-Step Guide to Law Firm Profitability*. 2nd ed. American Bar Association, 2003.

Jacka, J. Mike and Paulette J. Keller. *Business Process Mapping: Improving Customer Satisfaction*. Wiley, 2002.

Katzenback, John and Douglas K. Smith. *The Wisdom of Teams: Creating the High Performance Organization*. Harvard, 1993.

Kotler, Philip, Thomas Hayes, and Paul N. Bloom. *Marketing Professional Services*. 2nd ed. Prentice Hall, 2002.

Inside the Minds staff, eds. *Founding a Law Firm*. Aspatore, 2008.

Inside the Minds staff, eds. *Managing a Law Firm*. Aspatore, 2008.

Lauer, Steven A. *Managing Your Relationship with External Counsel*. Ark Conferences, 2009.

Law Firm Marketing & Client Development Best Practices. Institute of Management & Administration, 2008.

Leeds, Dorothy. *Smart Questions: The Essential Strategy for Successful Managers*. McGraw-Hill, 1987.

Lenskold, James D. *Marketing ROI*. McGraw-Hill, 2003.

Levy, Steven B. *Legal Project Management: Control Costs, Meet Schedules, Manage Risks and Maintain Sanity*. DayPack, 2009.

Lukaszewski, James E. *Why Should the Boss Listen to You: The Seven Disciplines of the Trusted Strategic Advisor*. Jossey-Bass, 2008.

Maister, David H. *Managing the Professional Service Team*. Free Press, 1993.

Maister, David H. *Strategy and the Fat Smoker*. Spangle Press, 2008.

Maister, David H. *True Professionalism*. Simon & Schuster, 1997.

Maister, David H., Charles H. Green, and Robert M. Galford. *The Trusted Advisor*. Free Press, 2001.

McConnnell, Ben and Jackie Huba. *Creating Customer Evangelists: How Loyal Customers Become a Volunteer Sales Force*. Dearborn, 2003.

McKenna, Patrick J. and David H. Maister. *First Among Equals: How to Manage a Group of Professionals*. Free Press, 2002.

Peppers, Don and Martha Rogers. *Enterprise One to One*. Doubleday, 1997.

Poll, Edward. *The Business of Law: Planning and Operating for Survival and Growth.* 2nd ed. American Bar Association, 2002.

Poll, Edward. *Growing Your Law Practice in Tough Times.* West, 2010.

Poll, Edward. *Law Firm Fees & Compensation: Value & Growth Dynamics.* LawBiz, 2008.

Poll, Edward. *Secrets of the Business of Law: Successful Practices for Increasing Your Profits!* LawBiz, 1998.

Rackham, Neil. *SPIN Selling.* McGraw-Hill, 1988.

Rackham, Neil. *The SPIN Selling Fieldbook.* McGraw-Hill, 1996.

Reed, Richard C. *Win-Win Billing Strategies: Alternatives that Satisfy Your Clients and You.* American Bar Association, 1982

Reichheld, Frederick F. *The Loyalty Effect: The Hidden Force Behind Growth, Profits, and Lasting Value.* Bain/Harvard, 1999.

Reichheld, Frederick F. *The Ultimate Question: Driving Good Profits and True Growth.* Harvard, 2006.

Robertson, Mark A. and James A. Calloway. *Winning Alternatives to the Billable Hour: Strategies that Work.* 2nd ed. American Bar Association, 2008.

Rouse, Peter E. *Every Relationship Matters.* American Bar Association, 2007.

Schmitt, Bernd H. *Customer Experience Management.* Wiley, 2003.

Shaw, Colin. *The DNA of Customer Experience: How Emotions Drive Value.* Palgrave Macmillan, 2007.

Shaw, Colin and John Ivens. *Building Great Customer Experiences.* Palgrave Macmillan, 2005.

Sheth, Jagdish and Andrew Sobel. *Clients for Life: Evolving from an Expert-for-Hire to an Extraordinary Adviser.* Free Press, 2002.

Schmidt, Sally. *Business Development for Lawyers: Strategies for Getting and Keeping Clients.* ALM, 2006.

Smith, Shaun and Joe Wheeler. *Managing the Customer Experience.* Prentice-Hall, 2002.

Sobel, Andrew. *All For One: 10 Strategies for Building Trusted Client Partnerships.* Wiley, 2009.

Sobel, Andrew. *Making Rain: The Secrets of Building Lifelong Client Loyalty.* Wiley, 2003.

Suskind, Richard. *The End of Lawyers?: Rethinking the Nature of Legal Services.* Oxford, 2009.

Zaltman, Gerald. *How Customers Think.* Harvard, 2003.

Zeughauser, Peter. *Lawyers Are from Mercury, Clients Are from Pluto.* Client Focus Press, 1999.

About the Authors

Carol Schiro Greenwald, Ph.D.

Carol Schiro Greenwald works with professional firms, practice groups, and individuals as a strategist and coach to help them develop business better. She uses marketing research findings as the basis for identifying key markets, effectively targeting prospects, and understanding perceptions of them held by clients and the marketplace. She works in three main areas:

> *Strategy*: uses research, targeting, and planning to reach identified market segments in the most effective manner
> *Marketing research*: creates and implements client interviews and focus groups with clients or prospects to learn what clients and/or what those in the marketplace say about you, your firm, and your services
> *Coaching and training*: works with professionals to develop personal marketing and sales skills that enable them to maximize their client relationships, develop stronger referral relationships, and identify and take advantage of new business opportunities

Carol graduated from Smith College, received an M.A. from Hunter College, City University of New York [CUNY], and a Ph.D. from The Graduate Center, CUNY. She held a post-doctorate Eli Lilly fellowship at the Bunting Institute of Radcliffe College. Visit her on the Web at www.greenwaldconsulting.com.

Steven Skyles-Mulligan

Steven Skyles-Mulligan is a branding, communications, and marketing expert who works with CEOs who want their people, products, and services to cut through the noise and stand out from the crowd. He has worked with clients of all sizes—from one of the world's largest financial organizations to solo practitioners—in a wide range of professions including law, accounting, education, financial services, healthcare, insurance, and strategic business consulting. Since 2001, he has been Executive Director of Evoke Strategies (www.evokestrategies.com), a communications firm that makes dull organizations interesting and interesting organizations irresistible.

Index